WE STILL LOVE FOOTBALL

Barry Hindson

©All rights reserved.

No part of this publication may be reproduced, stored in a retrieval system or transmitted in any form or by any means electronic, mechanical, photocopied, recorded or otherwise without prior permission in writing from the publishers.

Front cover photograph showing Steve Preen in action for Bedlington Terriers. Back cover photographs showing (top) the Prince Consort Hotel team, (bottom) Northumberland Senior Cup Finalists 1995, Blyth Spartans.

ISBN 0-9544091-2-4

© Copyright 2006 Barry Hindson

Published by
Baltic Publications, Baltic Business Centre
Saltmeadows Road, Gateshead
Tyne & Wear NE8 3DA
Tel: 0191 442 4001
Fax: 0191 442 4002

To Carol, Jonathan, Caroline,
Christian and sweet Madeline.

The Back Page

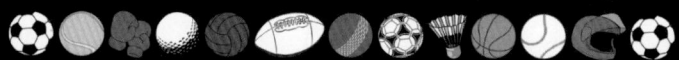

Sports books and football memorabilia

56 ST. ANDREW'S STREET, NEWCASTLE UPON TYNE NE1 5SF

Tel: **0191 261 5005**

info@backpagenewcastle.com

Monday-Friday 10am-6pm / Saturday 9am-6pm. Sundays 11am-4pm

www.backpagenewcastle.com

THE LARGEST SELECTION OF FOOTBALL BOOKS AND DVDS IN THE WORLD

(Including many North-East non-league titles)

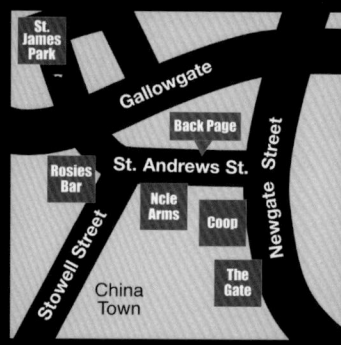

PLUS OUR WEBSITE IS OPEN 24 HOURS A DAY, 365 DAYS A YEAR

visit WWW.BACKPAGENEWCASTLE.COM <http://www.BACKPAGENEWCASTLE.COM> with FREE UK postage on almost every item, for a massive range of books, dvds, t-shirts, prints, photos, signed memorabilia, football programmes and much much more.

Foreword

By Paul Foster

As the manager of NonLeagueDaily.com I don't need to be told just how special non league football people are. In addition, being involved with Birtley Town F.C. for a number of years I know there are great characters involved in North East non league football. I enjoyed reading Barry Hindson's and Paul Dixon's book "We Just Love Football" so much that I knew the time was right for a sequel and I was ecstatic when Barry agreed to write "We Still Love Football".

"We Still Love Football" brings you some great tales and captures the poignant moments of characters that have given their all to local football. The anecdotes in this book span well over 40 years and it's likely that many non league fans, both players and fans, will relate to these stories in some way.

While speaking about the great characters involved in North East non league football, I have to give a special mention to the three Arngrove Northern League goalkeepers who all played in the Sky Northern Masters this year (2006). So well done to Simon Corbett, Kevin Wolfe and Ian Archbold for marking the event with a statistic unlikely ever to be repeated.

A special thank you must go to Brooks Mileson and the Arngrove Group for supporting the publishing of this book and, in doing so, he has yet again shown his support to grassroots football, especially within this region.

I am sure all who read this book will enjoy each chapter and the amazing characters who tell their own individual stories in their unique, inimitable way.

**NEWS...RESULTS...LEAGUE TABLES...FIXTURES...CUP DRAWS....
INTERVIEWS...COLUMNISTS...GUIDE 2 GROUNDS...BUSINESS FINDER
NOTHING BUT NON-LEAGUE FOOTBALL *EVERYDAY***

Contents

Chapter	Page
Introduction.	ix
1. **BROOKS MILESON.** Not bad for a lad from Pennywell.	1
2. **PAUL BRYSON.** Freezing cold showers and a tomato in the face.	10
3. **CAMPBELL MURPHY.** The man who almost met Marlon Brando.	17
4. **MARC IRWIN.** Watch out Exeter here I come.	25
5. **MALCOLM JAMES.** Chairman of the Fed.	33
6. **WILF KEILTY.** Robocop meets Captain Scarlet on the road to North Shields.	41
7. **STEVE PREEN.** Frosty the snowman.	49
8. **KEVIN WOLFE.** Captain Condom, a Mexican road sweeper and the odd psychopath.	57
9. **RICHIE BOND.** Whatever happened to Robson Green?	65
10. **SANDRA ORR.** Nobby Solano does not have to pay.	73
11. **JIMMY ROWE.** Swapping golf clubs with Jocky Wilson.	80
12. **RICHIE McLOUGHLIN.** Pulling up trees for Jarrow Roofing.	89
13. **KEITH MILLS.** The mysterious case of the disappearing crossbar.	97
14. **GRAEME FORSTER.** Was the whole of the cat over the line?	105
15. **PETER QUIGLEY.** A pantomime horse and one fight too many.	113
16. **RUSSELL TIFFIN.** Your cows are on my pitch.	121
17. **MICKY TAYLOR.** Bermuda shorts and a grass skirt.	129
18. **EVAN BRYSON & TERRY RITSON.** A suitcase full of money and an audience with the Queen.	137
19. **JOHNNY INNES.** The East End historian.	146
20. **TOMMY COONEY.** A policewoman and a spot of Morris dancing.	155

About the author

BARRY HINDSON is a former Head Teacher and for over twenty five years he has been a respected sports reporter and presenter with BBC Radio Newcastle where he is recognised as a leading figure in the world of non league football. He is married with three grown up children and lives in Newcastle. WE STILL LOVE FOOTBALL is his third book.

Introduction

I am delighted to have this opportunity to write the sequel to WE JUST LOVE FOOTBALL in which Paul Dixon and myself first wrote about some of the amazing characters who have populated non league football in the North East. Here are the stories of another twenty of the great characters and achievers from the grass roots in the area.

Non league people are a special breed with a deep and passionate love of the game as it is played at local level, and that devotion and commitment is typified by the people whose stories are told in WE STILL LOVE FOOTBALL.

You need a sense of humour to be a non league fan and there are some amazing anecdotes here to satisfy that need, but we also take our football very seriously. It is an enduring passion and whether our team is bringing glory to the region by achieving success in a national competition like the FA Vase, or struggling along on tiny crowds and minimal funds, we all have something in common. In triumph and in adversity WE STILL LOVE FOOTBALL

Barry Hindson
2006

I am grateful to all 20 of the people whose stories are told here both for their co-operation and for their generosity in providing photographs. I am also indebted in particular to Dave Anderson and Mervyn Hogg at m1capture-digitalphotography.com for permission to use his excellent colour photographs on the cover of the book and to Mick Worrall and the Shields Gazette for pictures of Mick Taylor.

x

Brooks Mileson

Not bad for a lad from Pennywell

Brooks Mileson was brought up on the Pennywell council estate in Sunderland, a place which he describes as 'quite infamous,' and when he was eleven years of age he shook hands with adversity for the first time when he was involved in a serious mishap which was to be a defining moment in his life. He was one of a bunch of lads who were playing in a sand quarry in Grindon where there was an overhanging ledge. They decided that it would be a good wheeze to have an avalanche, so Brooks and his pal George began to dig underneath while the rest jumped on the top of the overhang:

> "When it gave way the two of us went with it and I fractured the base of my back; the diagnosis was that I would not walk again. I had also twisted my hips and damaged my right kidney, which accounted for several problems in later life."

He was sent home from hospital with that depressing prognosis and while there was the minor consolation that the invalid, who was the oldest child in the family, was given his own bed for the first time to aid his convalescence, it really was a minor consolation.

Brooks turned the isolation to advantage, waiting until his parents went to bed at night then rolling out of his own small bed and crawling around the furniture until he became able to haul himself upright. His next step was to teach himself to walk again and the determination he showed in achieving that major goal was to be one of his principal characteristics as he grew up and made his way in the world. The problem with his distorted hips meant that he had to wear built up shoes, and the medical experts still took a gloomy view despite the progress his determination had brought about:

> "They basically said: 'All right, smart arse, you may have learned to walk again but you certainly won't be able to participate in sport.' I decided that no bugger was going to tell me what I could and could not do, so I started to run."

He was running as much out of cussedness as anything; to prove to the doctors that he could, and such was his commitment and dedication to his task that in 1966 he won the English Schools Cross Country Championships and he went on to represent England in the International Cross Country Championships (which evolved into the World Championships) in 1968. He finished in third place as the first English athlete home to collect the individual bronze medal and he led England to the team gold:

> "I had proved to myself what I could do, that I could run and that I could take part in sport, so I stopped. I actually hated running and had done from the moment I started. I was never happy until I had finished and I only did it to prove that I could."

When he was forced to admit to the doctors that he was passing blood, they told him he was training too hard, when the reality was that his damaged right kidney was becoming increasingly defective as a result of his childhood accident, and it was to have major repercussions in the 1980s when it became necessary to remove the kidney. His brief but spectacularly successful career as an athlete says a great deal about the kind of person Brooks is. He is a human being who will not be beaten and if that has meant learning to endure great pain and to show massive courage and determination, so be it. That 'no bugger tells me what to do' attitude has been his bedrock philosophy and it has allowed him to cope with the many physical hardships which have been cast in his direction.

BROOKS MILESON - NOT BAD FOR A LAD FROM PENNYWELL

As his athletic career blossomed Brooks was taking the first steps of his working life. He joined a firm of accountants with the aim of becoming a chartered accountant and then took four months off work to train because he had a deep desire to be successful in the cross country championship. His instincts began to draw him towards the building industry and he joined the Newcastle based builders merchants J T Dove. He was travelling twice a week to Billingham where his athletics coach Gordon Surtees was based and when J T Dove opened a branch on Teesside, Brooks left home at the age of seventeen to work there. He was poached by a Teesside building contractor but in the 1981 recession that firm closed down its North East operation, leaving him with the options of moving to London, joining the firm's overseas operation in Nigeria, or going on the dole:

> "I did not fancy any of those ideas so I set up in business on my own with a friend who was an engineer. We had no money and formed a £100 company with two £1 shares and we got a little job for a printer on the sea front at Redcar. We obtained the materials on tick, did the job quickly, satisfied the customer and were paid promptly, and that enabled us to begin the process of establishing ourselves."

In the mid eighties Brooks and his partner did a job for Arnott Insurance in Middlesbrough which involved forming a joint development company with Derek Arnott. The insurance side of the company needed some help which resulted in him becoming involved in that aspect of its work and soon afterwards he took over the firm, which he expanded to offer an extensive range of insurance products and thus it was that he began to build his extremely successful business empire.

It sounds simple, but it was extremely hard work which required seven days a week commitment, but Brooks responded to the challenge:

> "I have a theory about business that it doesn't matter whether you are selling insurance or beans, the ethos is the same. The difference lies with the technical side and you bring in technicians to deal with that. Basically, I worked hard and took some risks; in the early days my bankers called me The Cavalier and when I thanked them for the compliment they told me it was not meant as a compliment!"

In terms of sport, while the unique nature of Brooks Mileson's athletics career was actually more about proving others wrong than the pursuit of excellence, and was in no sense a quest for glory in the sport he loved – quite the reverse – his love of football was different. The people of the North East have football in their blood and when he was growing up in Sunderland in the fifties and sixties, football was the heartbeat of the town. He went to watch Sunderland play when he was a youngster and like the rest of us the love of the game was bred into him.

He had become aware of non league football as an entity when he was running for Billingham Harriers and had the opportunity to watch the successful Northern League side Billingham Synthonia occasionally, so he had some small understanding of what the game at that level meant to the people who followed it and played it. As his business began to flourish in the 1980s, he had a customer who was connected with the Vaux Wearside League team Marske United, and Brooks was persuaded to become their sponsor. It was an arrangement which endured for many years and it was the start of his real involvement in his support of grass roots football which reached another defining point when he extended his sponsorship to include Whitby Town:

> "Whitby is a little town I love. I have a fishing boat there and I love the area and visit it whenever I can. I began helping the football club with a board sponsorship, then sponsored their shirts and finally I sponsored the club itself and became its president. It was there that I learned to appreciate the real nature of the love and passion for their football which is such a characteristic of non league people. We reached the final of the FA Vase at Wembley on a day I will never forget. To be there and to watch your team win a cup final brings the passion home to you."

BROOKS MILESON - NOT BAD FOR A LAD FROM PENNYWELL

Brooks was an official guest at the final and he was invited to watch the game from the Royal Box, but the people in charge committed the cardinal error of outlining the protocol and, in effect, telling him what he could and could not do, so he said:

> "Bugger that. I'm with the lads, and I remember after the game dashing up and down the terraces like a raving idiot. It was a fantastic experience!"

They say that timing is everything, and at the height of his euphoria that day he was approached by the chairman of the Northern League, Mike Amos, who told him the league had lost it sponsor overnight and was in serious trouble. Brooks was asked for his help and he was so overjoyed by the cup final win that Mike could have asked him for anything and he would have agreed. It turned out to be a red letter day not only for Whitby Town but also for the Northern League because the tie up between Brooks and the league which has created such a happy and successful relationship for both parties had its origins in those post match celebrations at Wembley.

There was an official function for the winning team that night which Brooks did not attend because he was there with his family, but he had made an arrangement to travel back to Whitby the next morning on the team bus. Unfortunately he was the victim of the understandably robust celebrations which ensued and the bus left without him! When he crossed London to the agreed departure point it had gone, so he grabbed a taxi to Kings Cross, caught a train to York, took another taxi to the point at which the coach had to leave the motorway to make its way to Whitby, and waited by the roadside until the bus arrived to pick him up!

> "The whole weekend was absolutely unbelievable. We had the official functions, we did the open topped bus ride even though it was pouring with rain, and the whole town turned out. On the Sunday night at the official 'do' some of the fans got me in a circle and started to chant; 'Hero. Hero" because of all that I had done for the club, and that was the first time the game reduced me to tears. Now I really understood how much non league people loved their club and loved their football."

The iron was still hot a couple of days later when Mike Amos met Brooks at his office and they agreed the detail of his first sponsorship of the Northern League. He had been involved with a few individual clubs through his recognition that the grass roots was where help was most needed, and his decision to widen his support to embrace all forty clubs in the Northern League was simply an extension of that recognition and an understanding of the nature of the passions involved in the game at that level:

> "It is easy to be passionate on the terraces at Old Trafford or Arsenal, but the passion at non league level where people give up their spare time to their club is absolute, and while the players might pick up a few pounds in expenses, they are playing fundamentally for the love of the game and I have a real empathy with that."

One of the most pleasant by-products of his commitment to the Northern League has been the development of a deep and genuine friendship with the league chairman Mike Amos. He knew how much Mike had contributed and how much he cared and he also became aware of the fact that he was a real character:

> "He's a real tight arse who won't spend a bloody penny. We get together every Christmas to discuss my involvement for the following season and the first time we had such a meeting Mike arranged to take me for a lovely meal in a really nice restaurant in Darlington. I looked at the menu and asked him if we could go somewhere for a ham and pease pudding sandwich instead. Mike knew the exact spot and now we go there every year and talk about the deal over one of those sandwiches. It is our Christmas Dinner and it keeps Mike's costs down!"

There is obviously a close bond between the pair of them and Mike always manages to strike a suitably irreverent note at the Northern League's Annual Dinner where he has been known to present Brooks with such delights as a packet of cigarettes and a bottle of Lucozade as an oblique comment on his dietary habits, and a kiddies pull along phone in reference to his constant use of his mobile. It is good hearted and indicative of their mutual regard, though there is some accuracy in the cigarettes and Lucozade gesture because Brooks concedes that he does not look after himself as well as he might when it comes to the fundamentals of eating and drinking. Astoundingly, he did not become a smoker until he was 48 and he now feels the need to make up for lost time, and as an ME sufferer the Lucozade represents a helpful liquid intake. He is not at all interested in food and while he is content to eat once a day he is also capable of forgetting to eat for days at a time.

He is more meticulous in his attention to the needs of the Northern League. He realises that they need the money he gives them and he has also provided them with the security of a long term commitment which takes away the annual uncertainty over whether the deal will be renewed. He appreciates their need for his help but he is also buying into a way of life, taking a pride in the fact that he is supporting the second oldest football league in the world. He celebrates its great clubs and great traditions and in essence he believes that he is making a contribution to real football:

> "That is what you see on a Saturday afternoon in the Northern League. The crowds are small but the people are devoted. It is a million miles away from the Premiership but it is proper football. It is about local teams, local people and local pride."

Brooks has never stood still in any sense since he willed himself to walk again as a child, and after the euphoria of Whitby's triumph in the FA Vase and the inspiration he derived from that which gave him his desire to sponsor the Northern League, he moved in another direction to become involved with the then fledgling Scottish League side Gretna which is based a few miles up the road from his home. It has been another incredible chapter in the life of this amazing man. Although the town is on his doorstep and he frequently drove past it on his way to his business premises in Glasgow, he had never actually set foot inside Gretna football ground until five years ago:

"I had lived here for seven years and the only reason I went was to accompany Mike Amos who was there with some of the officials of the Northern League. In their Northern League days there was a great affinity between Whitby and Gretna because geographically they were the farthest teams apart in the league, and there were some of the Whitby people there that night as well. That was the only reason I went."

He was greatly taken by the warmth of the welcome he received at Gretna from people who did not know who he was; it had real echoes of the kind of hospitality he had become used to in the Northern League and he immediately felt at home. Things moved rapidly from that happy introduction and in a short period of time Brooks had taken over Gretna Football Club. From the first day he was careful to maintain and nurture that special non league philosophy which embraced warmth, passion and a sense of belonging on which he placed such a high value.

The importance of the close link between the football club

The Lord of the Manor.

and the local community which is at the heart of non league football is reflected at Gretna where they have carried their non league principles into league football and they have a series of ground breaking community programmes. They are the only club in England or Scotland which makes no charge for its Football in the Community programme. They have teachers attached to the club who teach football based numeracy and literacy skills. They run and finance a drugs rehabilitation unit in Dumfries and they pay for drug testing and screening for most of the major clubs in Scotland through a trust programme. All of these initiatives spring from Brooks Mileson's passion for non league football and while Gretna's rise to eminence in the Scottish League has been phenomenal and saw them reach the Scottish Cup Final and qualify for Europe last season, the philosophy behind the club of being an integral part of the community and in that sense belonging to the local people, is a consequence and extension of his non league background. It has helped the football club to stay focused throughout its heady success and prevented any possibility of them getting carried away and becoming Big Time Charlies. From the first he set about turning the club of hard up part timers into a full time community football club in the true sense:

> "Some clubs pay lip service to the community side of the game when in reality they are exploiting it as a means of getting hold of more money. I was determined that we were going to do it properly."

When it comes to assessing the reasons behind Gretna's virtually unprecedented success, Brooks talks about the importance of people and he begins with the manager, Rowan Alexander. He was the only full time person at Gretna when Brooks took over and as well as managing the team he cut the grass, maintained the ground, fought off the bailiffs and in many respects kept the club going single handed in a way which is another typical reflection of life in the lower reaches of the game. Brooks was impressed from day one and still holds his manager in the highest regard:

> "The most important person at the football club is the manager and its most valuable asset is its fans. We have been determined to retain our non league spirit because it is vital. We have done things properly and professionally and we have been successful. I have given them the means to achieve success but it still had to be achieved and they take the credit for that."

'They' include Ron and Helen MacGregor, the chairman and vice chairman. Ron had been a driving force in the non league days and in the transition to league football, and he stepped up from secretary to chairman at Brooks' insistence. He knew what he was doing both in appointing a very capable person to a key role, but also in relieving himself of the burdens of the job so that he could follow the team from the terraces where he felt most at home. Brooks is a football fan; he travels with the fans, particularly his mate 'Lofty' George Gordon who has supported Gretna for fifty years and Jack Gass, another long term supporter:

> "We go to every game together, have our fish and chips before the match and pay at the turnstiles. That is what I love and I will always do it that way."

As a successful and wealthy businessman whose love of the game was well known Brooks had received many approaches from clubs before he embarked on his Gretna adventure and at one stage he entered into negotiations with the flamboyant chairman of Carlisle United, Michael Knighton, to buy the Brunton Park club:

> "It was an unsuccessful experience but while Michael Knighton is not very popular in Carlisle after his involvement with the club I have to say I liked him because he was a real character and after all, he had rescued Carlisle from oblivion when he took over."

The Carlisle venture floundered and thanks to a combination of geographical good fortune which made him their neighbour and the warmth and energy of the people at the football club which had so impressed him, Gretna became the beneficiaries. The rest of the non league clubs in the area have not been neglected, of course, and as well as the forty clubs which benefit from his ongoing support of the Northern League he helps upwards of thirty others in various individual ways and he is a wonderful benefactor as far as grass roots football is concerned.

He is also involved in a number of football trusts which he regards as essential to the integrity of the game by giving supporters a say in the running of their clubs:

Brooks with the Scottish FA Cup. Gretna played Hearts in the 2006 final.

"That is where the help is needed. I even shirt sponsor the Nags Head pub team because they need the support. There is a lot of money in the game but it goes almost exclusively to the clubs operating at the top and does not filter down. Scottish football is in a state because nothing is coming through. The junior clubs need to be reinvigorated because that is where the talent comes from. When you think back to the Sixties, every club had a nucleus Scottish players; where are they now?"

Brooks desire to see the grass roots nurtured derives from his inborn passion for the game but it is important to understand that he is in it for the long haul. His sponsorship of the Northern League is unique in that sense. Mike Amos had an annual concern over whether Brooks was going to continue to support the league; there was always a natural anxiety which Brooks moved to allay by arranging to sponsor the league in perpetuity for his own lifetime as well as arranging a trust in the names of his two sons which will allow them to continue the arrangement. It is an incredibly generous gesture; generous in spirit as well as in kind, and the Northern League can count its blessings at having such a caring and committed benefactor:

"I want the Northern League always to have someone there, and not to have to worry about the plug being pulled on them. You cannot have the second oldest league in the world dying for lack of funding, especially with it being based in the North East which is the heartbeat of football."

Brooks Mileson loves the Northern League and believes it is a football institution. He likes their quirky independence and the charm of their parochial style. He grew up knowing about the league and the grand old clubs it contained and when he became involved with the people and developed his close friendship with Mike Amos he came to realise how much they cared about their league and its constituent members; the pride they have in its longevity, and the time, energy and money they spend ensuring its continuing success and good health. He shares their great desire to maintain the league's traditions and sees it as part of the social fabric of the region. He believes that if you can encourage young

BROOKS MILESON - NOT BAD FOR A LAD FROM PENNYWELL

Gretna's Scottish FA Cup Final team of 2006.

people into sport, whether it is football in the Northern League or any other sport, you are reducing the likelihood of them going astray:

> "One of the sadnesses is that while there are a lot of good people in the game, the bulk of the money is at the top and stays at the top. The sooner they realise that more of it needs to spiral down and less is gobbled up by the elite, the better. The game is not just about the Arsenals and Manchester Uniteds; it's about the people who are involved with their clubs at local level. It's about the integrity of the sport."

Brooks' first year at Gretna was their second as a Scottish League side and it was an unbelievable experience. He was able to 'muck in' and be involved on his own terms. His Saturday morning began with a trip to the supermarket to buy the ingredients with which he prepared the team's lunch. While the food was cooking he went to the ground and involved himself in power washing the terraces and approaches, then he returned home to collect and deliver the food before doing a stint selling food from the hot dog stand. He was, as they say, as happy as a pig in shit, but as the club grew and their incredible success was achieved he was forced to assume a higher profile and to employ others to carry out the basic tasks he had revelled in carrying out himself. He misses that level of involvement, but he still avoids the conventional trappings of a football club director. He is still a fan and he behaves like one. He has to strike a balance because of his position but he is still prepared to risk upsetting people by eschewing the warmth of the boardrooms for his place on the terraces:

> "I mean them no disrespect but I did not go into football to wear a tie and ponce around in boardrooms. I went to the Scottish Cup Final with the fans when we played Hearts and watched from the terraces. You cannot watch your team from on high and remain a fan."

His approach may be unconventional, but his success is recognised and admired in high places. He has addressed a House of Commons Committee about the way Gretna involves itself in the community. The club has produced a book telling the fictitious story of a young footballer who gets involved with drugs before joining Gretna's rehabilitation programme, getting clean, and scoring the winning goal in a cup final. Jack McConnell, the First Minister of Scotland, has asked to launch the book. What Brooks is doing at Gretna is having a wider impact and is laying down a positive model for others. He believes football clubs have a moral obligation to take these kinds of leads and provide these types of opportunity, and while he is a man who prefers a quiet lifestyle he now accepts the attention he receives and accommodates it in the hope that there will be positive outcomes:

> "I know the press are evil buggers and I like a quiet life, but I have to accept that there is an inevitability about their interest in the role I am playing."

There was another concern of conscience which Brooks had to deal with in his early days at Gretna when he became aware that like other professional football clubs they were bringing in youngsters when they left school and after three years of acting like surrogate parents they were releasing the vast majority of them:

> "It was a great moral struggle for me. We were taking over kids lives and then dumping them. So we moved our Academy to Central Lancashire University's sports campus in Penrith and now our kids train there and enrol in the University at the appropriate level so that they are continuing their education. If they fail to make the grade at football they can pursue their education at the University."

He has extended the scheme by endowing ten scholarships for bright youngsters who cannot afford a university education and for this and his work both in the local community and with deprived and disadvantaged children in Romania, the University has awarded him an Honorary Fellowship.

His commitment to the orphan children of Romania is something which Brooks takes especially seriously, and he has provided two flats in Budapest which serve as halfway houses between the orphanages and society to ease the process of rehabilitation. He is also a dedicated supporter of animal welfare and is a member of the board of the Scottish Society for the Prevention of Cruelty to Animals. As ever, his involvement is on a practical level. As a lifelong animal lover he had always had a desire to own a Shetland pony, so when he bought his present home with its twenty acres and a paddock he fulfilled his dream twice over by buying a pair. Word got out and he was asked to take in two more which had been abandoned. Then other people began to bring him a range of unwanted, abandoned and neglected animals so he increased his land holding to a hundred acres to accommodate them, and established a properly administered animal sanctuary which among its vast array of residents includes a hundred rare breed sheep, two skunks, a couple of massive South African horned tortoises, marmosets, ostriches, macaws, rheas which have been bred on site, alpacas, fallow deer, capybara rodents and a host of others! He becomes angry when he talks about people who buy exotic creatures they have no idea how to look after and he is scathing of the inadequate legislation which allows them to do so.

From his early working days as a budding builder when he enjoyed nothing better than filling barrows with sand and driving the lorry, to his time preparing the Gretna team lunches and his work with his animal sanctuary, Brooks Mileson has always been at his happiest when he could roll up his sleeves and muck in. He is not a conformist; he prefers his pony tail and jeans to a suit and tie and while he takes the pride to which he is entitled in his Honorary Fellowship and his place on the board of the SSPCA and says he has not done badly for a lad from Pennywell, he is still at his most relaxed when he is getting his hands dirty or standing on the terraces:

> "I don't believe in telling people to do what I can't do myself and I miss not being able to do as much of the basic, practical stuff as I did. People appreciate you more if they see you doing things yourself instead of sitting in an ivory tower giving orders."

He sees less Northern League football these days because of his involvement with Gretna, but his affection for the league has not diminished and his annual attendance at the league dinner is still a highlight to which he looks forward so that he can mingle with the people he values and hand out some of the awards. As far as the future is concerned, he is recovering from another of the major health problems which have dogged his life, and with the prospect of further surgery he is seriously involved in winding down his business interests so that he can take life a little easier and concentrate his energies on his football club, his charity and community work, and his animal sanctuary:

> *"It is logical that I should wind down and enjoy the rest of my life. I will enjoy looking after my animals and my footballers. They need me and if I feed them and look after them they will will give me my reward. That's where I see my future and I am looking forward to it."*

Paul Bryson

Freezing cold showers and a tomato in the face.

When young Paul Bryson was released by Middlesbrough and his dream of playing professional football was ended he thought his world had shattered. It's a scenario which many promising young players are forced to cope with because the fall out at that level is extremely high, and only a handful of hopefuls make the grade. Paul did what any sensible lad would do and went back to his roots to rejoin Redheugh Boys Club where he had learned his football and been spotted by Middlesbrough in the first place. He completed his career in junior football before moving up to senior level in 1982 when he joined Tow Law Town at the age of eighteen.

> "They were a lovely club and I had four very happy years there. The manager was Billy Bell who as far as I am concerned and from what I observed was light years ahead of his time as far as coaching was concerned. It was a privilege to play in his side. I was the youngest player in the squad and Billy used to pick me up in his car. I can't say I was in love with the James Last tapes he used to play but I have to say he was very good to me and he was probably the best manager I played under. Billy and his assistant Stuart Leeming were very good influences."

Billy Bell was also a great pioneer of junior football in the area; he was a visionary and Paul is not alone in his admiration of the contribution he made to local football at every level.

Tow Law was a successful side and as well as league success they had a significant run in the FA Cup. They beat Scarborough before being drawn against Bradford City at Valley Parade. Bradford were top of the old Third Division at the time and it was the kind of draw that non league clubs dreamed about. They had an impressive team which included the present Huddersfield Town manager and former Newcastle United defender Peter Jackson as well as player/manager Trevor Cherry, John Hendrie and Stuart McCall. Tow Law acquitted themselves extremely well and were just 3-2 down as the game entered its closing stages, but Don Goodman came on as a late substitute and scored a hat trick in the last twenty minutes. The final score was 7-2 which was harsh but even that did not diminish the satisfaction Paul and his team mates took from the occasion. FA Cup ties against league clubs are big milestones in the careers of non league players and the Bradford tie was no exception, even for as talented a team as Tow Law possessed at the time:

> "We were blessed with good players at Tow Law and we jelled very well. The two Haleys, Michael and Paul, played along with centre back Steve Webb, Kevin Campbell and Warren Pearson who played alongside me in central midfield. The two wide men, Danny Wheatley and Stephen Storey, were probably our most influential players and up front we had the choice of Stephen Turner, Kevin Blair and Paul Haley. It was a good side, well drilled and organised. We were not the best paid by any means but we competed with the best in the Northern League year in, year out."

After four years at Tow Law, Paul felt the time had come to move on and Terry Hibbitt, the former Newcastle favourite who was in charge of Gateshead, offered him the opportunity to play at a higher level in the Conference. It was a challenge and an opportunity to play for his home town club and he decided to take the plunge. What promised to be a great move did not work out however. Paul started a new job which made the greater travel involved in playing in the Conference a burden and after a few weeks he conceded

PAUL BRYSON - FREEZING COLD SHOWERS AND A TOMATO IN THE FACE.

that it was not possible to combine the two. It meant turning his back on an excellent team; as well as Terry Hibbitt who had been a hugely popular player at Newcastle. They had Simon Smith in goal, Dave Parnaby, Keith McNall, Barry Wardrobe and Martin Henderson in their ranks and it was a wrench to leave, but it would have been impractical to stay.

Paul Bryson was a player in demand and he was signed by another top side in Spennymoor United who were managed by Tony Monkhouse, a fearsome player in his day who was known as the "white rhino of Weardale" and was now a successful manager. Spennymoor have always been a well supported side and they had an excellent fan base when Paul signed for them. He settled well and stayed for three seasons:

> "Tony was excellent. He was a manager who looked after his players. He got the best out of us by telling us all the time how good we were as individuals and as a team. Players respond to that kind of encouragement and we finished third in my first season when we also had an excellent FA Cup run in which we played Frank Worthington's Tranmere Rovers in the first round proper."

There were some tough players as well as some skilful ones at Spennymoor, none more so than their centre half and captain Jackie Sheekey, and they did not like losing:

> "We were playing Newcastle Blue Star and we were winning 2-0 with ten minutes to go. We were really comfortable but we let it slip and conceded three goals in the last ten minutes to lose the game. Everybody was having their say in the dressing room after the game and I was a bit harsh in my criticism of the back four for conceding three late goals. I saw Jackie Sheekey coming over and he grabbed me by the scruff of the neck, lifted me off the ground and threatened me with a fate worse than death. I was shitting myself and I didn't say much to Jackie by way of criticism after that. Jackie was a great player and a great character and he did say sorry afterwards!"

After three happy and successful years at Spennymoor Paul had to leave because he was a contracted player and as such he was not permitted to play Sunday morning football, but as a player who loved the game and valued the friendship of his mates, he turned out with them on Sundays. Spennymoor found out and he was reported to the Football Association; he also had his contract terminated. So his indiscretion, based on enthusiasm for the game though it was, meant that he had to find another club.

His Sunday team was Sherburn where he played with the likes of Micky Taylor, Kevin Wolfe, John Cullen and John Milner and he recalls it as a time of great success but also of great fun in the company of some madcap mates. Typical of their antics was an incident when they won the prestigious County Sunday Cup:

> "We went back to the club with the cup; the place was absolutely choc-a-bloc so Micky Taylor decided to do his party piece. He went into the toilets and removed all his clothes then he walked through the middle of the concert room carrying the cup under his arm. Everybody was in hysterics and Micky shouted: "What's the matter, have you never seen the County Cup before?!"

Paul's 250th appearance for Eppleton. On his right is Marc Irwin.

11

PAUL BRYSON - FREEZING COLD SHOWERS AND A TOMATO IN THE FACE.

Stuart Sherwood was a good friend of Paul's and he was managing Eppleton in the Wearside League and he made that his next port of call. It was another successful move. Happy times and success on the field meant that Paul was content to stay at Eppleton for the next five seasons. The club moved forward quickly; if anything they moved too far in too short a space of time. Rapid success saw them winning the Wearside League, then winning the second division of the Northern League to be promoted again. It was heady stuff and they achieved another notable success when they won the prestigious Durham Challenge Cup by beating Consett 3-1 at Hartlepool United's ground.

Like every club, Eppleton had its share of characters, among them John Dow:

> "We had been training one night and John was in the showers. One of the other lads shouted: "What are the showers like?" and Neil Scott said: "They are luke warm." John shouted: "They might look warm but they're ******* freezing!"

John Dow was a lad, according to Paul, who would do anything for ten pence and like many teams the Eppleton lads went away on a trip at the end of the season. In their case the destination was Blackpool and on the first day the lads were walking past a fruit and vegetable stall, sharply dressed in their best gear:

> "John, whose Dad was a fruit and veg man, picked up this big tomato and said he would throw it as high in the air as he could and let it drop on his face if everyone gave him 10p. It was a bit like Gazza setting fire to his nose that time in a bet with Jimmy Five Bellies. He did it, and the tomato burst all over his suit. It made a right mess and we didn't give him the money. He was a crazy character."

The assistant manager at Eppleton was Tony Heslop and along with Deck Francis he was always taking the micky. The two of them were having an argument with the opposition dugout, going at it hammer and tongs and Tony shouted to Dougie Keys the opposing manager:

Paul holds the Durham Challenge Cup aloft after Eppleton beat Consett in the final.

> "I'm pleased you're standing up." "Why's that like?"
> "Because now I know what a pile of shite looks like!"

Unfortunately the club's finances were not strong enough to cope with the extra demands of playing at the higher levels and the rapid rise through the leagues on the playing side outstripped the expansion of revenue. It all fell apart despite the efforts of Paul and his team mates and the massive contribution of manager Stuart Sherwood:

PAUL BRYSON - FREEZING COLD SHOWERS AND A TOMATO IN THE FACE.

"Stuart was a great manager and a great motivator who loved the game. The success he achieved at Eppleton meant the world to him. He was a winner and a good guy to play for, and when I became a player/manager myself the first and best thing I did was to appoint Stuart as my assistant."

The financial problems at Eppleton and the club's consequent decline saw Paul Bryson move to Dunston for two years. It is a club with the highest of expectations and while the two seasons Paul spent there playing for Peter Quigley and Tony Heslop saw then finish in sixth place in each season and lose to Whitby in the League Cup final, that was not good enough to match the standard the club set itself:

"They are lovely people at Dunston; Malcolm James, John Thompson, Ian McPherson, Billy Montague, Alan Stott, Tommy Cooney – the whole committee. They are very hard working and it's a lovely, lovely club. They set the standard of how to run a Northern League club. Everyone does their fair share and the delegation is excellent. It's not just left to one person; everybody pulls their weight. I'm so pleased that when Bobby Scaife took over as manager he was able to bring the club the success it deserved."

Paul felt that he had performed well at Dunston in his time there but the opportunity came along to take on extra responsibility as player/manager at Chester le Street. Ironically he had also been contacted by the Dunston chairman Malcolm James and invited to apply for the manager's job there when Peter Quigley left. He was interviewed for the job, thought the interview went well, but in the end it went to Bobby Scaife:

"I was only thirty three and it was very flattering to be considered, but Bobby Scaife has done a great job and good luck to him. Besides I was happy to honour my commitment to Chester le Street."

So Paul took his first steps as player/manager and he did so recognising that he was embarking on possibly the toughest role in football, because it was actually two jobs in one and the interests of the manager might not always coincide with the interests of the player. It took some adjusting to, but that key decision to appoint Stuart Sherwood as his assistant stood Paul in very good stead. When a game was in progress Stuart was able to view it objectively from the dugout and Paul saw it at first hand on the pitch, and the combination worked superbly for the four years Paul was at Chester Moor. They took the club back up to the first division of the Northern League by winning the championship by twelve clear points. The secret had been to assemble a team of experienced players who knew their way around the Northern League and that experience, combined with Paul's skill and leadership on the field and Stuart's drive and enthusiasm from the touchline created a winning formula.

Winning promotion is a fine achievement, but the next task is to be successful at the higher level and that brings a whole new set of demands. Paul needed to strengthen the team, so he brought in a young Stephen Stewart, who went on the become an outstanding Northern League winger, and he also recruited the vastly experienced Micky Carroll:

"Micky came in when a lot of people had written him off and he had two absolutely fantastic seasons with us. He was thirty seven or thirty eight at the time but his attitude was brilliant. He was always there for training; he set a first class example and he was a lovely, lovely lad."

Typical of Micky Carroll's attitude, and unique in Paul's experience, was an incident in a game against Norton & Stockton Ancients. Micky was injured; he had damaged his right groin and could only make it as far as the bench. Chester were two goals down, Nicky Gray and Stephen Lewis had both been sent off and the situation seemed hopeless. Micky told Stuart Sherwood to put him on for the last ten minutes, during which Chester were awarded two free kicks; he curled them both into the net with his so called weaker left foot (though in reality he was a two footed player equally comfortable on either side). In the last minute

PAUL BRYSON - FREEZING COLD SHOWERS AND A TOMATO IN THE FACE.

Chester le Street's Northern League Division Two championship winning team of 1997-98.

Chester were awarded a penalty and up stepped Micky Carroll again to complete his hat trick and win the game for Chester le Street:

> "I have never seen that; a player come on ten minutes before the end of a game and win it by scoring a hat trick. It was phenomenal; the only other player ever to have done it was probably Roy of the Rovers!"

Paul obviously held Micky Carroll in the highest regard, and cites him as the perfect role model for any young player coming into Northern League football.

Chester le Street finished third in that first season in Division One which was an outstanding achievement and Paul Bryson had proved he had what it took to manage a club, but there was no thought in his mind of giving up the playing side to concentrate on his managing skills. He still enjoyed playing; he was fit and he was more than capable of holding his own in the top division of the Northern League.

Success brings its rewards and its satisfactions, but it also attracts the predators; the clubs with more to offer players financially or to tempt them with the opportunity to play at a higher level. It happened to Chester le Street just as it had happened to many a club before them, and they lost Ross Lumsden while Stephen Stewart picked up a long term injury. Chester found themselves without key players who had to be replaced with youngsters because of the club's financial restraints. The consequence was that the next two seasons were relatively mediocre with mid table finishes. Paul felt frustrated and his feeling was that the third place he had reached in his first season was the best he would be able to achieve.

Chester le Street has always been a club which has operated within its means and has recognised that they have to accept a mid table position in the Northern League first division as a reasonable and realistic target, and no-one can criticise

PAUL BRYSON - FREEZING COLD SHOWERS AND A TOMATO IN THE FACE.

In action for Chester le Street.

that. There have been a number of less wise clubs which have over-reached themselves in the quest for success and paid a heavy price. Paul Bryson understood Chester le Street's position and respected it:

> "I always got on really well with the chairman John Tomlinson and the major figures at the club like Joe Burlison. They were great guys and I felt that what I had achieved repaid the faith they had placed in me when they gave me the player/manager's job. As a manager, though, you want to be working with the best players. Sometimes we talk about great players, but the Paul Walkers, Kevin Todds and Bobby Scaifes of this world were very special players. So were Harry Dunn, Steve Baxter at Blyth, Tony Burgess and John Milner at Bedlington and Ian Nelson at Tow Law; they were exceptional."

The other factor which entered the equation was the recognition of Paul's skills as a coach which led to him being given the opportunity to begin working with the Academy players at Sunderland Football Club, and this combination of circumstances persuaded him that the time was right for a new challenge.

The Academy commitment virtually ruled out the possibility of playing in the Northern League with its midweek fixtures, so Paul decided to join Paul Foster and Dave Smith at Birtley Town in the Wearside League where he is playing now.. He led them to the Wearside League title before going to play for Ray Lish at Consett for a season in which he helped them back into the first division of the Northern League:

> "Ray is an amazing character; a dressing room comic. Billy Bell was ahead of his time, Stuart Leeming followed Billy and was superb. Stuart Sherwood was fantastically enthusiastic. I learned from them all and I am grateful to every

one of them, but I hope I am my own man in the end. I have thoroughly enjoyed the experience and now I am enjoying some good times at Birtley. If I have one ambition left it is to help them into the Northern League. After many years of effort they now have the grants to carry out the necessary ground improvements and if they can complete those and finish in the top two in the league they will fulfil their ambition. That would give me a very satisfying experience with which to end my playing career."

Paul knows that his work as an Academy coach will place restrictions on his future non league ambitions, and anyone who knows him recognises in him the quality of only taking on a commitment if he can devote the time necessary to do it justice. If an opportunity to manage one of the bigger clubs was to present itself it would interest him, but as well as working for Sunderland he is now employed at the very impressive new Gateshead College complex within the International Stadium, and to take on another major commitment would be unrealistic.

Paul has had some happy times playing Over 40s football at Heaton Stannington with old friends like Rob Carney, Billy Cawthra and Keith Mills but sadly that avenue is not one he expects to be able to extend when he finishes at Birtley because of his other commitments. Paul knows he would not be happy playing at a lower level, but he is sensible enough to be aware that the years are catching up with him in playing terms and while it will be a wrench, he is content to end his playing days, hopefully with success at Birtley. He will have had a career spanning twenty five years, filled with achievement and personal satisfaction and he has been a credit to the game.

Campbell Murphy

The man who almost met Marlon Brando

Campbell Murphy's career had its starting point in the 1967-68 season when he was playing for Forest Hall Juniors on North Tyneside. He was playing in midfield when he was spotted by the local Sunderland scout Charlie Ferguson, playing on the adjacent pitch to Billy Cawthra and Micky Spellman. Charlie was actually watching those two, but:

> "I must have caught his eye because I scored a hat trick that day; their goalkeeper was absolutely hopeless! Seriously, though, I had a wonderful game and Charlie invited me to Sunderland."

He was there for the remainder of the season and part of the next but he picked up an injury which affected his form and restricted his appearances, and he was called in despite playing well when his fitness allowed and had to face the heartache of being shown the exit door. Their judgement was that he was just short of the required standard for the professional game and Campbell was recommended to North Shields the year after they had won the FA Amateur Cup under the guidance of Frank Brennan.

Brian Joicey, the Shields centre forward, had signed for Coventry City and the plan was to groom Campbell as his successor, but he never got on with Frank Brennan, so there was a parting of the ways and he returned to Forest Hall for a while before moving across North Tyneside to play for Percy Main Amateurs where he enjoyed a number of successful years. They were not trophy winning years but there was plenty of fun to be had and the standard of football was good:

> "Teams like Carlisle City were in the league and there was some really good football played. Our biggest rivals were North East Marine who were another North Tyneside team. They had players like Mick and Billy Colwill and the games were like wars. The quality of the football was good and the commitment was better!"

After his lengthy stint with Percy Main, Campbell began to drift out of Saturday football and to interest himself primarily in playing on Sunday mornings. He does have one other vivid recollection from his Saturday football career, however, and that relates to playing in the final of the Northumberland Senior Cup and missing two penalties. He never took another penalty until a penalty shoot out in a Sunday Cup Final at Blyth Spartans where he had no option. He side footed the ball into the bottom corner of the net then ran straight off the pitch where he was physically sick from nervous tension:

> " I couldn't even begin to imagine how the pressure would effect a player in the 2006 World Cup Final shoot out when I contemplate what was at stake. It's a matter of not wanting to let your mates down. In my case we won the cup which made it better but the pressure players face in major World Cup and European championship situations is staggering and I honestly don't know how they do it."

He signed for his home team, Dudley, and had spells with the top teams in the area like Lemington Labour Club. He played in the Premier Division of the North East Sunday League against the likes of Lemington Comrades, Dunston and the Old Fold in what was a vintage era for Sunday football in the North East and invariably competed in matches which were not for the faint hearted:

> "I used to think I was a tough footballer and then I signed for Kenton Quarry. To say they were tough was a massive understatement. I was like a kindergarden teacher compared to those

guys. They were a rat pack, a real bunch of animals, but I had a really good season there before I returned to Dudley."

On the mike as Graeme Fennton presents the end of season awards at Dudley & Weetslade.

The Dudley side of the early 1970s was exceptional; they reached the semi finals of the All England Sunday Cup before being knocked out by a side from Liverpool called The Avenue. The setting for the match was strange one whereby one half of the pitch was in pristine perfect condition and the other half was a quagmire. Bobby Reid, a player of immense ability, played for Dudley and he dribbled the ball around the goalkeeper, pushed in towards the goal and turned away with his arm raised in celebration; unfortunately it stuck on the line in the muddy conditions instead of crossing it to put Dudley in front:

> "If you had seen it you would have thought that somebody's hand had come up out of the ground and stopped the ball. Then one of their defenders dived and punched a shot around the post. Everybody in the ground saw it except the referee. I'm not saying he was a homer, but he was a homer! There were ructions on after the game and even the home crowd said they they couldn't believe the referee hadn't seen it. Bastard."

The Avenue had Ken McKenna, one of the greats of non league football, in their team at centre forward and they were a very good side but Dudley matched them in everything except good fortune.

On another occasion Dudley played Prescot Cables, again on Merseyside, in the All England Cup and they were a really rugged side. If you played for Prescot and you had your face intact you were a cissy. You had to have a broken nose, missing teeth or a cauliflower ear to get a trial. They had an amateur international centre forward and Campbell was told to watch him because he was an exceptional player. The two of them clashed going for a fifty-fifty ball and Campbell nailed his man well and truly with a blockbuster of a tackle. The physio was waved on immediately and another character ran on with him:

> "It turned out this bloke was a hit man for a local gangster set up in Liverpool and he was an absolute psychopath. The physio was rubbing the injured player's leg and the henchman was watching him but talking to me. He never looked up once but his exact words which are immortalised in my memory were: 'If this guy doesn't play you will never play again.' I was willing the player to get up and thankfully he did. He actually had a great game and we lost 4-0. It's the only game I ever played in where I can honestly say I was over the moon to get beat. I didn't score an own goal but one of our lads did and I wanted to pat him on the back and shake his hand. It wasn't the Hand of God which decided that game, it was the Fear of God!"

Merseyside seemed to like Dudley as far as the All England Cup was concerned and on another occasion they were drawn away to a side called Canada Docks and after losing the tie 2-1 the Dudley team went back to the home team's none-too-salubrious pub on the Liverpool docks where the local punters were a rough lot to say the least of it:

> "They were sharpening their faces with their knives at the counter. It was like being on the set of 'On the Waterfront' and I kept expecting Marlon Brando to walk in; I must have just missed him."

CAMPBELL MURPHY - THE MAN WHO ALMOST MET MARLON BRANDO

Campbell shows his funny side to Richie Bond.

One of the customers started shouting abuse at the Dudley lads and being extremely offensive and although they were obviously a rough crowd there were some decent and respectable people in the pub, so Campbell took it upon himself to try to take the heat out of the situation. He did his proud Geordie act and asked the man why he found it necessary to be so offensive and to upset people. The man made it clear that he was not interested in engaging Campbell in a reasoned discussion, but he did invite him outside so that they could settle the matter between them. Campbell accepted without demur. He walked outside and when he turned round his potential opponent had six of his sidekicks with him to ensure an even contest! Campbell is not a man who is easily cowed but even he was apprehensive. As he waited for the worst to happen, however, the pub door burst open and the landlord who was built like a brick shithouse and looked capable of dealing with the whole gang single handed bellowed at the seven of them to go back inside. He could hardly squeeze his massive frame through the door and the not so magnificent seven went back inside without a murmur of protest. The landlord congratulated Campbell on his bravery – and his stupidity. Campbell simply took the view that it had been better to try to calm the situation down, but unfortunately there is no talking to some people:

> *"We got on famously with the landlord after that but it was one of those pubs where waving it goodbye was the most wonderful feeling in the world!"*

A team based in Durham provided the opposition on another occasion when Dudley had the much travelled Keith Jelly in their side. Keith was a wonderful lad and a famously prolific goalscorer who fancied himself as Sunday football's answer to the great German centre forward Gerd Muller. He had a high level of belief in his own ability but in fairness his goalscoring talent was second to none. He was like Muhammad Ali; he predicted how many goals he would score and more often than not he delivered. He played for Dudley in a sequence of fifteen matches and scored twenty four goals. When Campbell told him he had made thirty of them, Keith failed to work out the mathematics!

CAMPBELL MURPHY - THE MAN WHO ALMOST MET MARLON BRANDO

The magnificently named North Shields Terminus team was another of Dudley's keen rivals. The name evoked a colourful image and the rivalry was intense. Campbell believes the battles between the two sides should have been played on neutral ground in Beirut. The Terminus actually played on a ground in middle class suburban Tynemouth, somewhat improbably, and in one game the scores were level until Terminus went in front. Their centre forward had scored the goal and words were exchanged between him and Campbell; the Terminus player lost his self control and spat in Campbell's face whereupon Mr Murphy chased him off the pitch, up and over a fence and down the main street before the bloke disappeared at a rate of knots down a side street:

"I went straight back to the pitch and when I got there the stupid referee said; "Did you not see the flag?" I pointed to the spittle which was still on my face and asked the referee if he hadn't seen what had happened. I was very upset about it as anyone would have been. I told the ref I hadn't seen the linesman's flag because of the spit on my face. I apologised and suggested that we should forget it and just get on with the game. He wasn't having any of it, told me he was going to book me and asked me for my name. I said: 'C. Murphy,' and he went light. 'See Murphy,' he said, 'I'll not see anybody!' Then he sent me off. All of our people tried to tell him that C. Murphy was my name but he wouldn't listen. 'He's told me to see somebody and I'm not putting up with it.' He put his report in and I was hauled before the Northumberland FA. They said they couldn't believe it but because I had a bad disciplinary record I got a two week suspension for telling the referee my name! It was all reported in the local papers and I can see the funny side now but it seemed unjust at the time."

Campbell freely admits that most referees actually knew his name because they had written it down so many times in their note books. He could not tell you how many yellow cards he received but he reckons he supplied the local casinos. He was sent off twenty one times which if it is not a record it deserves to be.

Dudley and North Shields Terminus met again, this time at Dudley in the NE Sunday Cup and Campbell, who was returning from injury, was included among the substitutes, hoping to play for the last half hour. The plan was for him to go on and cause some mayhem against an old adversary, Tommy Gosling. He was standing on the touch line beside the dugout watching the game when an altercation took place just beside him. Campbell went to pick up the ball and Tommy Gosling attempted to pick it up at the same time with the result that Campbell accidentally stood on his hand. Unfortunately this provoked Tommy Gosling to punch him a couple of times in the face; he retaliated by punching Tommy so hard that he still had a handful of his shirt in his hand as the unfortunate Tommy fell to the ground; the referee came across and asked Campbell what had happened:

"I told him I didn't know; that I had suffered a brainstorm. I said if anyone had been hurt I apologised and I was sorry for the damage to the shirt. He said if I meant it that was alright and he took no further action!"

He also played in the Blyth Sunday League at one stage and went on a tour of Germany. He did not quite cause the outbreak of World War Three, but he gave it his best shot, finding himself embroiled in altercations on more than one occasion. The final of the competition in which he was playing was a massive affair by non league standards:

"It took place in a big bowl of a stadium in front of 40,000 spectators. It was like 'The Great Escape' - we should have had Sylvester Stallone in goal. It was in a place called Solingen which was actually twinned with Blyth. It was a beautiful place; they must never have visited Blyth before they arranged the twinning. The houses were beautiful and the place was wonderful. I honestly mean no disrespect to Blyth but this was a very different place. I think there might have been some hangovers from the war because we kicked each other more than we kicked the ball."

CAMPBELL MURPHY - THE MAN WHO ALMOST MET MARLON BRANDO

Campbell's caravan next came to rest in the area of Over 40s football with Killingworth alongside players like Billy Cawthra, Artie Lumsden and Wilfie Waite; all class players. It was some of the best quality football he was involved with; other teams had top players as well. Barry Dunn who used to play for Sunderland had a team in the Plains Farm area of the town and the confrontations between them and Killingworth produced football of the highest quality and a wonderful way of enjoying the final years of a career in which he also turned out for Dudley until he was forty nine.

Campbell even turned his hand to playing in goal for Dudley in the twilight years of his playing career and he once found himself in a one-to-one situation with an opposing centre forward who had broken clear. Campbell, all 18 stones and 4 pounds of him, raced out and hurled himself into the challenge:

> "The guy dived out of the way of my tackle and I nearly set my neck because I expected to collide with him but I hit the ground instead. I asked him why he had dived and he said: 'Kidda, I divvent get paid enough to get flattened by a big fat bastard like you hortling at us.'

A game against another good side, Newsham & New Delaval, saw Campbell called to the colours again because Dudley found themselves without a goalkeeper. Dudley were leading 4-0 when they were awarded a penalty and Campbell was persuaded to take it. He was hypnotised by the thought of local headlines relating the tale of evergreen Campbell Murphy scoring from the spot so he placed the ball on the six yard line. The referee asked him what he was doing:

> "I told him I didn't play very often and I wasn't sure where I should place the ball. He said: 'Here,' and plonked it down on the penalty spot. I said; 'Mind that's a long way, I can hardly see the goal.' The ball rolled off the spot and the ref said I had to put it back so I bent down and as I put my hand on the ball I saw the goalkeeper look the other way so I stuck it in the top corner of the net. I ran away screaming 'GOAL!' and the referee gave the goal. All of their team chased after him but he pointed to the centre spot and the goal stood. It was ridiculous."

Campbell eventually retired from playing, but he was unable to walk away from the game and certainly not from Dudley, so he stayed on to help run the team. It was a good side consisting primarily of youngsters from the Cramlington area. He had served his apprenticeship by running a team at Cramlington Juniors with a friend called Jimmy Snowdon who was one of Alan Shearer's mentors. He had very good young players like Keith Hall, Bobby Howe and Graham Fenton and they came up against a Wallsend Boys Club side which included future Newcastle United stars Lee Clark and Steve Watson. Wallsend also had a quick and useful winger called Trappatoni and not for the first time Campbell's tongue talked him into trouble in an incident involving the youngster. Dudley went into a 3-1 lead and Trappatoni was apparently having plenty to say so, trying to be the wag, Campbell told him to stick to selling ice cream because he knew nothing about football. It was an unfortunate remark, though one delivered without malice, but the boy's father and members of his extended family approached Campbell after the game, upset by his comments. He apologised and assured them that he had not meant to insult anyone but they were not to be placated. Campbell was not concerned for himself but felt he had to usher the watching youngsters away from the incident. The upshot was that a formal complaint was made and he was brought before the Northumberland FA once again. He apologised again for his unfortunate remark and resigned from his position at the Boys Club. He realised he had spoken out of turn with a joke which had backfired but his feeling was that in general he was being subjected to more grief from parents than he was from the youngsters:

> "One guy rang me at home at one o'clock in the morning before a match to complain that his son was not being given the chance to play. He was drunk but I told him not to ring me at home. I offered to talk to him about his problem before the match the following morning but he didn't turn up until half time. His poor son didn't know anything about it and he was embarrassed. You don't need that, and there was

another time when this bloke came up to me and started ranting and raving about how he was giving his son money to come to the Boys Club and he was not getting a game even when there were only seven or eight turning up for training. I told him he was out of order to talk to me like that in front of the lads and I asked him to name these occasions when only eight turned up. He said it had been every week so I informed him his son had only trained twice at the start of the season, once in the middle and I had never seen him since. The lad had used the money his dad gave him to buy tabs off his mates. The same boy could have been a great player; he went for a trial with a London league club but he bought a child's ticket on the train; he was thrown off at Crewe and had to make his own way home."

Campbell had his successes but he did not feel right in junior football. It should also come as no surprise that he was never seriously tempted to change from poacher to gamekeeper and become a match referee. True, he refereed the odd game, mainly for the young boys at Cramlington Blue Star when parents who knew him would ask him to step in if the official referee failed to turn up, but Campbell is realistic enough to admit that he does not have the temperament for the job:

"They were playing a team from Whitley Bay and one of opposing supporters was berating me something terrible so I stopped the game. Some of their people came over and said I was doing fine but I told this bloke if he wasn't happy with me he could referee the game himself. He didn't want that of course and made his excuses. I told him I thought his comments were a personal insult, that I didn't favour either side and I could only give what I saw in all honesty. He was shouting and bawling so I told him if I heard any more he WOULD be refereeing and he would be blowing his whistle from where he didn't want to. There were hoots of laughter and I think I embarrassed him because he shut up for the rest of the match. Actually, it's a terrible problem. These parents only see their own kids and what they are doing and they fail to see the wider picture. I think on balance that the evidence would be that I am temperamentally unsuited to the job!"

That aside, the great thing about Campbell is that he has nothing but happy memories of his life in the non league game. He values the friendships, most of which still endure. Despite a disciplinary record which he acknowledges was appalling he played with a smile on his face and had a great

Campbell receives the league championship trophy from his good friend Ray Kennedy.

talent for making people laugh. He remembers massive games like those involving Lemington Social and Lemington Labour clubs which were life and death to the people watching from the sides and where money changed hands in bets on the outcome, but the tension and hostility was secondary to the fulfilment he received as a player. Life long friendships with people like Wilfie Waite and Eric Daniels, and chance social encounters with former opponents in many parts of the world are part of a rich store of memories. Clashes with referees also feature prominently:

> "There was a referee called old Bunty and he was in charge when we played Bedlington in a cup final at Forest Hall. We were winning 2-1 in extra time and Bunty couldn't get the crowd to stand behind the touchline so he abandoned the game! He said the spectators had attacked him but they did not. We had to replay the game and Bedlington beat us which was doubly disappointing for me because I scored both goals in the first game. We had a great team with Billy Harding on the wing, and Ian Halliday who scored all the goals. Some of the players then were amazing characters and wonderful footballers like Eddie Alder who would have graced any league ground."

Tommy Mullarkey is another of the great characters in Campbell's extensive collection. The two of them were playing in a game for Stanley Bridges Tools against the United Services Club in a cup final at Wheatridge Park in Seaton Delaval is the early days of his Sunday League career; he reckons it was so long ago that Stanley Bridges Tools were pre-electric wind up models. United Services had a wonderful fast winger playing for them and Tommy Mullarkey played right back for Stanley Bridges. Tommy, who spoke very slowly and deliberately and had a Northumbrian drawl, saw this winger whip past him in the eighth minute and cross the ball for United Services to score. So Tommy told Campbell in his slow and purposeful way that the winger would not get past him again. The player tried a one-two so Tommy lashed him with a tackle which clattered him to the ground; his name went into the referee's note book. The winger got to his feet and tried to intercede with the referee on Tommy's behalf, saying he had not meant it whereupon Tommy punched him on the chin and knocked him out saying; "Don't you ever say I didn't mean it. I meant it all right, you bugger." He was sent off and Stanley Bridges lost the cup tie.

Then there was the time when a game against Wallsend Town turned nasty:

> I went in for a tackle and punched this lad purely by chance – he head butted my fist! However he got straight up and the referee asked me if I had meant it. I said; 'Referee, you know I didn't mean that; it was a complete and utter accident.' So he said: 'Well, I'll let you off this time,' much to the disgust of the bloke I had hit. Anyway, in the second half I hit the same player again so I said to the ref: 'I know you won't believe that was an accident as well' and I walked off."

Tales of Campbell's clashes with match officials are legendary but even he can claim that he was unique in receiving a provisional booking for Dudley before the game started. The referee came into the dressing room and said a comment he was alleged to have made had been overheard by a spectator and he was being issued with a provisional booking, which was a first even by Campbell's standards.

The response of those charged with dealing with indiscipline can sometimes give rise to raised eyebrows:

> "I was once sitting at a disciplinary hearing at the Northumberland FA for one of my many misdemeanours when one of the disciplinary committee members fell asleep. A few minutes later somebody sneezed and it woke him up and he shouted; "Guilty!" I hadn't even had my case heard; my reputation went before me! Another time I had to go with Tommy Brewis who was my manager at the time. It was upstairs in this pub in Bedlington. This bloke who worked with Tommy was having a drink in the bar and he said; 'I don't know what your mate's done, but the NFA officials have just walked in and they've got a rope!' Later on when I left the room where

the hearing had been held I slammed the door so hard that all the other doors in the pub opened. They thought the place was haunted."

Campbell did not receive a watch or a long service medal from the Northumberland FA when he retired but they did thank him for all the money he had paid in fines which helped towards meeting the cost of their new headquarters.

For all his early success and his days with Percy Main, Campbell's most magical and enjoyable memories are of Sunday football and there is no doubt that he is remembered with affection. There will be ex-players who can show you scars he inflicted on them, but you will be hard pressed to find someone who doesn't smile when they recall playing with him or against him. He is especially grateful to Tommy Brewis whose assistant manager he was at Dudley for many years and to David Dixon with whom he jointly managed the team for eight years. The committee at Dudley and Weetslade Club have always been very supportive of Campbell's efforts on the football team's behalf and he has great affection for them

Nowadays, he is not a very good spectator. He watched a number of games when his son in law Keith Sheardown was managing Newcastle Benfield and Lee Boyle was his number two, but he was disappointed with the general standard. Like the rest of us he looks back and thinks it was better in his day and I would hesitate to argue with him. He believes the teams at what he calls the shallow end of the league are poor these days and argues that teams from the Northern League did not disband in times past the way they are now, which he sees as evidence of decline. Finance is a real worry and when teams with the proud records of South Shields and Bedlington Terriers come within a hair's breadth of folding we need to be concerned. He still loves the game and is genuinely grateful for what it gave him but these days his passion is golf:

> *"Where would I have been without football? I would have been a nonentity. As it is people know who I am. They may not all like me though I hope more do than don't."*

I do not think he has anything to worry about.

MARC IRWIN

Watch out Exeter, here I come.

The Spennymooor United team which played Tranmere Rovers in the First Round proper of the FA Cup. Marc is on the back row wearing the headband.

Marc Irwin's first fleeting glimpse of the big time came when he was a seventeen year old and it is typical of him that he did not do it by halves; instead of a trial at Newcastle United or Sunderland he went to the other end of the country to try his luck with Exeter City. Never one to lack confidence, he was put on the train at Newcastle Central Station by his father along with a handful of other hopefuls from the Ashington area, dressed in blazer, slacks, white shirt and shiny shoes; smart as a carrot. By the time he reached Leeds he had changed into a crombie, a pair of half mast pants and a pair of Doc Marten's and he was ready to say: " Watch out Exeter, here comes Marc Irwin!"

He loved the experience, trained hard, and played in a midweek game against Swansea's reserve side, losing 2-1. Marc had what he believed was a decent game but he did not impress enough to be offered a contract, so he tried his luck nearer home at Hartlepool where Tommy Docherty's son Mick was the manager. The Linighan brothers, both well thought of centre halves, were at the club and there were other centre backs already on the books as well and Marc did not feel he would be able to overhaul them. Among those at the club at the time was Ray Kennedy who was sadly beginning to show the first signs of the debilitating disease which was to end his career and ruin his life. Marc's fears as far as a future at Hartlepool was concerned were confirmed when he was not offered a contract, and he moved to Gateshead Reserves.

While he was playing for Gateshead Marc was spotted by

25

the great Billy Bell who took him to Spennymoor United where he embraced his senior career in earnest and spent two happy and successful seasons, making lifelong friends among some of his team mates. One of the highlights was an FA Cup run which included a tie against Tranmere Rovers who were managed by Frank Worthington. The build up, the media interest, the atmosphere and the game itself made a great impression on Marc; it was like the big time:

> "We got beat 3-2 but it was a great game. There were no lasses hoying themselves at us or anything like that but it was a great day! I sat down with Frank Worthington afterwards and had a pint and he was good crack. It was a great experience for a nineteen year old."

At about this time his uncle, Cec Irwin, who had a great career with Sunderland and had been their youngest first team debutant at one stage, was still working at Roker Park in the youth team set up and he arranged for a Sunderland scout to run the rule over Marc and give an honest assessment. His opinion was that Marc was a very accomplished player, but he lacked that extra, vital, cutting edge – the 5% extra which makes the difference between the good non league player and the successful professional. Marc himself still felt that he had it in him, but realised that the odds were against him playing professionally with so many players falling by the wayside, so he resolved to keep giving it everything he could, hoping that another opportunity would come his way and knowing that he could have a very successful career in non league football if that chance failed to materialise.

He could not have started out in better hands than those of Billy Bell who was a renowned coach, ahead of his time:

> "Billy would go through his tactics on the bus, using 5p and 10p coins and it caused arguments because nobody wanted to be 5ps; we all wanted to be 10ps. Players swapped his coins around when he was not looking. I have to say, though, that his knowledge and his attention to detail were incredible."

One night after a midweek away match the team was travelling back on the bus and Billy Bell nodded off, so one of the players blacked his face with boot polish. Billy was dropped off at Wallsend Sports Centre where he worked and everyone gave him strange looks. He was totally unaware of what had happened to him and was wandering about like a black and white minstrel. That sort of antic was typical of the amazing bunch of characters which was assembled at Spennymoor, including Micky Bartlett who would take out a sandwich after games, spit on it, then ask if anyone would like a bite; he never ran short of food. Jackie Sheekey was a big, strong centre half and Micky Heathcote, who went on to play for Sunderland, was another; they were good times on and off the field. At the end of one season the while squad of eighteen first team players went to Blackpool for a weekend, during the course of which they all had themselves tattooed:

> "Every single one of the first team players had them done and when we came home we were dropped off at Low Fell. All the players were calling Paul Bryson 'Fred Flintsone' and his girl friend asked him why they were calling him Fred and her Wilma. He had to tell her that the shorts she had bought him with Fred Flintstone on had been used to model a tattoo on his arse. She threw her drink over him and told him he had scarred himself for life."

Shortly after the Tranmere cup game Billy Bell was sacked by Spennymoor and Marc decided it was time for a change. Peter Feenan who was the manager of Gretna came in for him and that was the start of eight great seasons over there. There were several changes of manager during his stay but the legendary Gretna committee led by Ian Dalglish stayed constant and they made Marc feel very welcome. He became great friends with another Geordie, Paul O'Hagan, and played in two championship winning sides as well as winning the Cleator Cup and enjoying another cup run which culminated in a tie against another league club, Rochdale. Unfortunately Marc was suspended for the cup tie:

> "You could still see me on 'Match of the Day' though. That was me in the dugout nearly crying because I couldn't play."

A creditable 0-0 home draw was followed by a 2-1 defeat in

MARC IRWIN - WATCH OUT EXETER, HERE I COME.

Marc is bottom right in Gretna's Northern League championship winning team of 1991-92.

the replay, but it had been another taste of the FA Cup and Marc' reputation as a player was blossoming:

> "Mick McCartney had taken over from Peter Feenan and he was later interviewed for the Carlisle United job. He told me that if he got it he would take me there but unfortunately they gave it to someone else so that was another lost opportunity to prove the Sunderland scout wrong. I must admit that I didn't envisage the subsequent success that Gretna have achieved in the Scottish League and Cup. When I think back to a time when Paddy Lowery asked me to play in a game they had to win to avoid relegation in the Northern League it shows you how far they have come. It's a fairy tale really. They tried three times to get into the Scottish League when I was there, and failed, so maybe fate dealt me a hand which said I wasn't ever going to be a professional footballer."

So Marc continued his factory work by day, trained at night, and played on Saturday. He was content with his lot, making many friends, enjoying great hospitality after games and having a lot of fun along the way. He was playing for Gretna at Guisborough once and managed to get himself sent off while he was in the showers! Jeff Winter was the referee and as Marc ran past one of his assistants he called him a cheating bastard, continued running until he reached the dressing room, took off his boots and went in the shower. He was washing his hair when the much beloved Mr Winter blew the final whistle:

> "One of the lads came into the showers and said the ref wanted to see me. I asked him what for and he said the ref had just told him to fetch number six. I said he couldn't mean me because I didn't have a shirt on. Winter told me he was sending me off for verbal abuse of the linesman and I got a one match ban."

When Gretna moved up a level to compete in the Unibond

League, Marc took the word 'compete' a little too literally and in his first season he was sent off twice and received fifteen yellow cards! He was called before the FA who sent an official from Torquay to the Station Hotel in Newcastle (and wasn't that typical of the FA) to speak to him:

> "There was only him and me in the room. I thought I was going to get bumped off. He asked me if I needed help so I said; 'I've got a big bill in the house; you can pay that for me."

Marc also told the FA official that he thought he was a victim and that referees had it in for him but the man pointed out, not without a certain logic, that he had been carded by seventeen different officials and they could not all have it in for him! He was fined £50 and banned for six weeks which meant that yet another chance of enhancement was lost because it coincided with an opportunity to go on trial with a team in Belgium.

He contemplated cutting his long blond hair and changing its colour so that he would not be so conspicuous, but he does acknowledge that he regarded referees as the enemy. Every decision they made against him was wrong, but it still meant a fine and a lengthy stay on the sidelines:

> "They called me the judge at Gretna that first season in the Unibond because I was on the bench so many times!"

Gretna played in a fund raising friendly against the Scottish giants Rangers in aid of the Lockerbie disaster victims and their families. Graeme Souness was the Rangers manager and as well as playing himself and putting in his usual quota of crunching tackles, his team included most of his regulars like Trevor Steven. Ally McCoist was present but he did not play, though that did not prevent him from locking the Gretna players in their dressing room. Against all odds, Gretna won the match 2-1 which prompted Graeme Souness to tell his players:

> "If we can't beat a team like that we are in ******* trouble!"

The Gretna people had laid on a sumptuous buffet after the game but Souness took his team straight to the bus and set off back to Glasgow:

> "They sent us each a Rangers tie and a pennant but I hoyed mine in the bin because I thought their behaviour after the game was so churlish. I also lost a bet because Paul O'Hagan and myself bet each other five pints on who would score first. He won but he only got three of the pints anyway."

After a happy and very successful time at Gretna Marc went to Tow Law where he captained the team to the Northern League title;

> "That was special for the people up there, old Mary and them. They deserved it because they had a great team. Stuart Leeming, the manager, had learned a lot about tactics when he was Billy Bell's assistant."

Marc celebrates Tow Law Town's Northern League championship win in 1994-95.

With respect, Tow Law is a cold place at the best of times, so Marc thought he should warm his team mates up by smearing the insides of their underpants with Deep Heat. He also had a habit of cutting holes in their socks and he had an endearing habit of peeing on players in the showers. They knew what he was up to but they could not stop him and he remembers one unfortunate wretch sitting in the dressing room with:

> "Two cans of lager straight from the fridge on his bollocks."

South Shields came next and Bobby Graham was manager. Marc admired Bobby's tactical ability but he did not agree with his philosophy of marking an area rather than a player. He believed it gave his opposite number an advantage. If he marked a direct opponent and that player scored it was down to him, but if the player was allowed the space to run and jump Marc believed it made his job as a defender more difficult, because he could not compete on equal terms. Marc's style was old fashioned; he kept it simple and he thought that managers and coaches sometimes complicated things unnecessarily:

> "I don't think you should disrupt your game to accommodate the opposition. You have to compete against your man and if you stick to 4-4-2 at this level and pick up the nearest man that's the way to do it."

Alu Bangura, Dave Thompson and Terry Baines were all at South Shields and they looked set to go places until Bobby Graham told the players before one game that they would have to take a pay cut. Thompson and Baines left on the spot and went into the bar to watch the game. Their argument was that you could not expect players to train twice a week and give you 100% on Saturday, then reduce their wages. Other players came in, however. John Outhwaite and "Porky" Brown joined along with Peter Kirkham and Shields were still a good side. They only lost four games all season which was less than any other team, but they drew eighteen so instead of winning the league they finished fourth and Marc felt it was time to move on. He was particularly disenchanted by what he saw as boardroom interference which made Bobby Graham's position difficult and he decided his future lay elsewhere:

> "To be honest, what some people who run teams know about football you could write on a fly's arse with a bingo pen and they should leave the playing side to the manager!"

Marc knew his time had come when his expenses packet was reduced and the manager and the chairman blamed each other. He believed he had given the team all he had and that his treatment had been unfair:

> "I was told I hadn't played well the previous week and that was the reason for the reduction but I said they had not given me any more when I had played magnificently and been named man of the match. I was worthy of my hire. I only knew one way to play and that was to win and when a club entered into an agreement with me I kept my side of the bargain and they should keep theirs."

Marc believes that players leave clubs either because those clubs do not want them or other clubs do, and all the evidence of his career supports that. Clubs have sought him out when they needed a player to spearhead a promotion or championship challenge or to get them out of trouble, and he has always answered the call and always delivered. His father always taught him to be a winner and would point out that his surname ended in WIN. He would, as the saying goes, kick his granny to win the ball and he takes the view that that there is no point in going through a season and not having a trophy to show for your efforts at the end of it; to be able to show his children what their Dad has achieved:

> "It also gives the girlfriend something else to clean!"

In his position as a central defender he took his share of physical punishment as well as giving it out, but he sees that as part and parcel of the game and just gets on with it.

Marc's next club re-united him with his old boss Stuart Leeming who was now in charge at Newcastle Blue Star and was building a team to challenge for promotion from the second division of the Northern League. As usual, he answered the call and, as usual, he delivered the goods helping Blue Star to promotion as runners up to an outstanding Brandon United side. Blue Star were no slouches themselves; they had a quality strike force in Peter Wetherston and Paul Hollier who complemented each other superbly, and with Paul Bennett in goal, Warren Fisher alongside Marc at the heart of defence as well as quality players like Johnny Niblo they were a good side. They were a team which played together, trained together and had a drink together after the game. The spirit and the desire to succeed were superb and allied to the manager's tactical know-how it was a winning combination:

> "It was great for the Blue Star people like Father Ted, Bobby Hunter and Jimmy Anderson to see their team promoted. Blue Star deserved to be in the top division for their facilities and for the people at the club."

Marc continued with his repertoire of dressing room antics at the Wheatsheaf ground; swapping track suits around so that small players were swamped in large ones and bigger players could not get into small ones was a favourite and it was part of the camaraderie as far as he was concerned. He carried it out onto the field with him as well, telling referees they had something on their heels so that he could make them stand like flamingos:

> "Some of them took it in good part but there were others who were not so amused. It's only a bit of fun and sometimes they should chill out a bit. I don't like referees who think the crowd has come to see them. A good referee is never seen or heard. I came to respect a few referees; I had a good chat once with Russell Tiffin and he turned out to be a decent bloke, so that was one less referee to shout at!"

Dialogues between Marc Irwin and referees have become the stuff of legend but in the bar afterwards it was more a matter of banter. He would cheerfully ask the ref to buy him a drink and expect to be told to **** off but it was just a matter of having fun.

The following season Marc received the call from someone close; his uncle Cec Irwin was managing Ashington and he needed a "winner" to bolster his side and he knew where to turn. It turned out to be a great move for Marc because he and his family are Ashington people and they could support him and Cec. The whole family would set off for Portland Park at midday:

> "Me fatha would feed his face and I would go and prepare for the game."

The Ashington fans loved him. he was one of theirs and they called him "Legend." They were some of his happiest times although there was extra pressure because he was the manager's nephew. He shared the captain's armband with Lee Anderson and he spelled out his mantra in the dressing room of not being there to accept second best. Lee and Marc became firm friends and he also got on well with Greg Peary who was a kindred spirit in every sense and is described by Marc as the only player he knew who could turn up drunk and put both feet in one leg of his shorts.

There was an extra intensity to the battle for the championship between Washington and Ashington as many of Marc's friends were in the Washington team. The last game of the season was away to Alnwick Town and Ashington had to win to clinch the title. They won it 1-0 and it was Marc Irwin who scored the winner, lashing a cross into the net in the 22nd minute. When he ran to his Dad and his Grandma in celebration it was a special and precious moment and his joy and satisfaction when Lee Anderson lifted the championship trophy were unbounded. There was, naturally, a celebration party afterwards and Marc reckons he got home a week later! Ashington is a football town and they know how to celebrate when their team wins the league. Marc's only regret in that respect lies in the fact that the town never gave his uncle Cec the credit he deserved for his long and outstanding career with Sunderland, feeling that the achievements of Jackie Milburn and the Charlton brothers overshadowed Cecil's:

> "That's a shame, though it bothers me more than it does him. When we won that second division title and I saw the look on his face it made it all worthwhile."

The euphoria did not last long. Once again Marc was annoyed by what he believed to be boardroom interference with Cec Irwin's ability to do his job,

He also found it difficult to work harmoniously with the club coach and the two factors persuaded him to move midway through the following season, secure in the knowledge that Ashington at least had enough points on the board to survive in the first division.

Once again the call came from a manager who needed a

MARC IRWIN - WATCH OUT EXETER, HERE I COME.

Marc in typical action as a guest for Dunston Federation in a pre-season friendly against Sunderland.

winner and a leader to head up yet another promotion push. This time it was Barry Fleming at Esh Winning who had been trying to go up without success for four years. Marc went to Esh and in return Cec Irwin received two tracksuits. There are no prizes for guessing who got the better of the deal. Marc led Esh to a run of fourteen games unbeaten and they duly clinched promotion. At the age of 36 Marc had convinced himself and a good many others besides that he still had what it took.

Barry Fleming started to bring in young players in an attempt to improve his squad and Marc, job done, went to play for South Shields for a second time but by his own admission it was a bad move:

> "The manager wanted to play a 3-5-2 system and in the second division of the Northern League that was absurd. You have to play 4-4-2 and scrap out results. He persisted even when we were losing week in, week out."

A 1-0 defeat at Washington was the final straw. Marc's typically unbiased opinion was that the referee had a nightmare and as he left the field told the watching chairman of the Northern League, Mike Amos, he should have a word with him. People accused Marc of swearing at Mike but common sense says that if he had he would not have been allowed to continue playing in the Northern League. The South Shields manager was not at the game so Marc rang him and told him that he wanted a move. The manager said there would be no problem and he would see him at training on the following Tuesday night. Come Tuesday and the manager said Marc was being released and when he was reminded that Marc had asked for a move four days earlier he said: "Oh aye, I forgot."

That was the end of the line at Filtrona Park and it coincided with yet another of those phone calls, this one coming from Vince Kirkup at Brandon who were second bottom of the Northern League and in need of help. Marc signed, took over as captain and led the team on a fifteen match unbeaten run:

> "Vince wanted to be everybody's friend and he needed a leader who had mental and physical toughness, as well as a positive attitude in the dressing room. It was time for some of the old Deep Heat treatment! They tried to get me back but no-one twigged that I always carried a spare pair of underpants in my bag to put on after the game. I used to empty ash trays into their sports bags so that when they got home they tipped a pile of tab ends on the floor; it was just harmless mischief and it kept the dressing room lively."

Brandon's problem was a common one; they simply did not have enough people to run the club and raise the revenue it needed to be successful. It meant that when Vince brought in three players to replace Marc while he was recovering from a hernia problem, he could not afford to play him when he was fit again, claiming that to do so would unbalance the books. However Marc did pressure Vince into playing him in a game at Whitley Bay whereupon Brandon, who had not won a game all season, beat Whitley 2-1. He played the following week at Chester le Street as well, but things were not right and he moved to Birtley Town at the start of the 2006-07 season.

Birtley have ambitions to move up to Northern League level and they have undertaken a comprehensive ground improvement scheme. They have also followed the very sensible example of previous clubs and signed Marc Irwin to lead their challenge for one of the top two places in the Wearside League which they must achieve before their application can succeed:

> "It's another challenge, so I'll see that out, help them up and maybe be able to hang up my boots and look back on my career with satisfaction. I tried to retire last year – I nailed my boots to a tree but I changed my mind and when I went back to collect them some bastard had pinched the nail."

Marc Irwin will be able to hold his head up high when he does find another nail. Seventeen red cards and countless yellow ones illustrate his do or die approach, his will to win and his hatred of defeat. He has helped teams to titles and promotions and saved them from relegation and he has rubbed shoulders with some amazing characters. Maybe none of them have been quite as crazy in the dressing rooms as Marc himself but Micky Bartlett at Spennymoor ran him close and on the pitch Ian Crumplin gave him a lot of grief:

> "He would talk about the weather or anything to try and put you off. I would get a headache and tell him to shut his hole but if you gave him half a chance the ball was in the back of the net. Dean Gibb and Micky Taylor were also top strikers who wouldn't let you settle; you knew you were going to get an elbow and they knew they were going to get a kick up the arse. Sometimes we would do each other before we went on the pitch to save all the hassle! After the game, though, it was always a pint, a laugh and some banter. Alan Shoulder was another tough player and a real character. He would chase people on the pitch with his todger and shout; "Come here, come here," but if you did the business for him as a player he made sure you were looked after."

Marc will have to make a decision about life after playing soon, and although the healthy disregard he has shown for authority throughout his career may not suggest that he has the temperament to be a successful manager, he did turn a team of Sunday morning no hopers into a winning side when he managed them at the age of 25, and with his experience and will to win, his ability to inspire belief and to motivate, it is more than likely that he could do it. If he can bring players in to a club who want to play for him he might just be very good. He recognises that it is about being able to commit the time the job demands and if he can do that he has every chance. Marc Irwin's record as a player speaks for itself; it speaks volumes and it has done for 21 years in the Northern League.

MALCOLM JAMES
Chairman of the Fed

The playing career of Malcolm James, the Chairman of Dunston Federation Football Club, had in it the seeds of the friendships which have led to Dunston becoming the very successful non league club it is today. Sunday football with Whickham Rose and Crown was the main strand; team mates included Billy Montague and Alan Stott – Alan is now Malcolm's vice chairman and Billy has for many years been one of the outstanding and best respected secretaries in the Northern League, and his efficiency has been a major factor in Dunston's recognition as probably the best run team in the league; the one which sets the standard. Malcolm also played in the Tyneside Amateur League before moving down south to work in 1971, returning six years later to play for Heaton Argyle in the Northern Combination before suffering the knee injury which forced him to call an end to his playing days.

He was then involved with Whickham Sports Club, again with Alan Stott and Billy Montague and also, significantly, with John Thompson and in 1978 he was invited to become a member of the committee. That was effectively the start of the amazing Dunston Fed story. Playing out of the Bay Horse in Whickham, the committee was for the most part also the team and they survived financially by selling pint draw tickets in the pub on Sunday evenings. They moved from Whickham down the bank to a new base at the Dunston Mechanics Social Club and played on Dunston park. The move generated an increase in interest in the team and they joined the Northern Combination League where they met with considerable success. The bulk of the players stayed with the club and as the years passed and their careers came to an end, the friendships which had grown continued to flourish as retiring players graduated to the committee in their desire to remain involved with the team.

This was unusual in the sense that traditionally, players play and committee men organise and raise funds; the roles are separate, but the bonds which had been formed among the Dunston people were strong and no-one wanted to break them, and that has been the main reason for their success and longevity as a football committee. They still socialise on a regular basis and the reputation for togetherness which has grown over the years has transmitted itself to many of the players at Dunston, who feel a great affiliation to the club and see it as much more than just another place to play football.

Dunston Mechanics evolved into Dunston Federation FC as it is now when the present ground at Federation Park was leased from Gateshead Council as a piece of fallow land which they fenced off and turned into a football ground. The ground was adjacent to the Federation Breweries which the club approached for sponsorship and the brewery agreed to a deal which involved the football club changing its name to Dunston Federation and christening its ground Federation Park. The deal was struck in 1981 and it proved to be mutually beneficial; it gave the football club a source of revenue and the brewery had the publicity factor of having its name attached to the local team and its ground. It was an arrangement which was to endure:

> "They were really brilliant with us. It was more like a friendship than a sponsorship arrangement and we had some great friends over there. Jimmy Ramshaw, sadly no longer with us, was a magnificent ambassador for the club and he did everything he could for us."

It must be said that the close relationship which was to develop between the two parties was put to the test almost at the outset. Dunston had just won the championship of the Wearside League which qualified them for promotion to the Northern League. The ink was barely dry on the sponsorship deal when club held its end of season presentation evening in the Federation Breweries and during the course of the celebrations one of the players set off the fire hose, sending foam in all directions. It made a terrible mess of the brewery boardroom and covered most of its occupants and the consequences could have been disastrous. A mortified football club committee insisted that the player involved sent a letter of personal apology to the brewery's directors and they reinforced it with one of their own, but it was hardly the most auspicious of starts to the new arrangement.

As if the fiasco of the fire hose was not enough, another catastrophe took place the same night. An arrangement had been struck that whenever Dunston Fed won a trophy it was placed on display in the Federation Breweries boardroom. It was a nice way of showing the close relationship between the brewery and the football club and it was also a sensible arrangement from a security standpoint because the breweries had excellent facilities for keeping the trophies safe. Unfortunately, when it came to the point when the Wearside League championship trophy had to be collected in order that it could be handed back to the league, it could not be found. The upshot was that Dunston Fed had to pay £500 for a replacement! The sting in the tail was that two years later when the boardroom was undergoing a refurbishment the trophy turned up in its brown wooden box behind the bar. Well, that LCL is strong stuff, after all!

There has always been a suggestion in some quarters that the Federation Breweries bankrolled the football club, but Malcolm is quick to put the record straight in that point. While the club was obviously delighted with the arrangement it had with the 'Fed' there were no blank cheques and it was a sensible business arrangement on both sides. For their own part the strength of the football club committee and their will to see the club succeed has seen them organise the region's most successful Sportsmens Dinner over many years as well as high profile fund raising nights featuring the likes of Alan Shearer and Les Ferdinand. Dunston is a football club which looks for help but which is also very good at helping itself. Success on the field has helped to attract investment as has the club's justified reputation for being very well run. Malcolm James stresses the bedrock importance of the brewery link, but believes it is important for people to be aware that aside from the single incidence of a one-off additional donation towards the cost of floodlights, the Federations Breweries, though generous, were also sensible in their financial contributions to the club.

Having a laugh as Jimmy 'Five Bellies' Gardner holds the FA Cup at Federation Park.

Welcome and indeed essential though finance is to the success of a football club like Dunston, the fact that it based on firm and solid foundations is the other principal reason for its success. Malcolm points to the stability which exists throughout the club and to the fact that as well as the long serving presence of people on the management committee, they have also had stability on the management side. When they first became Dunston Federation in 1975 John Thompson was the manager but he held the job only until the club was established. Alan Stott and Tommy Cooney were Liverpool-style boot room appointments before Peter Quigley's long and successful period of tenure, while the present incumbent, Bobby Scaife, is in his twelfth season in charge.

Dunston is also a club which has always made prudent and sensible financial management its watchword. Non league football in the North East can point to a number of clubs over the years which have found themselves in difficulties because they have existed beyond their means or been

MALCOLM JAMES - CHAIRMAN OF THE FED

unable to respond when a revenue stream has dried up. Dunston have never made the mistake of spending money they did not have and they have balanced their spending sensibly between the need to recruit and keep good players and the necessity of investing in their ground, the playing surface, drainage, the comfort of spectators and all the other components which together make a well run and successful football club. They have also been run immaculately in administrative terms with long serving secretary Billy Montague leading the way, and there is a general agreement in the area that Dunston provide the template for a properly run non league club. Malcolm is aware of the pitfalls and sympathises with the problems encountered by some clubs:

> *"I feel sorry for clubs which get into difficulties. The people who run them are almost invariably decent and honest and none of us takes any pleasure in their demise. It's simply that the income is not there and they do not have the manpower to generate it. That is where the long standing friendships that are at the heart of Dunston, and the way in which we have all bonded together, stand us in such good stead. There is also a problem in the way life in the area has changed; in particular the mining communities have gone now; they all had strong teams and it's a great shame. It's not all down to the wrong people being in charge, mostly it's to do with unfortunate circumstances."*

Dunston had to deal with a potentially threatening situation of their own when their long term sponsors the Federation Breweries sold out to the former Newcastle Breweries, the manufacturers of the famous Newcastle Brown Ale. It marked the end of an era and of a great friendship, but fortunately the new company agreed to continue the sponsorship deal, albeit at a reduced rate, on condition that the club and ground retained their 'Federation' name. This was agreed because the club felt it was in safe hands, and as the new company did not wish to include shirt sponsorship in the deal, Malcolm and his colleagues were free to make up any shortfall with new shirt sponsors. The transition therefore proved to be a smooth and amicable one.

Thus Dunston's is a continuing success story though it would be fair to say that for a club which possessed the positive range of ingredients it had, the ultimate success of winning the Northern League championship was perhaps longer in coming than it ought to have been. It was the fact that they insisted on operating within their means, progressing steadily rather than over reaching themselves by trying to buy success that made it take a little longer, but it was all the sweeter when it did come in the 2003-04 season and when they retained the title the following year.

Malcolm reinforces this point by pointing out that the budget for players was very tight in Peter Quigley's time as manager, as priority was given to improving and developing Federation Park to turn it into a worthy Northern League venue. There were good players who might well have joined Dunston if the club had been willing to exceed its budget, but they were steadfast in their determination to do things properly even if it took time. That principle still applies and while the club is relatively healthy with its combination of sponsors and self help, it still operates strictly within its means.

All smiles from Malcolm James (Chairman) and Alan Stott (Vice Chairman).

They are now one of the top teams in the region with those two Northern League titles under their belts, and people make assumptions about their willingness to invest in players, but as Malcolm says:

> *"There is more to success than buying it. Bobby Scaife built a team here to win the title but it took him eight years because it was done properly. Remember, some teams never do it; don't come close to what we have achieved. Take Tow Law Town for instance; it took them decades to win the title and they are one of the great Northern League clubs."*

The fact that Dunston have achieved championship status in itself makes it harder to sustain, because other clubs want to beat the best and they raise their game, but at the same time the two times champions take satisfaction from the knowledge that they have proved they are one of the best and have earned the admiration and respect of others. The levels of expectation have been heightened within the club itself; having proved to themselves that they can win titles their agenda now has the desire to sustain that level of achievement built in to it.

Malcolm makes another telling point that for five years Bedlington Terriers were so far in front of anyone else that no-one could touch them but during that period of unparalleled success Dunston did finish runners up to them once in 2001 and won the League Cup three times in succession. It was not under achievement so much as evidence of steady progress to the goal of winning the championship which they finally achieved in 2004.

The lesson of the sponsorship deal with Federation Breweries was that nothing stands still, and having achieved their primary ambition of winning the Northern League and then proving their quality and consistency by doing it again, Dunston and their chairman needed to address the issue of where they went from there. What level of football did they want to play at and what unfulfilled ambitions did they still harbour? High on the success wish list is the FA Vase, the national knockout competition which Northern League clubs enter. Their neighbours Whickham have won it, as have Newcastle Blue Star and Whitley Bay while Bedlington Terriers reached the final as did Tow Law Town, ironically under the managership of the former Dunston boss Peter Quigley, but success in the competition has eluded Dunston Fed. Malcolm James admits their record is disappointing:

> *"In terms of the FA Vase we have under achieved, of that there is no doubt. We have been beaten by teams we were expected to win against, though we did reach the quarter finals under Peter Quigley but lost down at Gresley Rovers. Since then, though, the nearest we have been is the last sixteen when we were beaten at home by Lymington; that was a game we should have won and our record is not impressive."*

The FA Vase is something of a Holy Grail for some local clubs but Dunston have accepted that as a knockout competition one miss, one error, one bad bounce, one wrong decision is all it takes to end your involvement. At the same time Malcolm makes it plain that success in the Vase is something which Dunston crave and strive for as hard as any other team:

> *"When we won the Northern League for the first time the euphoria was amazing and when we won the League Cup as well it was brilliant. I saw Bedlington's final at Wembley when unfortunately they lost in the last minute, and I saw Whitby win it and I thought at the time; "If that was only us!" You have to believe your turn will come and if it does this place will light up."*

The FA Vase may not have brought Dunston success, but like any other club they have had their moments on their travels in the competition. Even a club as respectable as this is not immune to outrageous experiences when the boys are away from home and one stand out incident took place when they were drawn away to Stourport and the party stayed at the Bromsgrove Hilton Hotel. They had travelled on the Friday, stayed overnight and played the Vase tie on the Saturday afternoon. Unfortunately they lost the match but they all went out on the Saturday evening for the obligatory night on the drink and returned to the hotel late. Malcolm James takes up the story:

> *"The Bromsgrove Hilton was really, really posh and we were sitting in the lounge having a nightcap. There was a big feature fireplace in the middle of the lounge and since it was November it was on. I went to bed, and the next thing I*

MALCOLM JAMES - CHAIRMAN OF THE FED

heard was the fire alarms going off. One of the young players had come down looking very pleased with himself as a result of a successful conquest of a young lady about which he started boasting. He was wearing a pair of trainers and someone took one off him and threw it on the fire. The rubber in the shoe caused smoke to engulf the lounge and the fire brigade had to be called. One of the players came down the corridor to see what was going on and he didn't have a stitch on. It was one of those situations which was hilarious at the time but really it was so irresponsible."

Young lads get into scrapes but Malcolm admits that the committee members enjoy a drink as much as anyone else, a fact which was well illustrated when Dunston were drawn away to the Cornish side St Blazey in the Vase. The late Harry Halfpenny, who was a magnificent Dunston committee man, was quiet as a rule, but when he had a few drinks he came to life. The squad were in a pub in Newquay and without warning he stood up and gave full voice to his version of 'Love is in the Air' much to the amazement and amusement of the other customers who were mostly young people and who were flabbergasted by Harry's spontaneous singing. They did not understand that it was the Fed and they had just won 5-1. If it had been the Dunston Mechanics Club nobody would have turned a hair!

Someone else who thoroughly enjoyed the St Blazey trip was the club physio Billy Thompson. Billy was a Scotsman who had previously been physio with Newcastle Blue Star when they won the FA Vase so he knew from past experience what was required on away trips. When the squad booked into their hotel on the Friday before the St Blazey tie, Billy immediately disappeared. He did not return until a couple of hours before team bus set off for the ground the next day, but when he did he had a very satisfied expression on his face.

The journey down to Cornwall was obviously a long one and it took place on a "dry" bus. There was no alcohol consumed on the entire journey or on the Friday night, but as soon as the game was over the beer started to flow. Dunston had plenty to celebrate having won the game, and their hosts provided excellent hospitality despite the disappointment of their defeat.

Dunston's lack of real progress in the FA Vase is mirrored by their experience in the FA Cup. Northern League clubs can and do win the FA Vase but they don't win the FA Cup. Their target is to reach the first round proper, pick up some decent prize money and hopefully get a big pay day against a league club. It is also about raising the club's profile through increased media attention and becoming known on the national stage. Malcolm again quotes the experience of Bedlington Terriers and the impact it had on their town and the region when they thumped Colchester United 4-1 in the first round.

Dunston committee members pose with the Northern League Cup and the championship trophy.

Despite their success over the years, including those two Northern League titles, Dunston has never succeeded in drawing large crowds. Malcolm puts this down to the fact that Dunston is not a big place, it has a modest population and it is in the shadow of Newcastle United. He does point out with some pride, though, that they have a good away following and he is also encouraged by the fact that sales of season tickets have improved year on year, providing up front income. Season ticket holders do not necessarily attend every home match and their commitment to buying a season ticket is to some degree a welcome gesture of support and a donation to the club.

Another issue Dunston have needed to consider is whether they should stick or twist as far as the level at which they play their football is concerned. The Northern League is part of a pyramid system and the opportunity exists for successful clubs to progress to the Unibond League. There are two fundamental reasons why Northern League clubs including Dunston have been reluctant to take the step up. One is finance; playing at a higher level requires a ground of a higher standard which implies additional expenditure; better players are needed so the wage bill rises, and with clubs based in places like Manchester, Sheffield, Peterborough and Leicester, transport costs escalate dramatically. The other issue is geographical. A midweek evening fixture in the Northern League might involve an hour of travelling time after the final whistle so that a player can expect to be home by 10:30. A coach journey from one of the Unibond venues is a different proposition and would turn the travel element of the game into a chore. The attraction of overnight trips down the country in the FA Vase or the FA Cup is obvious; there is an element of glamour and a possibility of glory, but it is also a one-off experience, almost a novelty, but if it was happening twice a week it would very rapidly lose its appeal. This applies especially if you are not doing very well. Driving back on a dark, wet night in February when you have just been beaten 4-1 by Colwyn Bay holds very few attractions. People involve themselves in non-league football and commit themselves in the wholehearted way that Malcolm and his colleagues have done because football is their hobby. They do it for their love of the game and because there is some fun to be had. If you take that away you diminish the experience and sap the enthusiasm.

Malcolm believes that any criticism his club or any other might receive for refusing to embrace the pyramid system is unjustified:

> *"The costs involved make it unrealistic. Clubs in this area are mostly strapped for cash and they simply cannot afford to contemplate it."*

Dunston's management duo of Bobby Scaife and Perry Briggs look on proudly as Malcolm, team captain Billy Irwin and club president John Smart display the Northern League championship trophy and the League Cup at the end of the 2003-04 season.

Dunston Fed prides itself in being a family club and their hospitality is of the best standard. Their pies, supplied by local bakery 'Superpie' are must haves and high on the list of the finest available in the league. Sometimes, too, there are unexpected fringe benefits for players and officials. When Ian Aitken, whose father was a butcher, played in goal for the Fed he was in the habit of bringing along wrap ups of meat for his team mates. Naturally, they were much appreciated, but manager Peter Quigley, who had something of a reputation for being a little squeamish, turned extremely pale when he opened his gift pack before a friendly against Spennymoor and found instead of a nice piece of steak or a couple of tasty pork chops, a blood drenched sheep's head!

The Fed have had their share of characters in their ranks

MALCOLM JAMES - CHAIRMAN OF THE FED

The 'off the field' team at Dunton parades thr clean sweep of trophies at the end of the 2003-04 season - Northern League Champions, League Cup Winners, BBC Radio Newcastle Team of the Season and Northern League Manager of the Year.

over the years. Ian Bensley was typical of those players who are massive jokers in the dressing room and very accomplished performers on the field and those kinds of players are great for team spirit. Keith Mills was another; one of the best Northern League players of modern times and one who enjoyed a pint, and occasionally needed to be poured into a taxi and sent home on a Saturday night. Keith was an exceptional player both at Blyth Spartans and at Dunston where he made a significant contribution on the field as well as to the bar receipts. Paul Hogg was another who enjoyed a pint and a laugh. He joined Dunston from Ponteland United and after a successful spell he went to Ashington but his love of the Fed saw him return to Federation Park at the start of the 2006-07 season. Dunston's claim to be a family club is borne out by the loyalty of players like these who come to regard the club as their home and it is another facet of the strength of the place.

Players can be outrageous at times, but so can committee men, even those bound by the rules of good sense and financial prudence. Founder member and former chairman John Thompson, for instance, excelled himself on a trip to Crook Town. John drove down with a couple of the players in his car and he pulled up to ask a local if he could tell him where Crook Town played. The man replied:

"I'll have to tell you where Crook is first – you're in Bishop Auckland!"

Malcolm James is a respected chairman and he is also passionate, especially on the touchline. He claims to have tempered his vitriol over the years but he has fallen foul of the football authorities on occasions. Things he has said have come out on the spur of the moment and they are not meant to be unpleasant or malicious:

"There was once a referee who checked the pressure of the balls before the game and said

they were fine, then three minutes into the match he said the ball was too soft. I reminded him that he had passed them fit three minutes earlier and he said: "Get out of the ground!" I stood at the car park gates and after the game he came into the office and said he wasn't going to report me. He said the inside temperature was higher than the outside temperature and that had effected the pressure of the match ball. I just told him he was talking bollocks, which he was. It would have been interesting to see what he put in his report if he had gone ahead with it."

The night Dunston won the league championship for the first time they were playing at Billingham and there were six minutes to play; nerves were extremely frayed and when the Billingham goalkeeper walked out of the penalty area carrying the ball, Malcolm bellowed at the referee, Russell Tiffin, to complain. Mr Tiffin shouted back: "Malcolm shut up, I've given a free kick!"

Malcolm is proud of what Dunston Fed have achieved and the professional way in which they have gone about their business. His record as a chairman is exemplary and the fine reputation of the football club is due in no small measure to his energy, drive and enthusiasm. Any success the club has achieved brings credit to a large number of people, but none more so than Malcolm James.

WILF KEILTY

Robocop meets Captain Scarlet on the way to North Shields

Tow Law Town - season 1981-82. Wilf is front row, second from the right.

As a schoolboy Wilf Keilty first demonstrated his aptitude as a footballer in an outstanding Lanchester St Bede's Grammar School side which swept the board in their part of County Durham, before graduating to Stanley Youth Centre in the town of his birth. His progress was rapid and the renowned South Moor junior side was his next port of call. South Moor was a club with a high reputation in junior football and Terry Liddell, their long serving manager, persuaded Wilf to leave the Stanley team where he was playing with his mates and join South Moor, where he linked up with some old school friends including Derek Wright who was to become the physiotherapist at Newcastle United in later years.

Wilf's growing reputation as a defensive midfield player brought him to the attention of the local scout for Arsenal who came to watch him and Derek in action, with the result that while Derek, an excellent athlete who could complete a hundred yards in less that eleven seconds, was signed by the Gunners, Wilf missed out: he impressed with his ability as a player but was judged to be too small to withstand the physical rigours of the professional game. Sadly, Derek Wright's fledgling career as a promising centre forward at Arsenal was also cut short when he suffered a serious knee injury, and he diverted to the career which was to bring him a different kind of success in the game.

41

WILF KEILTY - ROBOCOP MEETS CAPTAIN SCARLET ON THE WAY TO NORTH SHIELDS

Many of today's young players who fail to make the grade with professional clubs become disenchanted and turn their backs on the game altogether, but Wilf loved his football and although he was disappointed that the opportunity to play at the top level had eluded him he was anxious to continue playing at non-league level. The next stage in his development came when he graduated from junior to senior football and was spotted playing for a local team in the Stanley area by the legendary Billy Bell, then the Manager of Tow Law Town. He and his assistant Stuart Leeming were looking for a nursery side which could provide a source of talent for Tow Law's reserve side and they settled on the Sunday League team at New Kyo near Annfield Plain for which Wilf was playing. They took Wilf and Kevin Dixon, who later played professionally for Hartlepool United and York City, and that was the beginning of Wilf's three decades of involvement with the Northern League.

If you can play football at Tow Law you can play anywhere, in the sense that it is a bleak place in winter and it is archetypical non league:

> "We used to get really cold weather in Tow Law – in August! The practicality of just getting to the ground in the winter months was often hazardous. There were times when you drove up the roads and they were like bobsleigh tracks with six feet high snowdrifts on either side, but they were happy days. Tow Law was a lovely little club and Billy Bell was an outstanding coach."

Tow Law was the perfect place to learn what Northern League football was all about. So many good players came through Billy Bell's learning academy. In terms of how to play at that level and to cope tactically on a football pitch there was no better tutor than Billy Bell.

Wilf's departure from Tow Law came about following interest from Whickham which was not only nearer home but also had the attraction that several of Wilf's Sunday league mates from the Stanley Huntingdon pub side were playing there. He felt that the tradition and reputation of Whickham made them an attractive proposition; he also knew the manager, and it seemed a good move:

> "It was a move to warmer climes but Whickham had a slope on their pitch much as Tow Law had, so I did not have to make many adjustments!"

Wilf was only in his early twenties but he had already earned something of a reputation as an injury prone jinx which stayed with him throughout his career in which he stacked up an impressive catalogue of broken bones and limbs. However, the serious injury he sustained just a couple of weeks after joining Whickham came not as a result of some typically over-enthusiastic tackling on the field, but in a road accident:

> "I remember the day it happened distinctly. It was the day Kevin Keegan came back from Hamburg to play for Southampton, and his first game was at Sunderland. I knew nothing about the actual crash, but it happened just four games into the season. It finished me for the rest of season and at the end of it Whickham won the FA Vase!"

When Wilf was fit enough to resume, Colin Richardson had moved on the be replaced as manager by Billy Hodgson. Billy was a good lad and a sound technical coach, but he had a fetish for tea cups. If a player stepped over the line and failed to deliver to the level he expected, it was teacup time, and Wilf was a victim of the fetish on one occasion when Whickham played Tow Law. Whickham had an offside routine whereby the captain would shout the code words; "On Spelly" which was a reference to Micky Spellman and a signal for the defence to break out quickly and in unison to spring the offside trap. Unfortunately, Wilf switched off five minutes into the game and when the call of "On Spelly" came, all the defence moved out except Wilf who played six Tow Law players onside! The ball was in the net and the blame was entirely Wilf's. In the dressing room at half time he was on the wrong end of a fusillade of teacups:

> "It was like a war zone. Billy was ranting and raving like a lunatic and the teacups were whizzing past my ear. He said I had done it deliberately because I was from Stanley and I used to play for Tow Law. It's a wonder he didn't put me off tea for life."

WILF KEILTY - ROBOCOP MEETS CAPTAIN SCARLET ON THE WAY TO NORTH SHIELDS

The player Wilf enjoyed watching most and based his own game on was Bryan Robson, the former Manchester United and England captain who, like Wilf, more than compensated for his lack of height and weight with the tenacity and determination of his play. They both went in for tackles against physically bigger and stronger opponents showing no fear, sometimes to the points of recklessness. Wilf never pulled out of a challenge , but with that style of play there came a price tag; injuries were inevitable:

> "I made some crazy challenges and suffered the consequences. My team mates used to take the piss because of all my Injuries and they gave me nicknames like Robocop and Captain Scarlet. I hardly ever took the field without some part of my anatomy strapped or bandaged, but it was the way I played the game. I have broken my leg, my jaw, both of my arms, several ribs and my nose. I've damaged my medial knee ligaments; I've had the lot. It was so frustrating to miss games, and my focus was always to get back on the field as quickly as possible. I often played before I was ready and that was part of the problem."

Wilf had six seasons at Whickham; five successive years and then another year later. The FA Vase disappointment of 1981 was to repeat itself in 1984 when Whickham again made excellent progress, reaching the semi finals, then doing the hard part by drawing the away leg only to lose at home. He lays the blame for that devastating home feet very firmly at the feet of that most controversial of referees, Trelford Mills. Mr Mills was not the most popular of officials as far as North East clubs were concerned and he was fortunate to escape the wrath of the big crowd at the Glebe ground that day, many of whom were still angry from the occasion a few months earlier when his controversial decisions were perceived by the fans to have cost Newcastle United an FA Cup tie against Brighton: "The semi final was just another game for him and to be fair he gave his decisions as he saw them, but as far as I was concerned it was the biggest game of my life. It meant a helluva lot more to me than it did to him. The night before the game we were doing some light training and I was talking to our left back Keith Knox who had played in the 1981 final and he said; "You've always said how happy you are at Whickham but if we get to Wembley you will find yourself a real hot property. It will make or break your career and test your loyalty to Whickham to the limit. Instead of which Trelford Mills dropped me in it and my Wembley appearance never happened."

Of all the teams Wilf played for, the FA Vase team of 1984 contained the highest proportion of characters and head cases. They would fight and argue with each other on the field, or sing songs during matches. It was a bizarre experience:

> "There was a big crowd at the Glebe for that FA Vase quarter final and there was Keith Knox standing in defence singing Go West songs. I wondered what kind of nutters I was playing with."

Then there was Micky Spellman who was an ex-pro who could wind up anyone in the world. The number of players he got sent off and the times he was sent off himself was amazing. It was a team full of characters. Ian Diamond played in midfield and his attitude was "live by the sword, die by the sword" and he was the guvnor. Alan Barker and Billy Rafferty were both there and they helped to create the impression that Whickham was a magnet for characters:

> "We weren't a silky smooth team but we worked hard and we were a team full of daft lads – big Paul Herron up front was another one. It was great fun at Whickham."

Happy days at Whickham, but the opportunity to play at a higher level beckoned when North Shields came knocking. Shields were one of the biggest and most successful, clubs in the North East in those days and they were managed by Vic Hillier. Vic also ran a successful Sunday morning team called Winlaton West End and Wilf played against them many times for their arch rivals Stanley Huntingdon in the Derwent Sunday League. It was a standard comparable with the Northern League and Wilf's displays resulted in Vic Hillier pestering him to join North Shields. Tow Law and Whickham were lovely clubs which had given Wilf some very happy years but he felt he had to test himself with and against some better players, and he eventually bowed to Vic's pressure and signed for North Shields despite the fact that it involved more travelling. They were a consistently top six Northern League team, and having played at their Appleby Park ground on previous occasions Wilf knew he would enjoy the atmosphere and be happy playing there.

He felt a loyalty to the Whickham manager Billy Hodgson, but Billy did not stand in Wilf's way and respected his reasons for wanting to move, and so it came to be. It is easy to see why Vic Hiller would want to sign Wilf, because there were echoes of Vic's own tough and uncompromising style as a defender in his own. Wilf confesses to struggling when he first started playing for North Shields, playing in midfield where he had been so successful for Whickham. He had been a useful goalscorer as well but he had always felt that he was a better defender than he was an attacker. Vic spotted this as well and converted him into a defensive player, and Wilf believes that from being a decent midfield player he became a good Northern League defender.

Vic Hillier was a great one for a clip board and he always and he always had everyone totally organised. He took matters very seriously and was not a man who smiled a lot. Wilf did manage to get his face to crack once and to reduce the dressing room to hysterics when Vic arrived late one night for training:

> "He had been scouring the area for players and we knew he had been tracking a great player from Easington called Paul Pitman (who went on the win the Vase with Whitby). Vic came into the dressing room beaming which was an unusual sight, and said: "I've signed that Pitman from Easington." I said: "Which one was that Vic? There's hundreds of them digging for coal over there." Vic's smile faded a touch as the lads fell about laughing."

Once he settled in at North Shields Wilf was proud to play for them; they were a big club and he was enjoying his football. It must have made a special imprint on him because he is still there! After a successful run of three or four seasons the Keilty jinx reared its head again and he suffered a bad knee injury. He missed a whole season, during which time the club surprised him by resigning from the Northern League to move up to the next level in the pyramid in the North West Counties League. It turned out to be an ill considered decision and after two years of over investment in players the club was bankrupt; they lost their ground, potential investors either failed to materialise or did not deliver, and the club found itself in a perilous plight.

Wilf receives the North Shields Player of the Year trophy from club president Malcolm MacDonald at the end of the 2001-02 season.

Wilf got the phone call! He had recovered from his injury and there were local people who were trying to resurrect the club and who asked him if he could help out. So he went back in the early 1990s and played in North Shields' centenary season. The club held on by the skin of its teeth, playing out of a local pub on a parks pitch before they found their present home at Ralph Gardner Park. From the heady days of Vic Hillier, through a brief but very enjoyable spell under Jim Pearson, and through the dark years, Wilf Keilty has remained steadfast. He played regularly over the ensuing years until he reached the veteran stage, then graduated from player to player/coach and eventually to manager. It is fair to say that he did not seek any of these role changes; they just evolved through force of circumstances, particularly the manager's job. Wilf had actually helped the club to find his predecessors in the job, Terry Paddison, then a couple of lads from Peterlee.

Terry Paddison had been a good choice and he brought success to the club, but he left in frustration when the Northern League refused to allow the club to be promoted in spite of their success the Wearside League. The club's ambition was to return to the Northern League and by finishing in the top two of the Wearside they were entitled to do so. They finished runners up to Washington Nissan as well as winning two cup competitions, but their application was rejected. The following season Shields won the league and their ground matched Northern League criteria, and they were devastated to be informed that the Northern League was not accepting any new teams. It was a particularly bitter pill to swallow; the decision appeared to be an astonishing one and Shields could be forgiven for wondering whether they were being punished for their earlier defection to the NW Counties League. In the circumstances they could either throw in the towel on their Northern League ambitions or redouble their resolve. Thankfully they chose the latter course.

Nevertheless the decision defied logic and it cost Shields dearly. Terry Paddison resigned in disgust and frustration at the injustice and the whole team left. Wilf himself had stopped playing and the club was in disarray. The following season they were struggling at the bottom end of the league and the management team had been unsuccessful in its attempts either to bring players with them from the Peterlee area or to recruit locally, so once again the call went out for Wilf from club chairman Alan Matthews. Wilf took over the management of North Shields in a caretaker capacity with former players Paul Ross and Paul Hogg as his assistants and the team finished the season in the top half of the league and won a cup competition. Wilf agreed to stay on for another year and have a crack at the championship; the season was a magical one. North Shields lost just one of their thirty eight league games and romped to the Wearside League title. They were elected team of the season by BBC Radio Newcastle and they finally fulfilled their dream of returning to the Northern League, which Wilf still firmly believed they should never have left. It was the highlight of his career.

Since their promotion, their relationship with the Northern League has improved and league chairman Mike Amos has been extremely helpful and supportive. They have consolidated their place in the league and things are going well. They may be a mid table side, but they are happy to be so given their limited resources and the fact that they are playing in a tough and competitive league. The league may not be as good as it was in terms of quality teams, but the sides are well matched and there are no easy games.

Manager Terry Paddison flanked by Wilf and Ian Thompson with the Wearside League championship trophy which North Shields won in 2001-02.

As a football club North Shields has a reputation for being friendly and it has a family feel to it, and Wilf attributes this to the humbling experience of going to the brink of extinction. The people who kept the club afloat were local, old style non-league committee men, not business people or money people, and their homely feel for the club was a genuine one. They were honest local lads who did not want to see their football club, with its century old tradition, go to the wall. Their pride in the history of North Shields FC is massive and it was reflected in the 2006 reunion of the 1969 FA Amateur Cup winning team which was a wonderfully emotional and successful occasion.

North Shields' promotion team of 2003-04 were also BBc Radio Newcastle's Team of the Season.

The club is happy to milk the pride of having won the Amateur Cup, but it is not a burden that they struggle to live up to. They are proud that North Shields were the first Northumberland team to win the trophy, and rightly so, but it is not held up to the present team as the standard they are expected to reach; that would be unfair and unrealistic. Finance is a major issue for non league football in the area and North Shields receives a tiny slice of what is not a very big cake. If they can use their history and tradition to stimulate interest and generate revenue they will do so cheerfully; Wilf's budget is less than most clubs in the league and Shields have to battle hard and organise themselves well to get through on the field. Another positive factor is local pride, with local lads and long serving players in the team; the spirit is good and the mood optimistic.

Like everyone else Wilf has had to adjust to the fact of no longer being a player and he admits that in that respect managing is second best despite the satisfaction and success it has brought him:

"There is no substitute for playing. Once your lose your playing days nothing can replace them, but managing is the next best thing. The frustration you feel on match days on the touch line is awful. I came into it by default but I have become used to it and it gives me satisfaction but it is not like playing. I keep going because I don't want to let the lads down and there is also the pleasure of pitting your wits against the other teams and managers. It is an enjoyable challenge and I don't pick up injuries as a manager like I did as a player!"

One of the major plusses at North Shields is the presence at the club of their President, Malcolm MacDonald, the former Newcastle United hero. Malcolm still has a high profile on Tyneside through his media work and he is a busy man, but he takes his responsibilities very seriously and gives them real commitment:

"Supermac has been magnificent for us. He has never once let us down, whether it has been for a presentation, a fund raising event, or to meet the kids and sign autographs His commitment to the club and to my testimonial year in particular has been wonderful. We would not have reached our target without him, and he also brought Eric

> Gates along on several occasions. They never asked for a penny and I cannot praise them highly enough. He has been supportive in so many ways and it is so refreshing for an ex-player to put things back into the game at grass roots level. Very few of them do it and maybe because of his own humble beginnings in the game it means more to Malcolm, but he has been and still is superb in his support for North Shields."

The most recent highlight of Wilf Keilty's long association with North Shields Football Club came in 2006 when he was granted the above mentioned testimonial. His long and selfless service to the club made it an honour well deserved but Wilf took the decision that it offered him an opportunity to raise money for good causes rather than his own bank balance. He took his example from Niall Quinn whose testimonial at Sunderland raised a million pounds for charity, and Wilf set himself the target of generating £10,000:

> "I had been in non league football for over thirty years and I felt it should be marked in some way so I spoke to the committee and explained my thinking that Niall Quinn had set a marvellous example, but I knew of no-one in local football at our level who had done anything similar. This seemed like a good opportunity and the committee supported me. Alan Shearer did the same thing of course, but he came after me so I was his inspiration!"

The four charities which Wilf chose to support were Cancer Research, Meningitis Research, The British Heart Foundation and the Royal National Lifeboat Institution. His feeling was that they were great causes and everyone who was being asked to help and support would have been touched by one of them at some point in their lives. The target of £10,000 was set and at the end of the testimonial year a presentation night was held: Wilf reached his target thanks to a top up donation of £800 by his employers EDS and each of the four charities received their cheques on the night.

In some respects that magnificent achievement, coming as it did at the culmination of three decades in the Northern League, seemed a logical high note on which Wilf could end his career, and certainly his wife Keira made the point, ticking off his many achievements – the League and Cup double with North Shields as a player, a coach and a manager, and his hugely successful testimonial year itself. She had a point and Wilf did give it some thought, but he found reasons to stay because the club is in his blood and he feels there are still targets to be reached. He may make the decision to step down as manager in the not too distant future but he still talks in terms of going on to help the club with fund raising and ground improvements, so it looks as though Keira will have to do the weekend shopping on her own for a few years yet.

Wilf believes the game is there to be taken seriously but he also sees the value of humour to prick the mood when things are not going so well. There was an occasion recently when the team had played poorly and lost so Wilf decided that some light hearted punishment was called for. At home games he has the board up in the dressing room to discuss tactics and plan set pieces, after which he names the team. He has the best of attention because everyone in the squad wants to know if they are playing. Wilf is 48, Paul Hogg is 47 and Paul Ross is 39:

> "I told them that after their previous performance I needed to make changes and that I would be at number four, Paul Hogg would be number five and Paul Ross would be number six because I wanted to play three at the back and go for experience! The players bought it hook, line and sinker and there was a deathly silence until I told them I was joking. Then I told them that if they performed as badly again the joke would be on them. That broke the ice, the banter started and the players got the message."

Some of the most memorable incidents take place on end of season trips away and a couple of seasons ago North Shields had a trip to Edinburgh. The players were staying at the Heriot Watt University which was a fair distance from the station by taxi. Two of the younger players, Micky Kelly and Ian Dugdale, decided they would have no nonsense from any Edinburgh taxi driver and Ian said; "We know it's a canny way and we'll give you fifteen quid and not a penny more." The driver looked a bit sheepish but he agreed. When they reached the university there was £12 on the meter. Well negotiated Micky!

As well as playing for Whickham on Saturdays Wilf enjoyed a very successful Sunday morning career, playing at a good standard principally for the Stanley Huntingdon pub team:

> "The thing about the Huntingdon was that the manager of the team was a bloke but the person who really ran it was a woman. She was the manager of the pub which was a big concern with a restaurant, disco and so on, and she put decent money into the team. Her name was Brenda Thompson and she came to the games – though she never came into the dressing room! She was mad keen and she looked after her boys, but she had a ruthless streak. Our manager was an ex-pro called Gordon Carroll and we'd had a couple of ropey results; we were travelling back after one of them and I was in a car with the senior committee men and Brenda. She said; 'This isn't good enough. We're going to have to change the manager,' and one of the lads in front said; 'We'll have to set up a meeting and consult the committee.' Brenda said: 'I am the ******* committee.' They changed the manager! Brenda was a lovely woman and a class act."

There was no margin for error. The standard was good and the players were looked after but success was demanded in return. It was like playing for Real Madrid. Expectation was that you won every game, and three defeats in a row spelt the end of the road. One of the committee was a chap called Brian Richardson whose nickname was Giggles. Wilf had never known why he was called Giggles until he was on the bench for a game against their arch rivals Winlaton West End from which they needed a point to win the league. With five minutes left of the match Davie Johnson scored for Winlaton and Huntingdon were a goal down. Giggles turned to Wilf in the dugout and said: "That's it, we've lost the ******* league." Then he started to giggle like a machine gun. The poor soul could not contain his nervous laugh, and if the Huntingdon lads had not known about his affliction the sound of him laughing as their chance of winning the league disappeared could have landed him in a great deal of bother.

Wilf played hard and he has great regard for the people he played against who were his worthiest opponents. In terms of ability he would rate Bobby Scaife as the best and those who saw him would find it hard to disagree. There was Dean Gibb who was ruthlessly strong, Steve Pyle, a great striker who always kept you on your toes. Top ex-professionals tend not to come into the non league game at the end of their careers nowadays, but Wilf had the pleasure of playing against Frank Worthington and Stan Cummins and has great admiration for both. Willie Moat was always a handful and Kevin Dixon was an amazing player at Tow Law. He would play on Saturday afternoon, have fifteen pints in the evening, and play for Stanley Huntingdon on a Sunday as if he had iron lungs. Robbie Carney was also at Tow Law and Wilf rates him as such a good player that whenever he was in your team you did not feel you could lose. He has also taken things on board from the different managers he has played for (Billy Bell, Billy Hodgson, Jim Pearson, Terry Paddison), and found that a great help in moulding his own managerial career:

> "I was always lucky with managers and I hope some of their wisdom has rubbed off on me."

Wilf Keilty's story is one of love of the game, playing on the limit, enduring the pain of injury and the disappointment of missing out on the FA Vase. It is about the pleasure of learning from top managers and the satisfaction of achievements as a player, a coach and a manager. A story of pleasures and pains with every prospect of more of each still to come his way.

STEVE PREEN

Frosty the Snowman

Steve Preen is a Newcastle lad, born and bred in the West End of the city, and like so many Tyneside youngsters he nurtured a boyhood dream to play centre forward for Newcastle United. He never realised that dream but he has carved out a very successful career for himself as a centre forward in local non league football. It all began when he was playing under thirteen football for Montagu and North Fenham Juniors where his manager was John Carver, later to become Head Coach under both Ruud Gullit and Sir Bobby Robson at St James's Park:

> "I was absolutely terrified of him; he was a right monster, but he got the best out of us and it was great."

From Montagu he moved the short distance to West Denton Juniors where he began to collect winners medals and earn a reputation for himself as a prolific goalscorer. By the time he was sixteen he was introduced to senior football two years ahead of his time when he started to play for his father's favourite watering hole, the Slatyford Tenants Association, in the "D" division of the North East Sunday League:

> "That was where I first began to see some sights. There would be players we picked up from houses which were not their own, and others would be throwing up on the sidelines before we kicked off with the after effects of the previous night's drinking. It was a real eye opener."

Steve's nickname was Frosty because of his fair complexion and the fact that the sun bleached the hairs on his arms and legs white, and even though he was still a youngster he has allowed to go on the Slatyford team's end of season trip to Blackpool:

> "We turned up at the Tower lounge on the Friday after drinking eight cans of beer on the journey down. There was a karaoke going on and I heard my name called out. I got up on the stage and told the woman in charge that I couldn't sing, but she said I was on my own and they started to play "Frosty the Snowman." I was seventeen years old and I had to sing in front of nearly a thousand people in the Tower lounge. My voice had just broken and I had never sung at a karaoke in my life. I was absolutely petrified but I had to get on with it. I was not very good, but I was accepted as one of the lads after it."

Steve and his mates, who had been together since their schooldays and formed a strong bond, moved together to Morpeth Under 19s in the North Northumberland League. A "lovely old fella" called Geordie Bowey and his pal Derry Brown invited them to Morpeth and it was a big step because this was a Saturday league for senior players. However, the standard was modest and Steve was able to handle the extra physical element with such success that he finished the season as the league's leading scorer with sixty goals. The team won both the league and the league cup and were the beaten finalists in the Northumberland Minor Cup, which was a remarkable achievement for a new team packed with youngsters. Despite their initial success, however, the team disbanded, though they did undergo something of a reincarnation when Davie Huntley brought virtually the whole team together again to play for Manors Social Club in the NE Sunday League and they had great success, progressing through the leagues to the Premier Division before Steve moved to Lemington Social Club where he met up with Dean Gibb who taught him how to use his elbows! Before he left, Manors won the Sunday Summer Cup and his joy at their triumph almost had serious repercussions for the youthfully exuberant Mr Preen. It happened that John

Cummings, the League secretary and a member of the Northumberland FA council, was there to present the trophy to the winners and when the final whistle blew Steve ran over in celebration and jumped on John. Unfortunately John collapsed under the pressure and damaged his knee ligaments. Davie Huntley realised that there could be dire consequences and he immediately orchestrated a whip round among the players to buy John a bottle of whisky to ease the pain! Steve was required to write a letter of apology but he was too afraid to deliver it himself so Davie Huntley went to John's house with the letter and the whisky and apologised on his behalf. Poor John Cummings was in such a state of pain and distress that he was unable to come to the door and he was bedridden for two weeks!

Steve found himself sought after by Morpeth Town who were playing in the second division of the Northern League. He signed for Morpeth and to his surprise found himself playing right midfield, but despite being out of position he chipped in with fifteen goals and a successful season ended with Morpeth being promoted to the first division:

> "Being young and daft and not lacking in confidence, I decided to get my hair shaved down to the bone for the first game of the season. I was really hyped up for my debut which was against Darlington RA away from home. We were warming up on the side of the pitch before the game and I was dying for the toilet so I just had a wee on the corner of the pitch. Just before the game was about to start the referee took out his notebook and said: 'Baldy, come over here.' He took my name and sent me to the dressing room to fetch a bucket of water and a brush. While everyone was watching I had to swill the pitch; I was probably the only player to be booked before a game started and I still get stick about it to this day."

Whitley Bay were playing in the Unibond League at this stage and Steve signed for them because he wanted to play at the highest level of which he was capable, but he found the extra travelling involved to be a chore and it interfered with his social life, so after a month at Hillheads he returned to the Northern League to join manager Warren Pearson at Tow Law. It was there that he began to establish a reputation as a goalscorer in the Northern League and to attract the physical attention of opposing central defenders. He linked up with Trevor Laidler, an outstanding striker who had been the league's leading scorer the previous season. His team mates Keith Moorhead, Darren Darwens, Micky Bailey and Trevor were all Newcastle based lads and they travelled to Tow Law together. They formed a firm bond of friendship and Steve thoroughly enjoyed his time at the Ironworks ground.

He was just twenty years old and still learning his trade. The defenders took no prisoners and there was a game at Billingham in which a player grabbed his private parts really tightly; Steve thought the appropriate response was to smack him in the face, and the referee sent him off. He was given a sixty five days suspension for violent conduct:

> "The dressing rooms at Tow Law were very tight and it was common practice to piss on the backs of the legs of your team mates in the showers. It was just part of the camaraderie and I believe that is an important part of what makes a successful team."

He got his first taste of the FA Vase at Tow Law. They were a good side with a league championship under their belts which underlined their pedigree, and they fancied their chances in the Vase. They were drawn away to Brigg Town who were one of the favourites for the competition, and they beat them 3-1 with Steve among the scorers, though he admits that despite scoring and being voted Man of the Match he does not remember the match as vividly as he does the coach journey home:

> "It was the usual tale of people drinking, taking their clothes off and running up and down the bus. Keith Moorhead set my pubic hairs and chest hair on fire. I think he scarred me for life emotionally as well as physically! We'd had a good drink when the bus dropped us off, and I dived on Micky Bailey in my excitement. He fell over and cracked his head on the pavement, damaged his shoulder, and was out injured for three weeks!"

Tow Law did not win the Vase, though they did reach the final in a subsequent season under Peter Quigley. Meanwhile, Mattie Pearson, a good friend who was in charge at Spennymoor, came in and persuaded Steve to move to the Brewery Field, though when he signed he neglected to tell Mattie that he was serving a 65 day suspension:

> "Mattie was a hard, old fashioned boss; he was a great man manager and probably the best manager I've had. He knew I was inclined to be hot headed and he made it clear that I could not be successful if I could not control myself. He probably moulded me into the player I am today."

Steve was not overawed by the step up from Tow Law to Spennymoor; he took it in his stride and thoroughly enjoyed it. His growing maturity as a player and his continuing ability to score goals brought him the opportunity of a trial with Hartlepool United who offered him a part time contract, but Hartlepool were short of money and the offer was not attractive enough to tempt Steve to give up his full time job.

He was enjoying his time at Spennymoor, but when Mattie Pearson left to join Gateshead he wanted to go with him. The new Spennymoor manager was Colin Richardson and he phoned Steve the day he returned from holiday and told him he was required to play in a friendly against Newcastle Reserves even though he had arrived home at four in the morning and was not really mentally or physically prepared:

> "It was a boiling hot day and there was a packed house. There was a lot of expectation. Anyway, I played and scored and we drew 2-2, but it was my swansong and I moved to Gateshead. I had no problem with Colin who was great about it. He had a fearsome reputation and a fantastic aura in the dressing room. I remember at half time in one game he told a young centre half to get changed, pick up his boots and **** off! Colin didn't mess around but I found him to be a nice bloke and he didn't bear me any resentment."

Gateshead was the club where Steve Preen came into his own as a player and a scorer of goals. He scored seventy times in a hundred and fifty appearances. He loved the football club and formed a great affinity with the supporters as well as having a great relationship with the other players in the team. He also had the honour of captaining the side, which included Paul Proudlock and Kenny Lowe, two truly outstanding non league players. He also formed close friendships with centre half Sam Kitchen, Steve Bowey, Gareth McAlindon and Paul Thompson; all quality players. After away matches Gareth McAlindon's father had the unenviable job of picking them up and taking them home after their beer drinking sessions on the team coach and central to those homeward journeys was the Gateshead chairman John Gibson, a man for whom Steve has enormous regard and respect:

> "There were no Big Time Charlies at Gateshead and the crack on the bus was great. John Gibson would bring the cans of LCL and we made it a point of honour that they were all empty by the time we reached Gateshead."

Going for goal at Gateshead.

STEVE PREEN - FROSTY THE SNOWMAN

One of the real characters at Gateshead was their long serving physio Bev "Safe Hands" Dougherty, the only physio in the business who did not give players rubs and a man who took a genuine delight in inflicting pain. For example, Steve's mate Gareth McAlindon was suffering from a dead leg and Bev, sadist that he was in Steve's view, gathered all the players around to watch while he treated the problem:

> *"He was grinding his fingers into the bruise and the sweat was pouring out of Gareth. Bev kept us there while Macca screamed in pain; we were loving it, but not as much as Bev."*

He had two good seasons at the International Stadium before he had the chance to link up once more with his old boss Warren Pearson who was now a fitness coach at Queen of the South, who were managed by John Connolly. It was an opportunity to test himself again at a higher level and he had the pleasure of playing on one of the best surfaces he had come across at Palmerston Park. Things were going well; he liked the place and the people, but after playing ten games Steve broke his thumb and the injury, coupled with a certain amount of homesickness, caused him to have second thoughts, so he rejoined Gateshead and by the time he was fit again the Tynesiders were due to meet Billingham Town in the fourth qualifying round of the FA Cup. Steve scored after just eighty seconds to give Gateshead a flying start and to get his second spell at the club underway in spectacular fashion. Gateshead won the game and were drawn away against Cambridge United in the first round proper. Unfortunately a sending off against Telford meant that Steve was suspended for the Cambridge match which was a massive one for Gateshead. His only contribution was to make his radio debut as the match summariser for BBC Radio Newcastle's coverage of the tie. It was a poor consolation for missing out on a career highlight, and his manager's strategy for keeping his madcap antics under control was calculated to ensure that he did not interfere with the team's pre-match preparations:

> *"Mattie Pearson knew what a jumpy jack I was and he didn't want me anywhere near the players. The night before the game he actually paid for a taxi to take two of us who were not playing, plus the physio, into Cambridge town centre for a drink away from the hotel where the lads were staying. We had an eleven o'clock curfew; Mattie was taking no chances, but we still lost 1-0 to a disputed goal."*

The disappointment of missing out on the Cambridge game was relieved the following season when the club had another successful cup run and Steve was able to enjoy what he regards as the highlight of his career. Gateshead played at Halifax in the first round proper and won 2-0 with Steve playing his part by getting the Halifax centre half sent off!

> *"They treated us badly. They stuck us in a portakabin because they were refurbishing their stand and at half time they sent us to this mouldy old gym under the stand. We had a small pot of tea between the lot of us, and we were really pissed off so we went out and murdered them in the second half. It was a great career highlight for me. Absolutely brilliant."*

The win saw Gateshead paired with Swindon Town in the second round – another massive tie for the club. The trappings of success for a non league club in the FA Cup accompanied them; the trophy itself was brought to Gateshead for a photo shoot, there was increased media interest, and the mood was euphoric in the build up. The players had an early night before the game, with Steve and Steve Bowey rooming together as usual and everyone fearful of what antics they might get up to. One of the key players in the side was Paul Thompson:

> *"Paul was one of the clumsiest people ever. If we were playing cards on the bus you could see his hand without him knowing. He would drop his cards, spill drinks. One day he was having treatment on the coach and he leaned back and burned his backside on the hot drinks dispenser. We played at Queen of the South in a pre-season friendly and he bust his nose; he came off and went to sit in the dugout. He stotted his head off the dugout roof and split his eye open! I always made sure I was on the opposing team in five a sides because if I was on his team he would run into me, kick me or knock me over. He was such a clumsy man."*

STEVE PREEN - FROSTY THE SNOWMAN

After their early night the players had breakfast and as they boarded the team bus John Gibson approached Steve and demanded to know why there were three bottles of champagne and eight bottles of Budweiser on his room bill. He protested his innocence and later discovered that Phil Ross, who was suspended, and Bev Dougherty the physio had put their drinks on his bill. Steve paid the bill and he is still waiting to get his money back.

They finally reached the Swindon ground, and the atmosphere was remarkably relaxed. Steve admits he was more worried about getting the complimentary tickets he had promised to his friends than he was about the game. It was the biggest match of his career, demanding full concentration, and forty five minutes before the kick off he was running around chasing tickets he had promised his mates! Sadly, when matters did get underway Gateshead were beaten by four superb Swindon goals despite an outstanding display by their goalkeeper Adrian Swan. Once again, the most memorable moments came from the journey home; an integral part of the pleasure and the experience of big games like FA Cup and FA Vase ties:

"We were somewhere near Leicester when the bus broke down. What with drowning our sorrows after the match, we had all had a good skin full by this time. We had broken down at this service station and Steve Bowey and I were using traffic cones as megaphones to belt out songs. We pulled over this local bus and gave the driver a pound a head to take us to the nearest pub. There was a wedding on and Mark Donnelly asked if we could go in. We were made welcome and told we could get stuck into the food which was left over from the reception. Being footballers we demolished the food, then we took over the karaoke. John Gibson was singing Vindaloo on the stage and we had a great time, but after about three hours I was called outside by clumsy Paul Thompson because Wayne Edgecumbe had been making his mouth go. He tried to hit Mattie and smacked Thommo in the mouth before I calmed things down. Eventually, at five o'clock in the morning, a replacement bus arrived from Durham and we ended up sleeping on the bus floor and getting home at eight o'clock in the morning."

It was a great season for Gateshead and it ended with the customary trip away, this time to Edinburgh. Steve and Steve Bowey decided to liven things up in the quiet little bar they were in, so they went to the toilets where Steve took off his clothes, put his shoes back on and ran through the bar. He had toilet roll stuck up his backside which Bowey had lit, so this fearful sight of Steve Preen, naked and running at full tilt through the bar with flames coming out of his backside, greeted the locals. Then he ran out of the bar and up the street, to the consternation of the good people of Edinburgh. Later in the afternoon they pitched up at another pub where a group of rugby fans were watching an important end of season match in the television. Steve pinched the tv remote and switched the football channel on before hiding it down the back of Mattie Pearson's chair. The rugby lads were not best pleased and while the arguments were going on Bowey and Preen sneaked off to the pub up the road!

The downside of Steve Preen's career came when he broke his leg. Mattie Pearson had left Gateshead and Paul Proudlock had taken over with Gary Gill as his assistant. Steve had scored nineteen goals before Christmas and he was the league's leading scorer when he broke his leg against Altrincham. Actually, he took a whack on the leg and went off, but played against Runcorn the following week in the FA Cup. He was experiencing some pain but was unaware of the extent of the injury, but as he had a shot late in the first half he felt a numb sensation in the leg. It transpired that he had nicked the bone in his fibia in the Altrincham game and extended the break against Runcorn so that he finished up with a spiral fracture of the fibia; he was a victim of his own enthusiasm.

Paul Thompson, being the nice lad he is, was an early visitor as Steve began his rehabilitation:

"He came to the house with an armful of Kit Kats and Greggs cream cakes. I was lying on the floor with my leg out to one side and Thommo had orders to stay away from me because of his legendary clumsiness. He had backed this horse

so we switched the racing channel on; his horse won and as he jumped up the celebrate he kicked my toe. The leg was nicely on the mend but he put my recovery back three weeks. He volleyed my toe and I was in absolute agony. What a clumsy bloke."

The following season big things were expected. Gateshead had signed Steve Agnew and the pre-season had gone well, but the actual season began poorly with goals hard to come by. Disappointing results on the field were followed by disaster off it when the club's long time sponsor, Cameron Hall, brought their deal to an abrupt halt which caused massive problems for the club. John Gibson resigned and although a rescue package was put in place to keep the club afloat, things were not the same and Steve felt he had to leave:

"I was very reluctant; it was heartbreaking, but I couldn't see where the club was going and Tony Lee persuaded me to join Spennymoor."

Winning a heading duel for Blyth Spartans.

Steve left the International Stadium after four and a half happy years and took with him some wonderful memories, especially from derby matches against Blyth Spartans. He remembered winning 2-0 at Croft Park on Boxing Day for instance, to go top of the league, and the atmosphere at the Blyth ground for those derby clashes was always electric. He actually had a brief spell as a Spartans player, but his heart was always with Gateshead.

Spennymoor has been a club with a chequered recent history and the signs did not look promising when, no sooner had Steve signed for them than Tony Lee fell out with the chairman, Benny Mottram. However, Jason Ainsley took over and he brought in his pal Jamie Pollock. Jamie's professional experience proved to be invaluable and he turned the club around. He had a policy of rotating his three strikers which Steve was not very happy about, but the team went on a remarkable run of twenty eight matches without defeat and from being in mid table at Christmas they finished runners up. It was a tremendous achievement and it brought with it promotion. Then came another twist with Jamie Pollock falling out with the chairman and Tony Lee returning. Steve stayed for another season before Paul Baker, who had taken over at Blyth Spartans, persuaded him to go to Croft Park. His pal Gareth McAlindon was there and the pre-season went very well but unfortunately things failed to work out. Results were disappointing, Paul Baker left and Harry Dunn was brought in. Steve felt that Blyth would continue to struggle so he followed Gareth to Bedlington Terriers and so returned to the Northern League:

"Tony Lowery had been trying to sign me for Bedlington for about ten years and eventually I signed. I met Keith Perry and I liked him instantly. He did everything he could to look after the lads. It was also a reunion with Sam Kitchen and Dean Gibb. Dean is an absolute gem and a great player I admire hugely. Dean used to pick me up for games and we would have our own team talk on the way."

In management terms, the system at Bedlington was that Tony Lowery looked after tactics and Keith Perry was the motivator. Keith's dressing room style is unique and certainly Steve Preen had encountered nothing like it.

Celebrating victory for Bedlington over AFC Newbuury in the FA Vase at Welfare Park.

Bedlington had been very unlucky last minute losers in the FA Vase Final at Wembley in 1999 and from that point the Vase had become almost an obsession with the club. They desperately wanted to win it and when they reached the quarter finals in 2005-06 the whole place was buzzing:

> "Keith's team talk was one of the best I've ever heard. He told us we were gladiators, then he brought out a bowl of eggs. He said we were metal and they were soft like eggs, and he was smashing the eggs off the floor. He had us right up for it and we won 2-1. We stayed in Bedlington that night and you would think we had won the Cup. I got home at five in the morning. Sam had fallen out with his wife so I told him he could stay the night with me and when I had brushed my teeth and went to bed there was Sam next to my wife. Thankfully she was asleep!"

The subsequent FA Vase semi final was a heart wrenching affair. The Terriers were drawn against the favourites, AFC Sudbury, and they did the hard part by drawing the first leg away from home. Back at Welfare Park they had numerous chances to kill the tie off, but had to settle for a draw. They hit the crossbar, and in the dying minutes Steve turned his man and fired in a shot which hit the inside of the post and rebounded into the arms of the goalkeeper, who knew nothing about it. The game went to penalties and the Sudbury spot kick which won it was topped by the penalty taker and bounced three times before in crossed the line. The fates were desperately unkind to Bedlington that day.

The following season the Terriers reached the quarter finals again, and played Sudbury again. They were leading 1-0 when goalkeeper Marc Riches conceded a penalty from which Sudbury scored to take the game to a replay. To be fair, Sudbury were too good for Bedlington when the teams met at Welfare Park and once again their FA Vase dream was shattered. Worse lay ahead. Despite a battling league performance which saw them finish as runners up, the club was brought to its knees by a series of major administrative and financial disasters and only an eleventh hour rescue package by local businessman and former Terriers reserve team player Graeme Redpath kept the club alive. It was a sad chapter in the history of the club which had been incomparably the best in non league football in the North East for a decade. Managers Tony Lowery and Keith Perry, the committee and all the players left and long serving stalwart Mel Harmison began the very difficult task of restoring the club's fortunes.

On the bball for Bedlington Terriers.

Steve joined another top Northern League club, Dunston Federation at the start of the 2006-07 season at which point he was 31 years old. A red card in a pre-season friendly against Workington was not the most auspicious of beginnings but a typically committed and battling performance the following week in a splendid Dunston win over Newcastle Blue Star in the final of the Cleator Cup showed the Dunston fans what they were getting. Wherever he has played he has given 100% every time he has taken the field and he will continue to do so.

Steve has not gazed into the crystal ball to see what his future might be when his playing days are over. At 31 he still has a few seasons left in him at the top level of the Northern League, though he has given up on his Sunday morning football:

"I get up on Sunday mornings now and rigor mortis sets in, so I have to concentrate on Saturdays."

He may go into management, but knowing Steve and the type of character he is, he might be better suited to a role as Entertainments Manager, organising functions and keeping the dressing room lively in the Dean Gibb mould. He has some experience of the job from his brief time at Blyth Spartans where he was given the responsibility of organising the Christmas night out. He decided to make it a strippers night and kit man Tony Kennedy was given centre stage:

"Harry Dunn, the manager, knew I was daft and refused to come! We decided we would tie little Tony up for the strippers; he was all for it and he was tied to a chair in his string vest and pants. We blindfolded him and before they came on I went on stage wearing just my underpants. I started rubbing myself against him and he was loving it. I got this big bottle of baby oil from one of the girls and I was rubbing it into his body while he was moaning in ecstasy. We had it all on video and everyone was in hysterics. How he didn't know it was a bloke I will never know. Tony's a brilliant fellow and he took it all in good part."

So if you are looking for a modest and respectable night to celebrate Christmas, Steve Preen might just be your man!

KEVIN WOLFE

Captain Condom, a Mexican road sweeper and the odd psychopath

Sunderland Boys 1980-81. Kevin is second right on the front row with David Corner fourth from the left in the back row and Gary Porter second from the left in the front.

It was not Kevin Wolfe's idea to be a goalkeeper. He realised that his lack of pace prevented him from becoming a winger or a striker but his size suggested he had the potential to make a decent central defender. His teacher at Farringdon Junior School in Sunderland had other ideas:

> "He was a dear old bloke and he just said: "Wolfe, you're in goal. I attended a practice and he made the decision for me, though it turned out pretty well actually. I began by playing for my year at school and the next season I was nominated for the Sunderland Boys team and was selected."

It was a successful Sunderland schoolboys team and he vied for the goalkeeper's shirt with a boy called Alan Hope who went on to play for Sunderland AFC before retiring through injury. Gary Porter, who had a long career with Watford, was in the same side as well as David Corner, another who graduated to Sunderland's first team. Kevin's advance from primary to secondary school saw him selected for the town side again at Under 14 level, again competing with Alan Hope for his place in the side. Alan impressed to such an extent that he was chosen to play for England schoolboys, a development which, ironically, worked to Kevin's advantage, because the following season young Hope broke his finger on England duty and Kevin had the Sunderland

KEVIN WOLFE - CAPTAIN CONDOM, A MEXICAN ROAD SWEEPER AND THE ODD PSYCHOPATH

Boys goalkeeping position to himself as they reached the final of the English Schools Trophy competition. The first leg was played at Wycombe Wanderers ground and resulted in a 1-0 defeat while the second, a goalless draw, took place at Roker Park in front of a crowd of nearly 15,000. It was Kevin's first significant career highlight because the competition was the schoolboy equivalent of the FA Cup and as a Sunderland supporter, making an appearance at Roker Park was an extra joy for him. The Football Association, mindful of the susceptibilities of young footballers, had both sets of medals engraved with the word FINALISTS so as not to distinguish between winners and losers. Kevin gave the medal to his late father who treasured it, and it is now back in his possession; it is the only one of his medals he still has.

Kevin's prowess as a goalkeeper brought him to the attention of several professional clubs, and he had trials at Notts County, Luton Town, Ipswich Town, Sheffield United, Sunderland, Hartlepool and Darlington. He had realistic hopes of becoming a full time professional but despite all those trials it never quite happened for him; he was never offered an apprenticeship. So, he accepted his fate and took up an apprenticeship of a different kind as a sheet metal worker with Coles Cranes. While he was there he played for the company's youth team which had great success, sweeping the board in the area. He was spotted and given the opportunity to turn out for Darlington Reserves who played in the Northern League, and he made his debut as a sixteen year old.

"The call came from the manager, Cyril "Nice One" Knowles. He was the scariest man I have met in my life. I remember when I played my second game for the Reserves against Northallerton Town. The first team had lost their previous match and as a punishment he stuck most of them in the Reserves. I was just a kid and I was lining up with the likes of John Craggs, Kevin Todd, Bob Lee who had cost Sunderland £250,000 and Peter Johnson who had played for both Middlesbrough and Newcastle. I had a decent game and I was sitting in the dressing room afterwards when somebody said that Cyril wanted to see me and I was embarrassed because I had been up to no good the night before and I was covered with love bites! The lads were in hysterics, but he was OK about it. That game opened my eyes up; there are players who think they are hard but this bloke was in a class of his own. He was totally fearsome and I have never experienced anything like it. In later years I got to realise what a nice guy he was but he terrified the life out of me that night."

Kevin actually made one first team appearance for Darlington in 1985 in what was to be the biggest game of his career in the League Cup against Rotherham United, but that was the sum of his experience at that level and he soon moved on to join Newcastle Blue Star who were then a Wearside League team and managed, in Wolfie's words, by:

"Another psychopath, Colin Richardson, and you don't need to put that in inverted commas because he was!"

He went to Blue Star initially to help Colin out as cover for probably the best goalkeeper in non league football at the time or since in Tony Harrison. Kevin learned a tremendous amount about the job from Tony who has always made himself available when help or advice was needed. Despite Tony's presence at the Wheatsheaf ground Kevin did manage to play a fair number of games for Blue Star and they reached the first round proper of the FA Cup where they met York City. Unfortunately, with Denis Smith as their manager and players of the calibre of Keith Houchen in their line up, York proved to have too much for Blue Star and won the game 2-0:

"Newcastle Blue Star were a good team and they had a very large lunatic fringe. The king of the lunatics himself, Ian Crumplin, was there. Many a time I would go home with stuff in my bag that he had hidden – pint glasses, meat pies, plates, you name it, he put it there. Every night at training he would cut holes in your socks or cut your ties in half; he was a total idiot. Having said that, I have never seen a goalscorer like him. The

> *nearest would be Gary McDonald as a goal poacher but even he was not nearly as consistent as Crumpy."*

There were good players, proper players, at Blue Star like Crumplin, Brian Magee and Phil Leaver (another on Wolfie's psychopath list, but one who could really play). Unfortunately Kevin was not playing as regularly as he wished and so he move on in search of more opportunities and joined Seaham Red Star in the Northern League where his time, although it was again relatively brief, was extremely eventful. One of his team mates was the legendary Dean Gibb, an outstanding striker and a complete lunatic:

> *"Dean Gibb is a first class idiot. I first new him when we went on trial to Ipswich as kids when Bobby Robson was in charge. They put us up at this naval base called the Ganges which was about twenty miles from the town centre and there was nothing to do. All they had for amusement was these space invaders and my first experience of Dean was watching him taking the backs off them to get the money for free goes When we were together at Seaham, we were doing this passing and shooting drill in training one night which involved a pass, a lay off, a cross to the far post and someone running in to try and head the cross past me in to the net. It was a wet and muddy night and we were training behind the goal, which was like a cow pat. This cross came over and there was Dean Gibb charging in to meet it without a stitch on. Everyone was in fits of laughter and he dived and headed the ball past me. Obviously, I was distracted! He's a total idiot."*

One night Kevin and his wife to be (from whom he is now divorced!) were taking in the news that she was pregnant as they enjoyed a night out with Billy Cruddas, with whom he played for Dunston Social on Sunday mornings, and his wife. They were in Dunston Club and as they had no match the following day because of heavy snow, Kevin got home slightly the worse for wear and went straight to bed. His mother called up the stairs to tell him there was someone on the telephone for him from New Zealand; he thought it was a wind up by one of his mates but he eventually got out of bed and took the call:

> *"It was a bloke called Roger Wilkinson who was the only full time coach in New Zealand. He had heard reports about me from a friend of mine called Darren Melville who was playing for him; they needed a goalkeeper and he had recommended me. The upshot was that within a week I had left work, got married and was playing in New Zealand!"*

Life is never dull around Kevin Wolfe! He was on a two year contract and he played reasonably well without fully doing himself justice. There were other North East players there including Billy Wright, the son of the former Whitley Bay centre forward, who went on to play international football on the other side of the world. Paul Nixon, who had played for Chester le Street, was also there along with Darren Melville and it was something of a home from home. The team was successful as well, winning the league championship, but it was difficult for a newly wed twenty year old to settle so far away from his roots so:

> *"After a year over there I returned to play for another of my psychopathic associates, Billy Cruddas, at Durham City. It was one of my most enjoyable seasons because we reached the quarter finals of the FA Vase. It was actually the second time I had done that; I had been there with Blue Star a couple of seasons previously. We had a team at Durham who were not necessarily great players but they played for each other and there were no prima donnas. We had a couple of very experienced players in Peter Stronach and the player/coach Alan Scott who held things together, and a lot of up and coming players, and we did very well."*

Durham had played Tamworth at New Ferens Park to reach the quarter final stage. Tamworth were one of the fancied teams in the competition but Durham led 2-1 at half time; they then led 4-2 despite having two players sent off before Peter Stronach became the third Durham player to be dismissed, whereupon Wolfie shouted to Alan Scott;

KEVIN WOLFE - CAPTAIN CONDOM, A MEXICAN ROAD SWEEPER AND THE ODD PSYCHOPATH

Durham City's FA Vase Quarter Final team of 1988 with Kevin sixth from the left on the back row.

"What's the system now then, Alan?" Alan replied: "I'm ****** if I know!" So much for coaches.

Despite the handicap of finishing with nine men Durham won the game, but they lost the quarter final to Emley who scored twice in the last minute. Cue for another move and Kevin went back to Newcastle Blue Star for a second spell which did not really work out despite playing with outstanding talents like Kevin Todd:

> "Toddy was probably the best all round non league player of his time. In terms of his fitness and versatility he was exceptional. He could play anywhere. He would tell you he could even play in goal but I have my doubts! He was as brave as a lion and there really wasn't anyone to touch him. He would never tell me what he was paid but it must have been a king's ransom because he always went upstairs on his own to collect his money from old Billy Dryden. It doesn't matter what he was on, he deserved every penny. He was a great player."

Wolfie always enjoyed training and worked hard, but that was not necessarily true of everyone and one night at Blue Star one or two of the lads were taking it easily. John Reach and John Gamble were walking along the railway line behind the Wheatsheaf ground when they found a dead pigeon. They decided it was too good a pigeon to waste and too good an opportunity to miss, so they picked it up and stuffed it into Mally Newton's football bag. A couple of nights later Mally turned up for training with a different bag, but he refused to admit he had found the pigeon.

Another of the characters at Newcastle Blue Star was Ian Crumplin:

> "Crumpy was nuts. We lost a game at Dawdon in the Wearside League Cup and Colin Richardson in his infinite wisdom decided to fine us all a week's wages. The fact was that he had somehow got Trevor Brooking to play for us against Coundon the following Sunday and our wages went to pay him. Crumpy put two hammers above the door to welcome him and he sat blowing bubbles at him across the dressing room. After the game Brooking, who was absolutely immaculate, was getting ready and Crumpy had cut the toes off his socks. An England international and an immaculate bloke and he ended up with no socks!"

KEVIN WOLFE - CAPTAIN CONDOM, A MEXICAN ROAD SWEEPER AND THE ODD PSYCHOPATH

Wolfie's extended list of clubs grew yet again when he moved to Chester le Street where he was involved in an incident at a fund raising event for Comic Relief about which even he is uncharacteristically coy:

> "It was an incident with a stripper. It was Comic Relief Day and I had entered into the spirit of things by putting a red nose on the end of my manhood. There was more to it than that, but that's all I am going to tell you!"

The manager of Chester le Street was Barry Endean, a distinguished former professional. Barry was a very forgetful man and one Saturday the players were waiting in the clubhouse to travel to play a league game at Spennymoor. Mac Lumsdon was the assistant manager and he was panicking because there was no sign of Barry and the team really needed to be on the road, then Mac went down to the dressing room to collect something and there he found Barry in a state of great agitation because none of the players had arrived. He had to be told that they were playing away and not at home. As Kevin says:

> "He was a great bloke, but not the most organised!"

It was while he was playing for Chester le Street that Kevin was sent off on the first of many occasions in his glittering career. They were playing at Evenwood Town in a Northern League Second Division match and following a clash with a player called Tony Hodgson he had Hodgson in a head lock:

> "The referee sent him off then he told me I was going as well. There was this bloke behind the goal giving me some stick so in my infinite wisdom I whipped my top off and chased after him. What I had forgotten was that I was wearing a tee shirt underneath with 'Captain Condom' emblazoned across the front. Everyone was laughing at me and that made me even madder."

It would be fair to say that throughout his career Kevin maintained a hate/hate relationship with match officials, though he did believe that the higher level he played at the more likely it was that you could engage in banter with them. There was a more relaxed relationship with the referees in the Unibond League than he usually enjoyed in the Northern League. He took the view that the Northern League approach was out of date and that there was too much emphasis on discouraging bad language and not enough on controlling the game. He does not advocate wholesale and indiscriminate use of bad language but argues that some of it is part and parcel of the game. Referees at the higher level understood this and there was more scope for developing good relationships though:

> "I must admit I did lose my rag sometimes but that was because I was passionate about the game and hated losing."

Of all the teams Kevin played for the one he joined next, Workington, is the one he rates most highly, and he was later to return for an extended stay. In his first spell he signed for Alan Cook who had Stuart Sherwood as his assistant. Workington were blessed with their share of characters including Anthony Robinson and Wayne Walls but unfortunately they were not a strong side and they were relegated with the result that Wolfie responded to a phone call from Harry Dunn and moved to Blyth Spartans where his fortunes proved to be much brighter as he played in the Blyth side which won promotion to the Unibond Premier League and picked up the League Cup:

> "Harry Dunn was one of the most meticulous managers I have played for. It's a pity about his bad moustache which makes him look like a Mexican road sweeper. He also has the worst dress sense ever. I was sitting next to him on the bench once because Paul O'Connor was playing in goal and Harry said; 'Do you like me jeans lads?' They were Falmers jeans and nobody wore those! He said he had been able to get them for a fiver a pair and he had sold a pair to his missus for a tenner. The scary thing is he would have as well. Harry's dress sense was a disgrace."

Harry Dunn was an excellent organiser of teams and the squad he assembled at Croft Park was a very good one with good characters in it like Tommy Ditchburn, John Gamble and Steve Boon. It was a happy time which only ended when

KEVIN WOLFE - CAPTAIN CONDOM, A MEXICAN ROAD SWEEPER AND THE ODD PSYCHOPATH

Wolfie followed Harry to Whitby Town where they won the League Cup before yet another move took him to Harrogate where the chairman was a man called Maurice Hammond:

> "I have never met anyone like him. He wanted to pick the team and do everything because he had put a lot of money into the club, but to be fair we were successful and I enjoyed playing at the higher level of the Unibond League."

Tony Harrison then recruited Kevin for another spell at Durham City and he stayed on when a change of manager saw Paul Walker brought in. Paul was an incredibly skilful player and as a manager he brought the best out of Kevin. It was another team with its share of loose cannons including Gary and Alan Pearson who stuffed Paul Walker's head down the toilet before a match at Seaham causing him to throw up while he was giving his pre-match team talk.

There was a real togetherness in the Durham side for which Paul Walker deserved credit, but he was not immune to the wilder side of the dressing room antics which caught him out again when they played against Whitby who were a really strong side and won the Northern League title that season:

> "Paul Walker was giving his team talk and one of the lads had been polishing his boots and got black boot polish on his hands. He ran his hands over Paul's baldy head as we went on the field and he went out with a bonce like a minstrel. It was a really important game and he looked ridiculous with this black pate. We were all crying with laughter and the Whitby crowd thought we were barmy."

Next on the ever increasing roll call of Wolfie's clubs was Bishop Auckland where Tony Lee was manager and on the playing side he was reunited with his old friend Kevin Todd. The dressing rooms at Bishops' Kingsway ground were at the bottom of a flight of stairs and to reach them you had to pass the toilets. Kevin walked in with Kevin Todd for his first match and as they passed the toilets Tony Lee was relieving himself; Kevin Todd pushed him so that he soaked his trousers, then ducked into the dressing room leaving Wolfie standing sheepishly outside with the result that Tony Lee thought he was the offender. It was not the best way to impress your new manager on your first day! While Kevin was at Bishop Auckland Tony Lee signed Paul Dobson, the ex-Gateshead striker who, in Wolfie's terms:

> "Was a real nutcase! I always used to sit in the back of the bus with him and they always used to have a quiz on the way to away games. They used to call the two of us Dumb and Dumber because we never won. We played at West Auckland one night and it was absolutely chucking it down. It was a Durham Challenge Cup tie and it was 1-1 at half time. Paul Dobson was having an absolute nightmare and Tony Lee tore strips off him at half time. He went out in the second half, had three touches and scored three goals. When the final whistle went he couldn't get back in the dressing room quick enough! He said to Tony Lee; 'That's why I bought a three bedroomed house, Tony, to have have enough room to keep all my hat trick match balls in!" Tony Lee went berserk, but Dobber loved it; he was nearly as mad as Ian Crumplin which is saying something."

After his spell at Bishop Auckland Kevin was on his travels once again, this time returning to Workington where he had what for him was an incredibly lengthy stay of five years which he counts as the best spell of his career in playing terms. Tommy Cassidy, the former Newcastle United player, took over from Peter Hampton as manager while he was there and Kevin responded to Tommy and felt appreciated by everyone at the club. While he was there he suffered the only serious injury of his career when he damaged his cruciate ligament, causing him to miss a whole season, but he returned to complete a further two years at the club, enjoying himself playing for Tommy Cassidy:

> "We had a home game one night and Tommy had to be home early. He used to drive his partner's beautiful yellow Audi convertible and after the game he couldn't find the keys. He went absolutely berserk and held a steward's enquiry. They couldn't be found and he had no idea where the spare set was so he was stuck there until eleven o'clock at night when the AA came to sort him out. He blames me to this day but I can honestly say I was innocent. On the

KEVIN WOLFE - CAPTAIN CONDOM, A MEXICAN ROAD SWEEPER AND THE ODD PSYCHOPATH

Saturday we were playing at Harrogate and before the game all the lads put their keys on the dressing room table and asked Tommy to look after them for us. He was not happy; he had a bit of a twenty past eight face on!"

After his long spell at Workington Kevin was contemplating retirement, but Brian Honour persuaded him to return to Bishop Auckland before he wrapped his career up with a final spell at Durham City, playing first for Billy Cruddas and then Andy Toman. He had been taking his coaching badges and he was ready to move from the playing side to the coaching side of the game when he was contacted by Ged McNamee and invited to apply for the post of goalkeeping coach at Sunderland Football Club's Academy. His application was successful and he loves working with Sunderland's young goalkeepers and while it is not the same as playing there is great satisfaction in watching the progress of emerging talents. He admits that it probably surprised a few people in the game when he took his coaching badges with a view to developing his ability on that side of the game because of the image he built up over the years as a madcap character, who was always ready to mix it with the crowd behind his goal:

> "I always enjoyed a good rapport with the fans. I didn't mind if they took the micky and I usually gave as good as I got. Some of them, like the Tow Law fans, didn't give me the lickings of a dog, but I like to think they enjoyed the banter."

Kevin is keen to point out that behind the madness he was always a conscientious trainer and prided himself that he gave every aspect of his preparation and performance his best efforts. He tries to pass on that work ethic to the youngsters in his care and he finds that his natural sense of humour is not out of place. Goalkeepers are a crazy bunch anyway, and as long as they do their serious work properly he is happy to introduce an element of fun as well. He enjoys his responsibilities and sees what he does as life coaching as well as goalkeeping coaching; he encourages a healthy lifestyle and a respect for education and he believes that he is successful in his relationships with young players.

Kevin made a spectacular and unexpected comeback in the 2006 Northern Masters tournament which takes place

Kevin in distinguished company playing for Sunderland in the 2006 Masters tournament.

annually as a six a side contest for former professionals who represent their old clubs at regional level with the winners going on to the national finals. He was lying in his back garden enjoying a couple of cans of beer when he took a call from Tim Carter who is the goalkeeping coach to the Sunderland first team. Tim offered him the opportunity to play for Sunderland in the tournament against Newcastle United, Middlesbrough and Hartlepool because Mark Prudhoe, the original choice, had been forced to withdraw. He was happy to oblige and in doing so created a little piece of Northern League history because he was joined in the Newcastle and Hartlepool teams by Ian Archibold and Simon Corbett – the first time three Northern League keepers had competed together in the Masters:

> "It was very, very competitive but it was great. I met lads like Joe Allon and Brian Honour and played in the same team as Gary Bennett, Marco Gabbiadini and Paul Bracewell. I played against Peter Beardsley who is a world class legend. They were all down to earth people and it was a marvellous experience. Unfortunately we were beaten by the Mags and Middlesbrough; I was nutmegged by Peter Beardsley, but I wasn't the first!"

KEVIN WOLFE - CAPTAIN CONDOM, A MEXICAN ROAD SWEEPER AND THE ODD PSYCHOPATH

Kevin has no desire to go into management; he feels that football today has become too stereotyped and there are fewer characters around. He also argues that today's footballers often do not have the same attitude as those of past eras. His ambition is to become a full time goalkeeping coach with a professional club, though such opportunities are few and far between and he would need to relocate. He has made countless friends from his time as a non league footballer and he looks back without regret on a career which lasted until he was 40. To say that Kevin changed clubs frequently is a massive understatement and he reckons that was in part due to the fact that non league managers tend to change their goalkeepers regularly. He cites the experience when he was having his first spell at Newcastle Blue Star as an 18 year old:

> "Colin Richardson wanted his keepers to come for everything at the near post, but even top internationals cannot always do that. A couple of crosses came over and I didn't go for them. At half time I was sitting with all these top players like Kevin Todd, Peter Bragan, John Swinburne, Phil Leaver, John Reach, Phil Linacre and John Gamble, and Ricco said to me, in amongst a fair number of expletives, that he wanted me to come for every cross. I'm sitting there, naive as anything and I said; 'But Colin, I'm a bundle of nerves." The players put their towels over their heads because they were creasing themselves and they knew what was coming next. 'That's marvellous,' says Colin, 'what we'll do the next time they get a corner is we'll put Phil Linacre in goal and you can go centre forward you useless ******. Needless to say I was on my way two weeks later!"

In fairness to Kevin, although he changed clubs frequently it was often to play at a higher level and throughout his career he was a sought after goalkeeper. Clubs do not try to sign bad keepers, only good ones. He enjoyed a long career with just that one serious injury when he was with Workington and even that was sustained, ironically, at the end of a season when Workington's fixtures were finished and he was playing centre forward in a Sunday morning fixture.

It comes as no surprise that Kevin Wolfe believes that if you are enjoying your football you perform better, and he tries to inject the vitality and sense of fun which characterised his own playing days into the minds of the young players he works with now. Wolfie was a terrific character and a true crowd pleaser throughout his playing days and it will certainly never be dull at Sunderland Academy when he is around.

RICHIE BOND

Whatever happened to Robson Green?

Dudley Middle School team of 1976 with Robson Green standing in the middle of the back row.

Richie Bond first came to prominence as a member of the Dudley Middle School team which also included future England international Andy Sinton and Robson Green, who was to make a name for himself in another field of entertainment. They were a decent little team who did well, and Richie and Andy continued to play most of their junior their football together until Andy Sinton became a professional player with Cambridge United where he became first team captain at the age of eighteen. As for Robson Green, he became a porter in "Casualty" and never looked back:

> "They were both smashing, level headed lads and I'm delighted with the success they have achieved for themselves."

Richie moved to Cramlington High School where he was spotted by the distinguished football scout Jack Hixon who is forever associated with Alan Shearer. Jack spotted young Richie playing alongside his pal Andy Sinton for Cramlington Juniors, preferred Richie at that stage, and arranged for him to spend every school holiday from the age of fourteen until he was sixteen travelling to Southampton football club for coaching and assessment. He would travel on Saturday, meeting Phil Parkinson who is now a successful manager, on the platform at Darlington railway station, and picking up a young John Beresford at Sheffield on the way.

The youth set up at Southampton was very impressive; the standard was excellent and the level of expectation high, and Richie found it tough. Although he was doing reasonably well he was not offered professional terms and by the time he was seventeen he began to think that his chance had gone and he lost some of his enthusiasm and passion for the game. He took a year away from football after being released by Southampton, having previously had an opportunity to have a trial at Manchester United which had only served to reinforce his conviction that he "was a million miles away." Everton had actually offered him a two year contract which he thought seriously about accepting before deciding, wrongly as it turned out, that he had better prospects at Southampton.

Richie still retains his respect and regard for Jack Hixon, now in his eighties, and stays in regular contact:

> "Jack certainly knew a player when he saw one and I took it as a great compliment that he took an interest in me at such a young age. I still have a very high regard for him. He always encouraged me to keep my head up; he said I would get another chance and he actually came back into my career a few years later."

By the time he was eighteen he was beginning to get his appetite for the game back. He was playing Sunday morning football when Micky Dagless invited Richie and two of his Cramlington based friends to the North of Northumberland to play for Alnwick Town in the Northern League Second Division. The other two fell by the wayside, but Richie enjoyed life at Alnwick. Manager Micky Dagless had been a good player himself, notably with Blyth Spartans, and he gave Richie a great deal of encouragement as well as opening his eyes to the facts of life in the Northern League by bringing in some real characters to the club like goalkeeper Dave Clarke and Ian "Archie" Mutrie:

> "To have the opportunity of playing with people of that calibre, players whose reputations I respected, improved my own game enormously. I like to think it worked both ways because Paul Dixon was playing up front and he had a young buck to do his running for him. I would beat a couple of men and put the ball on his head for him to score, and he got all the credit!"

Richie enjoyed two seasons alongside Paul before Ian Mutrie, who had been a member of the great Blyth Spartans FA Cup team, joined the club. He was an amazing, refreshing character, full of antics and banter, but still able to deliver the goods on the field:

> "He was about 37 but he was great to play alongside. The camaraderie was excellent and we had a really successful side which ended up being promoted to the First Division of Northern League. For a little team like Alnwick Town it was a massive achievement. Unfortunately, the Alnwick people did not respond very positively to what we had accomplished. There seemed to be some resentment of 'toonies' playing for their team."

Despite the misgivings of the locals, Alnwick went on to give a good account of themselves in the First Division. They were a very well organised team and they had excellent individual players in Keith Muckle and Malcolm Crowe. Money was not an issue or a motivating factor for the simple reason that there was virtually none. They were just a good side, well managed and playing with belief in themselves, and it was a successful formula. Alnwick ended the season with a very commendable top six finish which included a 2-0 away win over Blyth Spartans at Croft Park. That is a game Richie still remembers because he played well on the night and Ronnie Walton, who had just been appointed as manager of Blyth and was looking to bring in fresh faces, contacted Richie with a view to him joining Blyth the following season.

There were still ten games of the current season left and he accepted an invitation from Bobby Graham to play them for Whitley Bay. Strangely, his form deserted him during that short spell and he was unable to do himself justice, but he did have one highlight when he played in a testimonial match against a Newcastle United X1 which included Paul Gascoigne:

> "Gazza had been doing a presentation at a local junior club and he got to Hillheads in time to play the second half. I went on at half time as well and I thought; 'Hang on, Whitley Bay are

putting Bondie on and Newcastle are sending Gazza on; that can't be right!' It was unbelievable to play against someone like that; I was 24 and he was a year younger and he was an incredible player."

That was actually Gazza's last game for Newcastle United. He visited the Whitley Bay dressing room after the match wearing a Liverpool cap and told anyone who would listen that he was going to sign for Liverpool. Richie told everyone he knew the exclusive news and a week later Gazza signed for Spurs!

At the end of the season Richie consulted Micky Dagless about the option of going to Blyth and was advised to take the opportunity of playing for a bigger club, so after four very enjoyable seasons at Alnwick he moved to Croft Park where Ronnie Walton installed him as his main striker. He played alongside Steve Cuggy:

"Anyone who follows non league football up here will know how well we did. It was just like salt and pepper. We clicked straight away. Steve was a young lad of twenty who had just been released by Sunderland – I was twenty four – and we just clicked."

There were some excellent, experienced players in the Blyth side like Jimmy Harmison and Steve Carney as well as the one Richie rated the best of the bunch by some distance, midfielder Nigel Walker:

"I was in awe of the bloke. I had watched him when he played for Newcastle and he was like a magician with a football. It was great to train and play with him and I felt that if he represented the bench mark for being a professional footballer the rest of us had no chance."

After Richie had been at Croft Park for eighteen months, Jack Hixon came back into his story. Jack knew a lot of people in the game and he had contacted a man called Jack Chapman at Bury to come and have a look at him. Blyth were due to play a Newcastle United side in a friendly at Croft Park and United's manager Ossie Ardiles and his coach Tony Galvin turned out for the black and whites, but it was Richie Bond who grabbed the glory with a classic hat trick including a thirty yards piledriver with his left foot. After the game Ardiles invited him for a trial with Newcastle where he played in a game behind closed doors at the club's Maiden Castle training ground:

"There were only eight people watching and they included Richie Kirkup and Micky Richardson; two blokes who went everywhere watching non league football. How they found out about the game I have no idea but they were there. I actually wore the number nine shirt – imagine that – and I played alongside another triallist called Alan Lamb."

The match was against Carlisle United but unfortunately from Richie's standpoint it came to nothing, though Alan Lamb was offered a three months deal. The two of them arranged to see each other that same night at Croft Park where Blyth were playing a league cup match against Brandon United. Richie played for Blyth and Alan was in the Brandon side, four hours after they had played together for Newcastle United!.

It was another disappointment that he was not picked up by Newcastle United but within a couple of weeks Jack Chapman invited him to Bury. Once again, it was a disappointing experience, in fact the entire exercise was an abortive waste of time for all concerned because Richie was under contract to Blyth Spartans which meant he was unable to play for Bury and could only spend the week training at Gigg Lane. Eventually, though, the lucky break which seemed destined to elude him finally came Richie's way in December 1991 when he went to Blackpool on the recommendation of Harry Dunn. Billy Ayre was the manager and as he was now out of contract with Blyth there was no impediment to Blackpool signing him:

"I did Blyth a massive favour. They were in dire financial straits so I said I would sign a new contract so that Blackpool would have to pay them a fee of £10,000. We struck a gentlemen's agreement that if the deal went through Blyth would give me a thousand pounds and two days later I signed professional for Blackpool for

£10,000. Blyth never gave me my £1000 which was very disappointing as they had gone back on a verbal agreement. I had done them a huge favour and they had failed to keep their side of the bargain, which left a nasty taste for a long time."

Richie signs for Blackpool.

Life goes on, and Richie began his professional career at Bloomfield Road. Blackpool were an established and successful side and he found it difficult. By now he had a young child and he was anxious to get home at every opportunity to be with his family, so that he was unable to devote his energies 100% to his football career. Although Blackpool beat Scunthorpe in the league play offs at Wembley to win promotion Richie was not enjoying life. He sat on the bench alongside an eighteen year old winger called Trevor Sinclair and he began to realise that he was likely to be overtaken by promising young players with Sinclair's ability. He also found the daily grind of training as a full time player tedious, and life in general as a professional footballer did not suit him. He knew he had been a top player at Blyth and he had enjoyed being in that spotlight and training just twice a week in non league kept his enthusiasm fresh. He was simply not getting the same pleasure from his football and he was also dispirited when he picked up a couple of niggling injuries. He was grateful to have had the chance to play professionally but his heart was not in it. He did try again with a short spell playing for David McCreery at Carlisle United:

"The Chairman was Michael Knighton; he was a character. He would come along to training and try to keep the ball up; the best he managed was eleven! He wanted to be involved in every level of the club and it was a strange set up. I left and reverted to non league again by signing for Bishop Auckland where I got Harry Dunn the sack! I was there a fortnight, played badly, and Harry got the bullet. He was replaced by the Penguin himself – Tony Lee."

Tony Lee brought the best out of Richie and put together a good side, but both of them knew that in his heart Richie's desire was to return to Blyth Spartans despite the stroke they had pulled when he signed for Blackpool. Ironically, Harry Dunn was now in charge at Croft Park and an arrangement was arrived at whereby Richie got his wish.

It was the dawn of a happy and successful era in which Blyth won the First Division championship of the Unibond League and moved up to the Premier Division. They reached the final of the Northumberland Senior Cup as well, and life was good. The basis of the success was the quality and genuineness of the dressing room. Players like Steve Pyle, who was professional in every aspect of his football, set a high standard and Richie learned good habits from him. Blyth also had their taste of FA Cup success later when they met Bury at Gigg Lane. The signs were not promising with the squad ravaged by injury to the extent that they only had thirteen fit players. They were down to the absolute bare bones, but the FA Cup is special for the Spartans and they managed the seemingly impossible by winning the game 2-0. Tommy Ditchburn epitomised the spirit and commitment in the Blyth camp. He completed a twelve hour night shift at Wilkinson Sword at eight o'clock in the morning, spent three hours being driven to Bury, trying to sleep on the way. Then he played in the match, giving an outstanding display and scoring one of the goals before getting straight back on the road after the game to be at work that night for another twelve hour shift!

RICHIE BOND - WHATEVER HAPPENED TO ROBSON GREEN?

Northumberland Senior Cup Final. Blyth Spartans team which played against Newcastle United Reserves at St James's Park in May 1995.

Richie scored the other goal as well as laying on Tommy's and both the home fans and the travelling Blyth supporters gave the team a tremendous ovation after the game. One of the Bury fans told Richie after the game that he remembered him from his unsuccessful trial week there; revenge is sweet. After the initial dressing room celebrations, the atmosphere went quiet when, to the astonishment and bewilderment of the players, the two club physios, Dave Robertson and Darkie Gair, announced that they had been sacked along with David McCreery who had replaced Harry Dunn as manager. The timing of the decisions was incomprehensible. It was one of the club's finest hours and the manager's reward was to be dismissed. Unbelievable. It took the gloss off the triumph and the journey home was subdued and flat when it ought to have been boisterous and exuberant. It was the highlight of Darkie and Robbo's careers and a great success for David McCreery and the three of them were distraught. The players did not want to be seen to be enjoying themselves despite their marvellous result and a wonderful achievement by Richie and his team mates was soured by the post match aftermath.

Two more successful seasons followed with top players like Lawrie Pearson and John Gamble playing alongside him. The social side of the team was as strong as the playing side and with Peter Harrison having replaced David McCreeery he and Richie had a good relationship. However, the next incumbent was John Burridge, and as far as Richie was concerned his appointment was a retrograde step. Richie and Budgie never hit it off, although Richie worked hard and that was a main plank of the manager's requirements:

> "He liked players who were not afraid to show a nasty streak if the situation required it but I wasn't that kind of player. I wouldn't put my foot in during the Hokey Cokey to be honest. The enjoyment level was diminishing and it

> *came to an end for me in a pre-season friendly at Workington when the manager shouted from the goals to me in the opposition half: 'You'll never play for Blyth again, Bondie."*

That was indeed Richie Bond's last game for Blyth and he was saddened by the circumstances of his dismissal. He regarded it as hurtful and unprofessional and knew it was time for him to move on. He joined Whitley Bay in a straight exchange for Glen Renforth who was a similar sort of player to himself. For the second time things did not work out at Whitley Bay. He was desperate to do well for the manager, Paddy Lowery, who had put great faith in him and he did have one memorable appearance against Netherfield in which he scored five goals, but he felt he had not produced his best form or repaid Paddy Lowery's faith in him. He apologised to Paddy at the end of the season and among the phone calls to the Bond household in the close season was one from Keith Perry who invited him to join Bedlington Terriers:

> *"Keith treated the club as his family and they were on their way to great things. He had recruited some other Blyth players and he saw me as the next one who could help the team to make further progress. The result turned out to be the most enjoyable and successful year I have had in football."*

There were some exceptional players at Welfare Park. Martin Pike was there for instance, and he had played 500 league games as a professional but he expected no special treatment. Richie's job was to play wide right to supply and support the outstanding strike force of John Milner and Dean Gibb; two players he rated extremely highly:

> *"It was a privilege to pull the Bedlington shirt on every week and know you were part of a team which played great football. It was so enjoyable and we kept winning and winning. It was incredible. I felt like I was a supporter who happened to be playing for this great team."*

Many of the games from that great season were to stay in Richie's consciousness. A magnificent performance at Bamber Bridge in the FA Cup was a particular highlight which ended in a 4-4 draw followed by a penalty shoot out. Dean Gibb took what was to prove the winning penalty and after having taken a lot of stick from the home crowd during the game he took his penalty, scored the goal, then dropped his shorts!

> *"The referee gave him a red card. I couldn't believe a player was sent off during a penalty shoot out but Dean, being Dean, just brushed himself down and walked off. We had won, so he had the last laugh."*

The atmosphere was fantastic as the team made progress on three fronts. They were closing in on the Northern League title and winning ties in both the FA Cup and the FA Vase. One particularly memorable game for Richie was the first leg FA Vase semi final against Thame at Welfare Park in which he was on the bench. Bedlington led 1-0 at half time and Keith Perry told him he was going on for the second half. He scored twice and laid another two on for John Milner. Bedlington won the leg 5-0 and knew that they were going away the following weekend under no pressure whatsoever with a trip to Wembley in the final virtually guaranteed. The week was interminable as the players waited to complete the formality with a boring 0-0 draw at Thame.

Richie was made redundant from his job around this time and he decided to take advantage of the situation by relaxing and enjoying the process of preparing for the final. He enjoyed every aspect of it including the social side as the FA Vase finalists found themselves in great demand:

> *"Asda wanted the team to model some of their clothing range so they got the good looking ones like Lee Ludlow, Mel Harmison, Gary Middleton and me involved! We modelled their 'George' range with some of the lasses from the cheese counter. It was an hour long show culminating in the swimwear, which appealed to Gary! I have to say some of the girls should have been modelling balaclavas, but it was great fun."*

There was something happening nearly every day, with heightened media interest, interviews and photographs and Richie, who was thirty four, realised that this could be his final chance to enjoy the limelight and the attention. Despite the heartbreak of losing the final to a last minute goal, it was an incredible and memorable experience. Bedlington's league, FA Cup and FA Vase success was unparalleled and Richie was proud to be an integral part of it.

The disappointment of the FA Vase final was devastating:

In action for Bedlington Terriers at Wembley in the final of the FA Vase.

"You are playing at Wembley in front of your family and friends and you are desperate to play well and to win. After the game we all shed tears because we were gutted for ourselves and all the people who had supported us along the way. Afterwards we went to a pub where Keith Perry had organised a room for us; we had a drink and slowly we began to unwind. The worst of it was getting up the next morning. We had an early flight from Heathrow and some of us were really shabby from drowning our sorrows the previous night. We were waiting on the plane and everything was going smoothly as we bombed along the runway at over 200 miles and hour, when Lawrie Pearson suddenly started pulling the emergency brake cord. The emergency lights started flashing, the pilot pulled off the runway and aborted his take off and Lawrie had to be taken off the plane because he was ill from the drink the night before! I roomed with him because I liked a good sleep and Lawrie's stories were guaranteed to send you to sleep."

Despite their friendship Richie refused to get off the plane to stay with him because he had arranged to pick his little one up from school when he got home, so John Milner stayed behind and the two of them had to catch a later flight.

Dean Gibb was a key player at Bedlington where he was a fearless strike partner to John Milner. He was also one of the players who lit up the dressing room with his crazy behaviour:

"We were warming up with Mel Harmison in the centre centre circle one training night at Welfare Park when Dean came across wearing absolutely nothing and riding Micky Cross's bike. He said we would do a few laps and pedalled off around the pitch. He was still last, even on the bike!"

The following season he linked up again with Paddy Lowery who was managing Gretna and who showed his faith in Richie by coming in for him again despite the disappointment of their spell together at Whitley Bay. Sadly, it was another let down as Richie failed to find his spark and he moved on after four months. By now he was beginning to involve himself in the coaching side of the game with Cramlington Juniors, and thoroughly enjoying the experience, but there is no substitute for playing and he accepted chairman Ken Beattie's invitation to play for Morpeth Town. However, what he regarded as an average season forced Richie to contemplate the prospect of hanging up his boots, when out of the blue an offer came from Newcastle Benfield to join them and lend his experience to their rapidly developing Northern Alliance side. It was a move which rejuvenated his career. He had never played at that level but he played regularly and helped the young players to the extent that they won the league championship and were promoted to the Northern League for the first time in their short history. Once again Richie Bond had proved his value as a player.

Father and son. Richie and Chris with the Wade Associates Northern Alliance trophy won by Newcastle Benfield in 2002-03.

A change in management in the close season saw him part company with Benfield along with Alan Bell and he went to Newcastle Blue Star where his former Bedlington team mates Warren Teasdale and Dean Gibb had taken over. He joined as their number three and a bit part player which suited him perfectly at that stage in his career. He helped to create the good dressing room atmosphere which is essential for success, but Blue Star had high expectations and a fourth place finish meant that they just missed out on promotion to the Northern League First Division, so Dean, Warren and Richie left. He had a very brief spell as a manager which he did not enjoy before linking up with some more old mates including Gary Middleton, Dave Robertson and Darkie Gair helping to run West Allotment Celtic at the start of the 2006-07 season.

Richie played for twenty two years and he can look back on an excellent career; like everyone who has played for any length of time in the Northern League he made lifelong friends along the way. Someone once told him that good players can sometimes have bad games but bad players cannot have good games and as he looks back he hopes he will be remembered as one of those good ones who had a few bad games rather than one who never played a good one.

He hopes to remain involved in the game helping another generation of players to make their mark. He is conscious of the transient nature of the game and of how you are not necessarily aware of your good fortune at the time, but he has more than his share of wonderful memories from an outstanding career:

> "It's great to have played with outstanding players and when they pay you a compliment it is very satisfying. John Milner was one of the very best and he once said that I was one of the best players he had played with which was enormously pleasing, especially as he swore it wasn't the drink talking!"

Richie Bond was an extrovert; he played his football in a flamboyant way and he had a magnificent rapport with the fans:

> "Once I crossed the white line I wanted to do my best, but I also wanted to entertain and have a good relationship with the crowd. I would take the micky, but in a nice way, and I never complained when I got kicked by opponents or took stick from fans. There is no point in playing if you don't enjoy it. I played with a smile on my face because that it the way I am."

SANDRA ORR

Nobby Solano does not have to pay

The remarkable story of Sandra Orr and Blyth Town started in Bedlington! Sandra's son Richard was nine years old and together with two of his friends he had joined a junior football team which was based in Bedlington. He was not the greatest footballer in the world but he loved playing the game and his Mum went along dutifully to watch him in action. It was a brand new team and like many an emerging side they found victories difficult to come by. As the end of the season approached they had not won a single match, then their day of destiny arrived with a 2-1 win over Wideopen:

> *"I will never forget it. It was like they had won the World Cup. It was worth losing all of those games just to win that one; it was magnificent. The opposition couldn't believe our delight and our celebrations because they didn't realise how important that first win was for us."*

Sandra was hooked, and she made it her business to help bolster the team for the following season by recruiting more of Richard's friends. Most of them were from Blyth and as they went through their Under 11 and Under 12 phases there were growing numbers of Blyth based youngster turning up and wanting to play, so that eventually the parents of the Blyth contingent decided that it made sense for the team to relocate in Blyth and that was how Blyth Town came into existence. The group of parents met in Sandra and husband Geoff's house and put up the necessary money to get the team off the ground. There was already a junior side in Blyth which existed to give local youngsters the opportunity to play football; it was run by nice people who were happy to function at their own level and did not have ambitions to expand and develop. Sandra had other ideas, and the club started to grow:

> *"At that stage we had three age groups. We had Under 13s who were 'my boys' as I still call them and we also had Under 11s and Under 10s. The following season we pulled in the missing age group so that we then had 14s, 13s, 12s and 11s and we were on our way."*

From the inception at that meeting in Geoff and Sandra's lounge there were certain basic principles put in place. It was a fundamental rule that all the youngsters should be regarded as equal regardless of their social backgrounds and academic levels. They would be turned out properly so that when the Blyth Town teams took the field they would look the part and take pride in their appearance, the club they were representing, and where they came from; a fact which was reinforced by the fact that they all had the town crest embroidered on their shirts.

The club wanted to be ambitious; it was located in the biggest town in Northumberland and the management committee could see no reason why they could not compete with the highly successful clubs at Cramlington and Wallsend. The founding of the club also coincided with a time when the competitive side of sport was being frowned upon in schools where the Corinthian spirit of taking part was being regarded as more important than winning was in vogue:

> *"Children were encouraged to come top of the class in Maths but they were not encouraged to win races."*

Blyth Town filled the void; they wanted teams which would compete and that was what they encouraged. Times change, and today schools are trying to address issues of obesity and solitary computer based play by encouraging competitive exercise, but a decade ago attitudes were different.

The town of Blyth also suffered from an image problem. It had endured some adverse and often unfair criticism as the drugs capital of the region, and Sandra and her colleagues believed it was important that their boys were encouraged to conduct themselves properly and portray a positive image. Their resolve has made a significant contribution to the perception of Blyth; as they have become better known and people have looked at the way that they do things, the local population has taken pride in Blyth Town. The club simply grew as each year passed and interest and the demand to play grew and spread, so that the club developed at a phenomenal rate. The reputation of Blyth Town has expanded and interest has spread like wild fire to the extent that at the start of the 2006-07 season they were fielding 27 teams including girls, ladies, men and boys.

There had always been interest among some of the local girls and the club felt that at some stage it might expand to meet that particular demand. Blyth Town had been established in 1995 and at the start of the 1998-99 season the decision was taken to form a girl's team and they rapidly reached the stage where they were a major force in girl's football in the region.

When the original team which had started it all grew older, bigger and stronger and reached the point where they were eighteen and too old to continue in junior football, the committee discussed the option of forming a senior side because there was no league for the team to play in and they began to disperse in pursuit of senior football. It was a major step for the club to contemplate but the decision was forced up them by the fact that the oldest of the girls were now sixteen and they too had run out of junior options and were looking elsewhere. Sandra and her team did not feel comfortable with the thought that sixteen year old girls were no longer under the umbrella of the club and they felt compelled to grasp the nettle and embrace the challenge of moving into senior football.

The decision needed to be even handed which meant not only forming a ladies team to accommodate the older girls, but also forming a men's team in order to encourage the original lads back to the club. They returned almost to a man and Sandra and her close colleague Margaret Nicholls applied for a place in the Wade Associates Northern Alliance which they thought was the appropriate level at which a young team containing two schoolboy internationals could compete. They had been together for ten years and they had a tremendous bond, and there were no fears that they would

be able to survive at that level. Many of the boys who had come through the ranks had never played for any other team and most of them had received the club's award for ten year's service. That special loyalty is the bedrock of the fantastic success which Blyth Town has enjoyed in its decade of existence and it saw some players who, frankly, were not very good, develop into top class players by the time they made the senior side.

When the team took the Northern Alliance by storm and quickly established themselves at the top end of the spectrum, they provided yet further evidence of the club's progress. They had adapted very quickly and all the evidence points to the fact that Blyth Town has the potential to go further. The next level could be the Northern League, which is an ambition they could never have dreamed of in the past. The players can achieve it and they now have the senior teams to carry things forward. When Blyth Town Reserves entered the Tyneside Amateur League at the start of the 2005-06 season the original Under 11 side had achieved senior status as the club's development side. Both senior teams have been supplemented by players from other age groups as the strongest players gravitate to the top, but essentially they are the original squads. The success Blyth Town Reserves achieved in that first season was phenomenal. The club was confident that they would do well, but not only did they romp to the league championship, suffering only one defeat, but they reached the final of the Northumberland Minor Cup, beating sides from the higher grade Northern Alliance in the process before going down in extra time in the final against Ashington Colliers. For a team of nineteen year olds it was a remarkable achievement, and they came close to emulating the feat of the first team, which won its first senior trophy in 2004 when it lifted the Minor Cup. It was the first time in 98 years that a Blyth team had lifted the trophy and it was particularly sweet for Sandra because the players were the ones she calls 'my boys;' the original team which started the whole fairy tale.

While the senior men met with instant success the ladies have taken a little longer. They had been dispersed as sixteen year olds to such an extent that fourteen members of the quad had left to join the professional clubs at Newcastle, Sunderland and Middlesbrough in pursuit of senior football:

SANDRA ORR - NOBBY SOLANO DOES NOT HAVE TO PAY

Sandra celebrates as 'her boys' win the Northumberland Minor Cup. It was their first senior trophy and the first time a Blyth team had won the Minor Cup for 98 years.

"I was upset because we had brought them through. They had beaten all three of those clubs and it was a pity to lose them to professional sides. We had really acted as their development side because we received no recompense."

Before they went their separate ways the girls had won promotion and Blyth Town were now in a position of having to play fourteen year old girls at a good standard of senior football which simple was not sustainable. They claimed a couple of notable scalps but lost regularly. Thanks to the positive role of the team manager and the support of the club they have turned things round and are now pursuing success in a more realistic environment.

The club has grown to such an extent that they now need two end of season presentation ceremonies to meet demand. The seniors have theirs one night, but some of them attend the junior night as guest presenters to preserve the spirit of one-ness which the club values so highly. The continuity means that the young players aspire to play for the seniors in due course, and while other senior teams in the area have difficulty in recruiting juniors, Blyth Town have done it the other way around. They began as a junior side and have grown into senior sides to which today's junior players can graduate.

The togetherness which lies at the heart of the club is cultivated carefully. At club meetings the coach to the youngest team is in attendance as well as representatives of every age group – boys, girls, men and women – right through to senior management, and every aspect of the club is discussed. There are no separate bank accounts, just a deposit account for savings and a current account for the day to day running of the club on every level. It really is one club. Another of its enormous strengths has been the efficiency of its administration which has principally been

Celebrating the Football Foundation grant and the beginning of a new era for Blyth Town.

the responsibility of Sandra and her colleague Margaret Nicholls who have worked tirelessly to ensure the smooth and efficient running of the club. It is a vital and sometimes thankless role which Margaret in particular has carried out with superb dedication while Sandra has been the dynamic driving force with her determination and strength of personality. The pair of them have the same ideals which are passed on to all newcomers; they have open minds and admit to past mistakes as they have learned the business, but they and their management committee colleagues know how to run a football club.

It is inevitable that in such a large club there are occasionally people who fall by the wayside, but the discipline within the club and the disciplinary record of the teams on the field have been remarkable. Continuity has had a crucial part to play in this; Blyth people have a spirit of togetherness, a characteristic which Sandra describes as clannishness, and this has been in evidence as people at every level have remained at the club throughout the years and the club's disciplines and ideals have remained intact. In short, it is a family club.

Within that family atmosphere there is one family which predominates, for not only is Sandra Orr now in her eleventh season at the helm, happily presiding over 27 teams and watching with justifiable pride as Blyth Town's new ground grows at the end of her street, but her husband Geoff, who has also been a stalwart from the start, is manager of the very successful Blyth Town senior team and her father, George Vennard, is the team's physio and prime character:

> "He's a bit of a loon. He's football mad; a big Newcastle supporter, and he has always been there for his children and his grandchildren. When we went senior he began helping with the first aid of which he had experience from work. He is a great character and when the FA launched their 'Get Into Football' campaign in the North East at the time of the 2006 World Cup we sent George along to the meeting."

It took place and St James's Park; Michael Owen was involved and when the photo shoot took place the photographer saw the potential in George's face:

> "We had trimmed his nose hair, tidied his hair and made him put on his best suit so that he was as smart as a carrot. We made sure he showed off his Blyth Town tee shirt in the pictures and they made him the face of the campaign. He went around sticking posters with his picture on them all over Blyth. He thinks he is a superstar now and when Nobby Solano came to watch a game George told him he wouldn't have to pay to have his photo taken with him!"

George has supported Newcastle United 'for ever' but this season he has given up his season ticket to be with his boys – who are also Geoff and Sandra's boys. At 69 he is involved in local football and it is wonderful.

Blyth Town has always enjoyed a close working relationship with the Northumberland FA which is the sport's governing body in the region. Their County Development Manager, Stuart Leason, has been especially supportive and his positive imput has now developed to the level of a two-way dialogue whereby he will discuss with Sandra strategies which are successful at Blyth Town and which may be appropriate to pass on to others. In the area of discipline, for instance, the club has a written constitution with sets of rules for players and for parents, and great care is taken at the start of each season for team managers to sit down with players and parents and talk them through the rules so that when they sign up they know they are buying into Blyth Town and are bound by the rules. Other comparable clubs have similar systems and the wellbeing of junior football depends of everyone concerned understanding and accepting their responsibilities. That is certainly the case at Blyth Town where the players and their parents understand their obligations in terms of the way they conduct themselves, the respect they show to match officials as well as other players and spectators. There may be some rough diamonds at Blyth Town but they know they are part of something special:

> " We have to have standards. We cannot and will not have our kids running out like Raggy Arse Rangers. They play in quality kit and they wear the town crest with pride, and that's the way it has to be."

The local football community is now aware of Blyth Town and parents contact the club asking if their children can join because they have been told it is the best place to take them in the locality. Feed back is good, and the fact that Blyth is a football town helps; Blyth Spartans has a long and distinguished history and is currently a team in revival, and there is a comfortable co-existence between the clubs. Blyth Town can accommodate a higher proportion of home grown talent because of the level at which it operates and there is no rivalry for talent. After a successful friendly between the two teams during the pre-season of 2006-07, plans are afoot to make it an annual fixture to benefit a local children's charity. Whether Town will ever play at the same level as Spartans remains an open question:

> "Never say never. If anyone had told me eleven years ago that we would be at the level we are now I would not have believed it. When we started out we didn't aspire to this but as we grew and at the same time maintained our standards, we were striving to give the kids something in our town to be proud of. I am proud to be a Blyth lass myself and it was important to do something positive for the town. It has developed naturally and it can go on, so who knows where we might be in the years to come."

The successful way in which Blyth Town was run received official recognition when they responded to the challenge of applying for the new FA Community Charter status. They became the first club in Northumberland to achieve the kite mark by virtue of having satisfied the criteria in terms of equity, child protection and administration:

> "It's a template for all clubs to adhere to if they are going to do things properly, and you have a dossier of evidence which proves you are doing things in the right way. People ask us for guidance now in terms of how to apply for charter status, how to get grants and so on. People were very helpful to us in our early years and we are happy to help others if we can."

After eleven years of playing on any available pitch in Blyth and dealing with the logistical nightmare that it created, Blyth Town now looks forward to the opening of its own new home facility. Over £900,00 is being spent creating a complex at South Newsham with an annexe at South Beach. Margaret Nicholls had the major headache of matching fixtures to venues for all those years and she has managed it superbly; now she will have the luxury of allocating pitches on the club's own site.

The fact that the club was able to secure Community Charter status alerted Sandra to the fact that grants were avaiable from the Football Foundation for the development of grass roots facilities:

> "There were 180 clubs out of 43,000 nationwide which had the charter and we were the first in the county, so I went to the council and told them there was a large grant available if they would gift us the land as matched funding. The council pointed us in the direction of South Newsham."

There was development money attached to the site, which was allocated for community use and it meant that if Sandra could put together a suitable plan she would effectively have £300,000 of matched funding to carry the project forward:

> "It's a beautiful site; it's not big enough for 27 teams of course, but we'll manage! We have now got a satellite site close by which is easily accessible and it is a wonderful opportunity."

The club will soon have a home for the first time and after eleven years of extremely hard work it is just reward for Sandra and her team, who have knocked on the council's door from day one. The local MP, Ronnie Campbell, has been very supportive and the council have put in the time and the professional expertise to draw up the bid, and the status of Blyth Town has enabled them to secure a grant of £575,000 from the Football Foundation. All the appropriate people and organisations in the town have worked together to make the South Newsham facility a reality. Sandra is right, it is a wonderful opportunity to develop a community facility, to bring the local schools on board, as well as providing quality, supervised conditions for 400 Blyth Town youngsters.

The process of draining the fields at the South Beach annexe is due to begin in Autumn 2006 and by Christmas work will have begun at South Newsham, so that by the start of the 2007-08 season Blyth Town teams will be playing at home in the truest sense of the phrase. The next phase will be to develop one of the pitches to Northern League standard so that another hurdle can be negotiated: Blyth Spartans watch out!

It is an inspirational story and the hardest aspect of it for the diehards to grasp has been that it has been spearheaded by two women: Sandra Orr and Margaret Nicholls:

> "I was once over at Harraby in Cumbria looking after the team because Geoff was working. My Dad, who is 69, and myself were in charge. I went on to give the lads a pep talk at half time and the whole of the Harraby team were standing around open-mouthed. People just don't expect women to do stuff like that."

Sandra's Dad, George, with Nobby Solano.

Actually, the women who help to run Blyth Town take their football very seriously, and all of them are qualified referees. The club has recently taken a Sunday morning team under its wing and Sandra describes Sunday morning football as 'another planet' where traditions die hard:

> *"There was this hairy arsed centre half once who shouted across; 'Why don't you go home and wash the dishes?' at Eleanor, the club's Child Protection Officer, and myself. I shouted back; 'Never heard that one before. Are you going to tell us to make the dinner next?' All the people on the sidelines were cracking up, and he was suitably embarrassed and started to laugh. Eleanor has actually taken a Yorkshire pudding for the referee before now!"*

The lads have grown used to Sandra's presence at games; she has, after all, been there from the outset, and they always insist they are decent if she asks to go in the dressing room:

> *"I know for a fact they are not; I can sense it and there is no way I will go in. As the kids get older your relationship with them changes. You go to their 18th and 21st birthdays, their weddings and their children's christenings."*

Football is a serious affair at Blyth Town but they have their moments, young as they are. When they went to Germany to play in a tournament they had the good fortune to be based next to a tennis club populated by lots of young German girls in their short tennis dresses, and a mutual admiration society developed very quickly with the girls following then players everywhere:

> *"When we got home I received a call from the mayor's office asking if we had a member called Patrice. We did have Patrick who had bribed all his mates to sleep on the balcony while he had his wicked way with one of the girls. That's lads from Newsham for you! Thankfully it wasn't the German CSA on the phone, just one of the girl's trying to get in touch with him."*

Some of the boys have never been abroad or away from home when they go with the club, and the way they respond can have a potential for problems, but they are made aware of their responsibilities, reminded that they are wearing the club crest, and watched like hawks!

"I remember once I took charge of all their passports because most of them were going abroad for the first time. There was only one lad who insisted he was all right, and what happened? He lost his passport on the plane!"

For all their trips to overseas tournaments and competitions in other parts of Britain, Sandra firmly believes that their toughest opponents are always the teams closest to home; Cramlington Juniors, Wallsend, Walker Central and Redheugh. She believes the local professional clubs are missing a trick because the best players are still up here. Nor does she subscribe to the view that junior football is in crisis, an opinion voiced in some quarters. She argues that while there are one or two excellent clubs like New Hartley, which remains successful because of the dedication of John Maley, the trend is towards the expansion of the big clubs at the expense of the small individual outfits. Sandra also believes that while Saturday football is in decline the game is expanding in a healthy way on Sundays. The tradition of Saturday afternoon football is dying at grass roots junior level just as the Premiership is moving away from its traditional pattern, but it is being replaced by another thriving game on Sunday mornings and Blyth Town is at the heart of it.

The small family of Sandra and Geoff Orr and father George has had a magical journey and come a very long way in the eleven years they have been part of the big and growing family which is Blyth Town. Sandra's contribution has been massive and it was officially recognised at the end of the 2005-06 season when she was surprised at the senior presentation night with an award of her own. She received the prestigious Billy Bell Memorial Trophy which is awarded annually for a major contribution to junior football in the region. She was only its second recipient and after extolling her many qualities the presenter told the audience that while she had achieved great things at Blyth Town; "She has not finished yet, not by a country mile she hasn't." Believe it.

JIMMY ROWE

Swapping clubs with Jocky Wilson

Jimmy Rowe was never a serious player; he made his reputation in the field of management, and it began thirty eight years ago at the Corner House pub in the Heaton suburb of Newcastle. In his younger days he used to look after the doors when the pub held disco nights:

> "When I worked on the doors at the Corner House in the early days I used to get calls from other venues to help out. One of them was the Swallow Hotel in Jesmond and my job was to be the presence at the outside door. I had people - hard men – inside to stop any outbreaks of trouble and keep the place calm. One time I brought in young Steve Black, who was then just an up and coming kid, to help. I sent him and Eddie Bruce inside to make sure there was no trouble. They were supposed to ask anyone who stepped out of line to leave, or to escort them to the door. After an hour I heard an almighty scream so I went in and there was Blackie fighting with this kid on the floor. I separated them and reminded him he was there to prevent trouble, not to dig everybody in sight! A couple of minutes later there was this massive brawl. I had to put those two on the outside taking the money and the tickets while I kept order inside, but the next I knew Blackie was at it again at the door. He just wanted to fight people; it was crazy. I love Blackie to bits, but he worked for other people after that!"

One of the Corner House regulars had the notion of starting a football team The basics were undertaken; raising the necessary finance through sponsorship, buying the strips, recruiting the players and joining the Sunday morning North East Heating Trades League. As is usually the case, the first two years saw the team struggle to establish itself, but gradually the reputation of the Corner House grew, fund raising nights based at the pub raised the team's profile, and better players were attracted.

Success came and, more important, it was sustained over an extended number of seasons, with trophies coming their way consistently. They played their early football at Paddy Freeman's Park at the top of Jesmond Dene before moving to Walker Park and they attracted players of the standard of Lou Henry, Geordie Parker and Harry Thompson. All the while they continued to carry all before them and Jimmy was in charge of the Corner House team for a highly successful period of fifteen years before leaving:

> "I went to run a team with little Danny Gates at the Prince of Wales pub on Shields Road and we had some good seasons there before I moved to High Heaton Tenants Association which was close to where I lived."

Jimmy admits to having what he calls 'a short passion fuse.' In a cup semi final at Gosforth his team murdered the opposition but lost the game because they could not find the back of the net. He heard the opposing manager and bench making disparaging remarks about his team, saying they were not as good as they thought they were. His 'passion fuse' came to the fore and he threw a full bucket of water over them, and soaked the referee who happened to be in the vicinity as well. He claims he controls himself better these days. I am not so sure!

There was also the odd time when it was not his lack of self control which caused problems but that of his players:

"We went to Blackpool at the end of the season once. It was always the rule that the players stayed in a different hotel from the committee because young footballers can be difficult to handle when they are away from home. When we went round to collect them in the coach on the Sunday

Jimmy, in civvies, with the Corner House team which swept the board in the 1980s.

morning for the journey home I told the manager I was there to collect the Corner House football team and he said: 'You're the ****** who sent them here are you? Get in here and see the state of my hotel.' They had absolutely wrecked the place. I got a summons to appear in court to answer a claim for £50,000 to put the damage right, but the booking had been made in the Corner House's name. Then they tried to hit the Corner House for the money. In the end it was scrapped; the case I mean, not the hotel!"

It is a fact of Sunday morning football life that match officials do not always turn up and sometimes club officials, however reluctantly, are forced to officiate, and it is not easy!

"You are never right. I was refereeing this game and I was trying not to be biased. I was favouring the opposition if anything. I blew up for something and this massive blond lad started running at me. He was running so fast I thought he was going to clock me, so I nutted him! I knocked him out. There was a local paper reporter at the game and I was asked for a comment but I refused. The next day the 'Andy Capp' cartoon showed Andy nutting a player so I suppose I got some sort of recognition. I was up before the league disciplinary committee and they banned me from refereeing, which was probably best for all concerned!"

JIMMY ROWE - SWAPPING CLUBS WITH JOCKY WILSON

The Corner House team of 1990-91.

One season the Corner House swept the board, winning the league championship and all three cup competitions and Jimmy proudly received the four trophies at the end of season presentation ceremony in Newcastle city centre. He came outside at the end of the evening to put the trophies in the boot of his car and had to pass a coach containing a contingent from rival club Winlaton Vulcans:

> "They jumped off the bus and started to set about me; even some of the women. I had high heel shoe marks on my face. Some of our lads saw what was happening and pulled me out and I spent two hours at the hospital getting stitched up. Nowadays my son Mark looks after me. He is a big lad and I have no worries!"

All of his Sunday morning success cemented Jimmy Rowe's reputation as someone who knew how to run a winning football team, and when another High Heaton based club, the famous Heaton Stannington, found itself in difficulties, their legendary supremo Bob Grounsell approached Jimmy to take on his first Saturday team and attempt a rescue act.

Heaton Stann. were in a desperate plight, and Jimmy had just two weeks to assemble a squad of players. It was a tough call and although Heaton survived Jimmy drifted out of football after a season in charge. He had been running football teams for twenty five years and he needed a break to recharge his batteries and restore his enthusiasm, so that when Danny Gates approached him again he was ready to respond. Danny's proposal was for Jimmy to become the

JIMMY ROWE - SWAPPING CLUBS WITH JOCKY WILSON

The Prince of Wales team in 1986.

chairman of Newcastle Benfield Saints football club and in the twelve years of their existence, with Jimmy at the helm and Danny lending invaluable support, Benfield's progress has been nothing short of staggering.

Benfield was in many respects an extension of the old Corner House team, with many of the original people still involved, and Jimmy was returning to his roots, though the significant difference as far as the new challenge was concerned was that Benfield were a Saturday afternoon team like Heaton Stannington, and Jimmy's decision to become involved brought to an end his lengthy connections with the Sunday morning game. The other sea change was a financial one. Instead of a Sunday team which cost a couple of hundred pounds a season to run and players were happy to be rewarded with an end of season trip to Blackpool, Jimmy was now embracing the world of non league football at a higher level with its cost implications in terms of ground maintenance, players expenses, the cost of match officials as well as all the ancillaries such as supplying kit, paying for heating and lighting, providing match balls and so on. It was, very literally, a different ball game and a budget of £2,000 was an absolute minimum requirement for financing a team in the Northern Alliance. Jimmy Rowe has always been a determined man; a winner who would not settle for mediocrity if he took on the chairmanship of the club and he was determined that Benfield would be a success. With the help and support of a committee of experienced football people, he made it happen. What they have achieved in their twelve years of existence is almost unique and it is a great

Newcastle Benfield Saints. Wade Associates Northern Alliance Champions 2002-03.

tribute to the small band of people who have been with the club since its inception.

They have not been content to stand still; they had a good ground at the old Sam Smith's playing field adjacent to Benfield School, but they have made it their business to develop it over the years with the help of ground improvement grants to finance the provision of floodlights, hard standing, a covered seating area and an outstanding playing surface as well as top class modern dressing rooms. Each year they have set themselves a target in terms of improving the facilities in some significant way, and each year it has been achieved. They recently installed a metal perimeter fence and their future ambitions include a second stand as well as a clubhouse which will provide an essential regular revenue stream to run alongside the sponsorship deals which currently provide the club with its only significant source of income:

> "It has been hard work because we don't have our own clubhouse. Effectively, we just have a refreshment hut, but we really need the security of the income a properly run clubhouse would provide if we are to realise our true ambitions."

The committee has undergone a number of changes over the years, with only Jimmy, Danny and John Colley of the originals still in place, but whoever has been involved has worked hard and that has been the basis of the club's success. In the early days they recruited expertise from another team, Wallsend St. Columba's, which was folding. St. Columba's had some experienced committee members who had the vital Saturday football expertise which Benfield lacked and, equally important, they had some good sponsors. In particular they had been sponsored by a local company called NFL, and their managing director agreed that if Benfield incorporated the word 'Saints' in their title he would continue to give the team his backing:

> "You have to be realistic in life and if you have to compromise with things like the name of your team to secure finance you have to do it. If Bolton could call their ground the Reebok stadium we could be perfectly relaxed about

calling ourselves Newcastle Benfield Saints! It was the first realisation we had that without a clubhouse we would have to work very hard to generate revenue from other sources"

The Wallsend St. Columba's people did Benfield proud in those formative years as they came to terms with the different administrative and organisational requirements of Saturday football, but gradually they faded from the scene and now, their work gratefully done, there are none of the original incomers on the Benfield committee.

As chairman of the club Jimmy believes in leading from the front "I need to do it that way. My nature is that I have to be a winner. There is no place in my make up for mid table finishes. I have always been at the top end of whatever I have done."

That sentiment does not apply only to his involvement in football. In the days when he was pursuing his interest in another of his passions, the world of darts, he did not compromise and he succeeded in persuading the former world champion Jocky Wilson to play for him. He has always set his sights high and he even left Jocky out of his Monday night team at High Heaton Tenants Association once because in Jimmy's words he was 'playing shite!'

"Jocky lived nearby in Wallsend at the time, so I approached him and asked him to play for us in the Super League on Monday nights. He agreed, but a couple of times he turned up late so I dropped him! He was world champion at the time but he just shrugged his shoulders and we went for a drink. I remember a time when my wife and I were out with Jocky and his missus at North Heaton Sports Club and droves of people were leaving the concert room while the turn was on and coming upstairs to get his autograph. He would sign half a dozen then get on with his drink, and the queue was getting longer. The turn was doing his act but nobody gave a toss. He eventually signed all the autographs but it took ages and he wasn't keen on doing it; he just wanted to drink his Brown Ale. I had to tell him the time to worry was when people stopped asking him."

Jimmy and Jocky became firm friends and there was an occasion when Jimmy took him up to the golf driving range in Gosforth Park. Jocky had never played golf in his life but he borrowed some of Jimmy's clubs and proceeded to belt ball after ball down the driving range with unerring accuracy. As they passed the golf professional's shop afterwards Jocky decided to have a look around and his eye caught a set of clubs priced at £1,000. Jimmy advised him to invest in something more modest for £200 as he was a complete novice but Jocky said:

"I couldn't do that. If I start going to pro-ams with a £200 set of clubs, Eric Bristow and that lot will just take the piss."

He bought the expensive set of clubs and went back to the driving range with a new basket of balls to try them out; he could not hit a ball! He went back to Jimmy's clubs and immediately started hitting screamers again, so he offered to swap clubs. He had paid over £1,000 for a new set of top of the range golf clubs and half an hour later he had exchanged them for Jimmy's:

"Jocky was a really funny man and it is a tragedy that he is not still playing darts. I went to see him about a year ago and he is back living in the same dwellings in Kirkaldy where he started from. I offered to sponsor him for a year if he would come back, but he wasn't interested. He would not even come to the pub for a pint. The publican told me that he had started playing in that pub. That was where it all began for him, but now he is a virtual recluse. It's a shame."

Winning is Jimmy's motivation and he is instilling that attitude at Benfield as the committee grows and the team continues to progress:

"We performed well last season, especially in the FA Vase, and this season's team is better. Our manager, Paul Baker, and his second man Paddy Atkinson are excellent coaches. We have made great progress but we are still miles away from what I want to achieve."

They may have a distance to go, with the pace of progress now dictated by their ability to attract still more revenue and to continue upgrading the ground. Striking the correct balance between the competing financial demands of the playing side and the desire to improve the ground and its facilities is an art in itself and Jimmy Rowe takes the view that at present the balance needs to lie in favour of the off-the-field aspects of running the football club:

> "Ground improvements are a must if we are to make progress and attract the sponsors who will bring in the sort of money we need to realise our ambitions. It will come as long as we work together. To be fair, we give the manager a decent budget but we are not yet in a position to compete with the top Northern League clubs financially. In playing terms we are not a long way behind the long established clubs like Durham City and Newcastle Blue Star and we also have one of the top playing surfaces in the league, but we still need to press on in terms of ground improvement."

While it might be a long term ambition to test the temperature on the water in the Unibond League, the more realistic goal, and one which should be achieved more quickly, is to become consistently one of the top teams in the Northern League and to enjoy a taste of the success and recognition which come with decent runs in the FA Cup and the FA Vase. In those respects Benfield share the same ambitions as the top clubs in the Northern League, and being up there with them to the extent that they are capable of winning the championship is very definitely on the Benfield agenda:

> "We need to win that title and we will. I cannot say when it will be, but it will happen. I don't think it is far away because we have the right people in place."

Jimmy keeps referring to his nature as a winner, and it is fair to say that when his team fails to reach the standards he sets, and of which they have proved themselves capable, it effects him emotionally. There was case in point in the 2005-06 season when Benfield had a successful and impressive run in the FA Vase, but let themselves down when they lost away to the Blackpool side Squires Gate:

> "We should have beaten them. We had already knocked out better sides. We let ourselves down and I was so emotionally distraught that I couldn't go out that night with the lads and enjoy a night in Blackpool Rather than go out and sit there like an arsehole, I stayed in and sat like an arsehole! I couldn't cope with the fact that we were beaten by a poorer team. If they had been better than us I would have been disappointed but I could have accepted it, but they were not and I could not."

Jimmy Rowe is a successful businessman as well as a successful chairman and he is as driven with his 'City Signs' company as he is with his football. He is adrenalin driven; if his order book is not full he has to go out and get more work and he has the same energy and drive with Benfield. He is a hands on chairman who attends most training sessions and is a high profile presence at matches. He is also surprisingly old fashioned; he hates diving and cheating:

> "In my day if a player went down it was because someone had nutted him. Now you only have to breathe on some of them. That's not football."

The knock on effect of this single minded desire to succeed and to drive his club forward is that it makes him, by his own admission, hard to work for. He is demanding and he has no time for what he calls 'bullshitters' of whom he has had some experience during his many years in the game:

> "People have sometimes come along and thought they could push us to one side and run the football club their way, but it does not work like that with me. Maybe we have lost some people because I would not let them have their own way but I have no regrets about that. I have a responsibility to see that things are done properly and I have no doubt there are people who are not happy with the way I do things, but as chairman I believe I have to be strong and not waver."

It is important to understand that while Jimmy has no time for people who either fail to deliver or who he perceives as negative influences on his football club, he also places great store in loyalty. For instance, he has had a great relationship with Danny Gates over the years, based on mutual respect. It has had it moments, as you would expect when people with strong and forthright personalities are involved, but it has stood the test of time and they have had some wonderful times together in football and achieved outstanding success. He looks for the right kind of people at every level – he knows the value of a good player but also looks for good characters who will contribute to a harmonious dressing room. The same applies to managers. Over the years he has sometimes had to deal with managers who, no doubt for good reasons from their perspective, believed that their needs and priorities should come first. That simply does not happen at Benfield:

> "Managers are natural whingers; they are never satisfied. I can understand where they are coming from, but I have to look at the over all picture and they are just a part of it. We try to accommodate them, but they have to realise that there are other aspects to running a successful club. The present manager seems to understand that and we will push on with him."

Jimmy believes it is important to let the manager manage, the coaches coach and the players play. He mixes with the players and he is a familiar figure on away trips, but that it part of the social inclusion he also considers vitally important. He does not want or need the pressure of being involved in the management side of the club. He knows that he contributes to the pressure the manager and players are under because he and his committee have high expectations, and tough decisions sometimes have to be taken. Managers sometimes have to be told that things are not working out and changes have to be made. He acknowledges that hiring and firing are part of his business life as well as his responsibility as chairman of Benfield, but he does not enjoy that aspect of his work or find it easy. He values the relationships he has built with managers but he realises that sometimes the bond can become strained or stale:

> "Sometimes you can see that things are stagnating. Managers can be inclined to think things grow on trees and that spending money always solves problems. We are still quite a small club with limited resources and there are limits to how much we can spend, but I have backed every manager to the hilt. None of them can could argue otherwise, and I will continue to do so because we will always strive to get the best within our budget."

The lack of a clubhouse at the Benfield ground is something Jimmy keeps coming back to and it has assumed the proportions of a priority for the club to have its own base, but another issue is the fact that despite being in close proximity to a large volume of inner city housing which means there are a lot of potential supporters on their doorstep, that has not been reflected in the size of the crowds the club attracts the Sam Smith's. A marketing job is needed to raise the awareness of the club's existence in the local community, and that is one of the tasks facing the newly appointed commercial manager, Paul Taylor. Jimmy believes that the club's extremely rapid rise has compelled them to focus on other priorities, which has meant that they simply have not had the time or the people at their disposal to work on building their fan base. A new hospital is under construction across the road from the football club which will bring large numbers of additional people to the area and the intention is to target that with publicity material, along with the local housing, in order to raise the football club's profile in the local community:

> "I am over the moon with the fact that we have just sold our first four season tickets, thanks to Paul Baker. We have never had that before and I am really delighted. Our challenge now is to build on that so we can bring in regular, up front money season on season. We have to get out there. We are the senior team in the East End of the city and we need to attract gates which reflect that."

It will be hard work, because non league football in the region is no longer watched by large numbers of people, but there are few clubs better placed to attract fans than Benfield. Jimmy also sees their neighbours at Benfield School as potential partners, both as a source of support and as a source of future talent. At present the senior team stands alone, but the recent recruitment of people with local junior

Walker Central Juniors, sponsored by Jimmy's company, City Signs.

football backgrounds underlines the club's desire to extend their activities to include junior football, providing a potential stream of the talent of the future:

> "We have to have young players coming through and at present they are going elsewhere. The East End has always produced top quality footballers and we must attract them to Benfield."

Jimmy Rowe does not stand still. His talk of a clubhouse, junior teams and ongoing ground development is more than talk. He is still restless and ambitious and he retains his desire to reach the top, which he would measure in terms of success in the Northern League and the FA Vase. The club's successful FA Vase run in 2005-06 whetted his appetite and he was excited by the atmosphere their progress in the competition generated for the club. He has had a taste of it and the continuing progress the club is making encourages him to believe that here is more to come. The rapid rise of Newcastle Benfield, driven forward by Jimmy Rowe, supported by Danny Gates, John Colley, Trevor Atkins, Stan Gate and the rest of the Benfield crew, has been as impressive as it has been speedy, and Jimmy Rowe's energy and his gnawing desire to win suggests that the Newcastle Benfield story still has some exciting chapters to unfold.

Jimmy's company 'City Signs' sponsors the local junior team at Walker Central as a way of putting something back into the community in Newcastle's East End. He is also giving the local people a senior team they can follow and respect, and given a fair prevailing win, the loyalty of those around him in which he places such store, and his own drive and will to win, it will not be long before they have a team of which they can be proud. Then they will have no option but to go along to Sam Smith's and support Newcastle Benfield.

RICHIE McLOUGHLIN

Pulling up trees for Jarrow Roofing

Richie McLoughlin was a regular soldier and when he returned to civvy street he found work on South Tyneside and looked for a local club where he could continue to play football as he had in the army. He joined a Sunday team called Boldon Mechanics which was part of the Boldon Community Association where his close friend Brian Marshall was a player. He started to help Brian run the team as well and having found his feet again after army life, he formed his own company which he called Jarrow Roofing and he began again the work he had been doing before he joined up.

He was working seven days a week to establish his business and it was demanding work which left him no time for football, so he decided he had to compromise by sponsoring a team and reducing his work commitments from seven days a week to five. He needed the time away from the business to recharge his batteries and he devoted his weekends to football:

"Brian and I had a decent little side and we had won quite a number of trophies in the Business Houses League, but we decided we wanted to push on. Brian was connected with Boldon Community Association so we approached them with the idea of developing a piece of unused land at the Welfare into a football ground. Our proposal was discussed by the management committee and they gave us the go ahead as long as we met all the costs and carried out all of the work."

The arrangement suited Richie and Brian and the deal was agreed. Richie began the huge task of clearing the site by hiring a vehicle and a digger 'for next to nowt' because it was the Easter holiday weekend. Sites were not working and equipment was lying idle, so Richie was able to strike a good bargain. He worked the whole weekend, three days solid, stripping out everything from trees to shrubs to undergrowth and at the end of the weekend he had cleared an area the size of a football pitch. That was the basis, and the next step was to fence off the area and begin turning it into a football ground:

"I was working on some big sites by now, and everywhere I went I picked up anything spare I could lay my hands on. People knew what I was trying to do and they were very helpful. I scavenged metal sheeting and stuff like that and I was able to build a stand. I picked up bits and pieces wherever I could to get the job done."

How it all began...

So it was that in 1984 Jarrow Roofing Football Club came into existence; Richie was the scrounger in chief but his pal Brian Marshall was invaluable. He worked at the colliery and when it closed down it was a disaster for the local workforce, but it proved to be a perfect piece of timing for

RICHIE MCLOUGHLIN - PULLING UP TREES FOR JARROW ROOFING

Jarrow Roofing who were starting just as the pit was finishing, so they were able to get their hands on surplus materials which were scheduled for scrapping, dumping or burning. This included the wooden pylons for the club floodlights and with the assistance of a grant a set of lights which would otherwise have cost close to £50,000 to install were constructed and erected for a fraction of that amount:

> "I had a little bit of spare money which I hoyed in; we got the pylons for nothing and with the grant we were able to have floodlights, which would have been out of our reach financially otherwise. We were very lucky."

Richie believes that good fortune was on their side and that the establishment of Jarrow Roofing was meant to be. He was able to accomplish it without a massive financial outlay because he and Brian had the right contacts at the right time and they were not afraid of the hard physical slog the job entailed.

Jarrow Roofing began life as a Saturday team in the South Tyneside League where they operated for a few seasons, but Richie had higher ambitions. He felt the club was capable of operating at a better standard and he developed a two step long term strategy which involved joining the Wearside League from where he could build a side capable of winning promotion to the Northern League. Once the first stage was accomplished and they were admitted to the Wearside League, Richie embarked on a policy of watching as many midweek Northern League second division matches as he could, building up a dossier of information on clubs and players at that level, so that if Jarrow Roofing won promotion they would know what to expect at the next level and be equipped to cope with it.

He was determined to achieve Northern League status, and nothing he saw during his extensive scouting missions discouraged him from his ambition. He felt it was within his, Brian's, and the club's capabilities, though there were plenty of people who told him it could not be done:

> "People from some of the top clubs in the Northern League told me it was impossible but I always believed we would do it some day and, as a matter of fact, it came sooner than I expected. I thought it would take us ten years but we did it in less than that."

Jarrow Roofing's great rivals for promotion from the Wearside League were Marske United and while the teams were very well matched on the field Jarrow had a massive advantage, thanks to those early scrounging efforts, as far as meeting Northern League ground criteria was concerned. They had floodlights and Marske had not. Richie was confident he could carry out any other ground improvements the Northern League stipulated, so it was a matter of finishing in the top two places in the league:

> "I really wanted to make the step up because while I respected the standards in the Wearside League I had seen enough Northern League football to know that the standard was higher. I also liked the way the game was played in the Northern League and I wanted us to be part of it."

Once again, as it had been when the club was formed, so it was as they sought to fulfil their Northern League ambitions, the fates were generous to Jarrow Roofing. Nothing stood in their way. If Richie needed something to use at the ground he would find it on a job he went to. He put his scavenging talents to good use once more, and while he will say that he found the task of preparing the ground

Ready for the first game.

Jarrow Roofing after winning the Sunday Business Houses League. Richie is second left with a hand on his shoulder, and Brian Marshall is standing third from the right on the front row.

for the Northern League easier than he had expected and easier than some other teams have found it, he and Brian put in an enormous amount of work themselves. They were determined that nothing would be allowed to stand in their way and their resolve, and their sheer hard graft, paid off. The Northern League had laid down their ground criteria a year before when they carried out their inspection, so Richie knew what was needed in that respect and he was able to concentrate on making sure the team was good enough to finish the season in a promotion spot.

Finding talent has never been a problem for Richie. Right from the first he went out at every opportunity looking at players. He had been away from the area for several years and he had no contacts and knew no players so he had to work as hard as a talent scout as he did as a construction worker at the ground. He knew there were a lot of good players on South Tyneside, so he signed the best he could to consolidate the team's position in the Wearside League, then he widened his net as he searched for even better players who could help the club to mount a promotion challenge, and help Richie achieve his dream of bringing Northern League football to the club. He assembled an impressive squad which included good players like John Caffrey, Paddy Liddle and Lee Young; he had brought in a number of players from the Sunderland area to supplement the South Tyneside contingent and the result was a successful and exciting team. They played the kind of attacking football

Richie advocates and he was confident that they were good enough to win promotion. He was right:

> "We were lucky in a way, because we had signed Paul Tinmouth from Shields and I was still a bit naïve in those days; I did not realise that he was suspended. I played him and we were deducted three points which cost us the league championship. We finished second, but we knew that Marske's ground was not yet up to Northern League standard so we were confident we would go up."

Nevertheless, Richie was taking nothing for granted and every Saturday he travelled down to Marske, had his lunch in a café near the ground and made sure there were no signs that they were working to complete the necessary ground improvements!. The Marske people were sick of the sight of him, but he need not have worried; Jarrow Roofing were promoted to the Northern League, and happily Marske followed them the following season. Marske has mixed memories for Richie; it was a place where his famous touchline antics got him into trouble more than once:

> "They had this bloke in the crowd who was there just to provoke me; they did that down there and stupid me fell for it every time. He was giving me stick all afternoon and eventually I lost my rag and went to punch him. Unfortunately there was this low barrier and when I threw my punch my momentum carried me over the barrier. I hit fresh air and landed on my face. I was grappling with this bloke and the crowd was in hysterics."

The hours he had spend watching Northern League second division football paid rapid dividends. Richie knew the precise nature of the challenge the new league presented and he put together a team to meet it, then he undertook a similar exercise, spending all his spare nights going to watch Northern League first division games so that when Jarrow Roofing cleared the next hurdle and moved up to Division One, he again had his dossier to tell him what the standard was like, how the teams played, and what he would need to do to compete:

> "When we played in the second division in our promotion season we had to play at Billingham Town in our second last match and we had to win it to go up and so did they. We produced a great performance and we beat them; everybody was jumping up and down and celebrating and loads of people wanted to shake hands with me and have a word, so by the time I got to the dressing room it was a while after the final whistle. Eventually I went charging down the corridor and burst into the dressing room shouting and cheering like a crackerjack but when I looked around the place was totally deserted and there was complete silence. I was bewildered and I felt a fool, but the showers at Billingham are set back from the actual changing area and all of a sudden all the players jumped out from the showers and started spraying me with champagne. I was absolutely soaked but it was one of the greatest nights of my life."

Richie talks about the good fortune he has had along the way and the help they had when he and Brian were starting out, how their timing was right, but it was hard work and attention to detail on his part which formed the foundation of the club's success. Having become a Northern League side and quickly moved up to the first division, Richie has made it his business to sit down at the start of every season and plan his strategy for staying in the top division:

> "We had worked very hard to turn ourselves into a Northern League first division club in a short time and I was determined that it was not going to be a temporary thing. The target I set myself each season was to produce a team which would keep us there and we have been successful in that. It was hard to get there and I am determined that we will always have a team which will keep us there."

The need to concentrate on achieving consistency and respectability at league level meant that Richie paid scant attention to other competitions which to some extent would be distractions from his prime purpose. Jarrow Roofing were used to being knocked out of the FA Cup and the FA

Vase at the early stages and it was never an issue. They were a small and homespun club which had made rapid strides to be where they were and they were not really inclined to look beyond that to see what might be over the horizon. That attitude changed dramatically in the 2004-05 season when Jarrow Roofing embarked on a remarkable journey which was to take them to the semi finals of the FA Vase. The North East was also represented at that stage in the competition by experienced Vase campaigners Bedlington Terriers and local non league fans savoured the tantalising prospect of a final of a national competition between two teams from the region; as it turned out, neither team reached the final but both came mighty close. For Jarrow in particular, with no tradition in the Vase, reaching the last four only to lose to the eventual winners of the trophy was a monumental achievement.

The further Roofing progressed in the competition, the more people came to watch them; crowds turned up for their home games at Boldon in unprecedented numbers and they had good support in away ties as the unsung and unfashionable team from South Tyneside went through round after round, beating several fancied teams along the way. It was different from any previous experience Richie had enjoyed in football and it was his finest hour:

> "I began to believe that if we could get our best eleven players on the pitch we could do really well in the competition. We had our best eleven players available for every round up to the semi final and that was how we got so far."

Richie was performing a precarious balancing act. With a small squad he needed to protect his first choice players and in the later rounds of the Vase that meant that meant rotating them and putting out weaker sides in league games, putting his prime objective of preserving the club's league status in jeopardy. The fact was that events overtook him and he changed his priorities for the second half of the season. He realised that it might be a while before a comparable opportunity came again and he had to focus on the Vase. In doing so he saw Jarrow struggle for league points and there was a stage when relegation looked a distinct possibility:

> "Once I got the feeling for the Vase and started to enjoy it, I put our league priorities on the back burner. We had a lot of games in hand because of our Vase involvement and I was confident that we would be able to put a run together which would keep us in the first division. We were picking up odd points here and there which meant that things were not desperate, but I admit that our league position was not strong."

Richie is known throughout non league circles in the North East as a passionate, volatile, argumentative touch line observer who can say rash things in the heat of the moment which make him an easy target for wind up merchants from other clubs. He has been in hot water with the Durham FA and the Northern League on many occasions, but his finest hour, or his most infamous experience, depending on your point of view, came in the FA Vase quarter finals when Roofing met Tipton:

> "They were a rugged team and a lot of the Tipton folk were not very nice people. We scored a late goal in the home tie which sickened them because they thought they had the game won, and they were gloating in the bar afterwards about what they would do to us in the replay. They had this big centre forward called Royston who had been making his mouth go all week in their local papers and when we went out to play the crowd was extremely hostile and abusive. This Royston was mouthing off again and getting me going and he came over to get the ball off me to take a throw in. I held it behind my back and he went mad. After the throw in he clipped me on the back of the head, so I smacked him one. That set everything off and there was mayhem. I was sent off and the police came and wanted to arrest me and escort me from the ground. Things calmed down a little bit and when the game restarted we were transformed. We had been terrible and we were going out, but the fracas changed everything. The big centre forward lost it; he got sent off

and the game went to penalties. I went to the toilet before they started and the big bloke followed me and threw a punch; I hit the door and if I hadn't I would have landed twenty feet away, then their committee came along to see what the commotion was and hauled him off. They ordered me to stay in the dressing room and when the players came in I said: 'Never mind lads, we did our best.' 'What do you mean you daft bugger?' one of them said, 'We won!' I had not seen the penalties and I didn't know the result. I was ecstatic. It wasn't in the coaching manual but that set to on the touch line changed the game for us. None of their people would speak to the centre forward in the bar afterwards because he had cost them the game and we were through to the semi finals."

Richie's attempts to protect his strongest team came unstuck at the semi final stage when he found himself without both his captain Martin Thompson as well as Craig Nelson who had been their outstanding player throughout the Vase run and had scored a number of important goals. His best eleven was not available to him despite his best endeavours and they lost both legs 1-0, though there was certainly no disgrace in either scoreline. Didcot were a good side and they proved it by beating Sudbury in the final, but Jarrow ran them close and the Didcot people were full of praise for their efforts and rated them as much the hardest opponents they had met in the competition.

Actually, Richie believed that four or five of his players froze in the first leg which was played in front of a massive crown compared to what they were used to and some of the players failed to produce their lest form. Nevertheless, they had done their homework and they shackled Didcot's two highly rated strikers who had scored freely throughout the tournament but failed to find the net against Jarrow in either leg of the tie. Despite a below par performance in that first leg Richie felt that his team was still in with a good chance as they were only behind by a single goal. The Roofing fans turned out in their hundreds for the game at Boldon, but to their credit Didcot repeated their 1-0 win in a very tight game. They just had the edge and there was a tinge of relief as well as praise in the Didcot manager's post match compliments regarding Roofing's performance. Didcot had swept teams aside throughout the Vase run with three or four goal wins, but they only just squeaked past the Jarrow lads.

Having entered the competition with no real expectations, Richie had taken his team to within a whisker of the final and while it was a bitter blow to be knocked out at that stage, he believed that what they had achieved was an outstanding advertisement for Northern League football. Looking back, he takes great satisfaction from what his small club achieved, and it had the effect of putting Jarrow Roofing on the national stage:

> *"It certainly put us on the map. People still contact us asking for badges and programmes and wanting information about Jarrow Roofing, and that is a direct result of what we did in the Vase. I was surprised at the impact it had and it certainly opened my eyes."*

The success had a positive effect on attendances because people were attracted by success, but that kind of support is inclined to be transient and fickle. However, in Roofing's case there is still a residue of fans who first came to watch them in the Vase and who still attend matches. Others, who are not 'every week' supporters, swell the ranks when the bigger games come along.

Jarrow survived the season in the first division of the Northern League, so Richie's strategy paid off in that sense, but he had savoured his team's experience in the Vase and wanted more of it. Unfortunately, the following season they were knocked out in their first game, which brought them down to earth and reminded them to respect the competition, but they have learned that lesson and they will be ready next time. They will not be complacent again; they will be properly prepared.

Richie's pitch side behaviour has him marked as one of the league's real characters, but he is not the only one at Roofing:

> *"We were playing at Chester le Street once and our physio Alan Leslie, who always wanted to be the fastest in the league, was not his usual self.*

He seemed a bit sluggish and I made a comment about it. It was a really muddy day and when one of our players was injured right on the centre spot Alan was obviously determined to show me. He picked up his bag and plastic bucket and he was off like a greyhound out of the traps. Then one of the straps on his bag came loose and he got it caught around his foot. He tripped, and took off. He flew through the air from the edge of the centre circle and landed on the centre spot then he slid slid along in the mud clinging to his plastic bucket. The crowd were bad with laughing and as he came off they gave him some terrible stick. He was so confused and embarrassed he sat down in the opposition dug out and started watching the game. It was hilarious."

Outsiders look at Jarrow Roofing and see it as a one man show, and it is certainly true that Richie has been the principal force behind the club, but his friend Brian Marshall has been with him from the very beginning and shared with him the vision of creating a respectable Northern League club. They both had ambition and for the first two seasons the two of them carried out the bulk of the work before they began to recruit others on to their committee to share the burden. The two of then are still the main movers and their involvement and commitment has never wavered, though Richie does say he is disappointed at what he sees as a lack of commitment on the part of some of the younger players, not just at his club, who seem to prefer a Friday night on the town and will look for excuses not to play on Saturday. He also believes that a lot of young players are not as good as they think they are and that the general standard has declined because young lads have lots of leisure options to distract them away from football.

Richie has always worked hard to uncover talent before other people spot it, but has sometimes suffered because bigger and financially stronger clubs have tempted players away from Jarrow. He realises that this will continue to be an issue unless he can move his team up a notch; players will stay if the team is successful and this was clearly underline by the successful FA Vase season when no players left. Occasionally, good players will show loyalty. Paul Chow, for instance, was a prolific goalscorer who was coveted by all the top clubs in the area but he stayed with Jarrow Roofing for several years and when he did move there was no resentment on Richie's part because he appreciated what Paul had given the club. Ironically, his move did not work out and he was back at Roofing a year later. Another of his star talents is Craig Nelson and he, too, has been very loyal, resisting the temptation to go elsewhere. It is a quality any manager hopes for in his best players and there must be something about Jarrow Roofing which keeps players of the quality of Chow and Nelson on side.

Richie holds the starting gun as international athlete David Sharpe and Shields Gazette reporter Mick Worrall prepare to compete against each other in a race for charity.

Richie is willing to concede that his passion and commitment during matches has got him into his share of disciplinary trouble and cost him a fair amount of money in fines, but he can record one small victory over the system:

> "I have been in loads of bother but the last time I was up before the league they let me off. I had been warned about swearing previously and I was sent off for abusing the referee in a cup game against Dunston and fined £50 by the Durham FA. That meant an automatic appearance in front of the Northern League but I pleaded my case that although I had criticised the referee I had not sworn and I should be given credit for trying. They saw the funny side and let me off."

Richie's first priority is still to achieve Northern League respectability every season, but he has looked beyond, and he would certainly be interested in taking his club to the next level if the Unibond League made a commitment to a more tightly regionalised system, perhaps in conjunction with the Northern League, so that travelling distances were realistic. It would drive up standards and while there would be cost implications Richie would be firmly in favour of a regional league with an eighty or ninety miles travelling radius. Midweek trips to Manchester, Sheffield and such like, however, are very definitely off the menu.

Conversations which Richie McLoughlin inevitably include recollections of his brushes with authority which he admits are usually self inflicted:

> "I don't keep a record of how many times I have been disciplined, but I have always been in bother. When I was playing in the South Tyneside League years ago this experienced old player flattened a young kid who was playing for us so I hit him over the head with a plastic bucket full of water. That was my first £50 fine and another time I was running the line but the referee was ignoring my signals so when he came for his flag after the game I snapped it in two. I told the disciplinary hearing I had dropped it accidentally, but they fined me £50. It must have cost me a fortune over the years: I have been in trouble so many times. Mike Amos once told me I would be banned from the dugout and I would have to watch games from the tea hut if I didn't improve. Just after that this referee was coming off the pitch in front of the players and there was this big goalkeeper right behind him. I called the ref a cheating bastard and he reached for his notebook. I knew I was in trouble so I told him I was talking to the goalkeeper, not him. He told me later he knew I was talking a load of shite but he had let me off because I had changed my mind at the last minute. It was a close shave because he knew I had been talking to him and I could have ended up in the tea hut. People come deliberately to wind me up and I never learn. There was this bloke last season and he started mouthing off so I responded. He offered to take me outside so I agreed, but he chickened out, then this massive bloke came across and said he would take his place. It was ridiculous but it happens every time. It is my own fault. I know some teams cannot stand me, but I don't mean anything. I am just passionate and I won't back down. I have had some right ding dongs with some of the top teams because I always want to get a result against them. I respect them and I know I should keep quiet, but I can't. I say good luck to them but I still have a go at them."

He has abandoned the arduous and soul destroying business of trying to squeeze money out of reluctant sponsors and no longer knocks on doors in the area selling draw tickets to raise funds. He is sensible enough to welcome revenue from programme advertising and boards around the ground, but he bears the brunt of the expense himself thanks to his successful business. People who know Richie and are aware of the level of his investment of every kind in Jarrow Roofing are full of praise and he has twice had the satisfaction of having his work for the football club publicly recognised in the South Tyneside Local Sports Personality of the Year awards. It is not the reason he does it, but it is nice to be acknowledged occasionally. It is no more than he deserves, and long may it continue.

KEITH MILLS

The mysterious case of the disappearing crossbar

Keith Mills is an East End lad who began to play football at West Walker Primary School where he received early encouragement from a teacher called Mike Bell who was 'a proper football man.' Mike was also in charge of the Newcastle Boys side and he selected Keith for the city squad where he first came into contact with young players like Derek Bell and Neil Rowe. Next came secondary school which in Keith's case meant Walker Comprehensive School where he played in the school side which won the league championship for each of the five years he attended the school. He continued to be a regular in the city boys side, though there was a period when that accolade was taken away from him:

> "I was chucked off in the third year because I went a little haywire. I was not turning up for training and I was missing games. The teacher in charge actually taught at Walker School and he said I was not playing for the city any more. I got a good rollicking off the old man and I pulled myself round. I realised you cannot take the micky out of decent people and I got myself back into the city side. It was a case of a lesson learned."

Keith was never one of those young talents who were chased by professional clubs, which was something of a surprise and a disappointment because he felt there were players less able than himself who were being given opportunities to go away on trial. He was philosophical about it, however, and when the time came to leave school he graduated to local football. On Saturdays he played for Walker Sporting, a team which was run from Walker Youth Club and despite being only sixteen he was also playing Sunday morning football for the Walker Turbinia pub side.

It was while he was playing in a five-a-side competition at the Lightfoot Stadium that he was spotted by Dave Robertson who used to referee at the Lightfoot on a regular basis. Dave was connected with Bishop Auckland and he invited Keith to try his luck at Kingsway playing for Brian Newton. After initially agreeing to join Bishops Keith changed his mind and it was not until a year later when he was again playing in an indoor tournament at the Lightfoot Stadium that his next opportunity came along:

> "I was playing for the Locomotive and the winners of the competition each received ten pints. Obviously that meant we had to win it, and we did!"

Dave Robertson was now associated with North Shields, which was a much more convenient location for a Walker lad than Bishop Auckland, so Keith decided that this time he would accept Dave's invitation and give it a go. It was a shock to turn up at the old Appleby Park ground and to realise that it was a proper football stadium; Keith had no previous experience of playing in that kind of environment:

> "Bobby Elwell was the manager; a bloke I have a great deal of time and respect for. The first time I went they had a friendly against Percy Main; he played me on the right wing and I did OK. I signed for Shields after the game."

What Keith had failed to mention at this juncture was that he was carrying a suspension and would be unable to play in the opening game of the season the following Saturday. He was compelled to reveal the fact on the morning of the match and to his credit Bobby Elwell told him to continue training with the club for the duration of his six weeks ban. He liked the club, enjoyed the surroundings of Appleby Park, and held the manager in high regard; a happy player is a loyal player and Keith Mills laid down roots at North Shields.

KEITH MILLS - THE MYSTERIOUS CASE OF THE DISAPPEARING CROSSBAR

When his suspension was completed, it coincided with an injury to another Shields forward, Ian Mutrie, and the opportunity of Mutrie's misfortune gave Keith the chance to establish himself in the team. He was joining a good side which included quality players like Peter Stronach, Dave Varty, Tim Gilbert the former Sunderland player, Bede McCaffrey and Jimmy Harmison. They were all respected players of the highest calibre and Keith regarded himself as fortunate to be in a position of learning about the game from so many good players. He made his debut when he was chosen as a striker against Horden, and he scored:

"I was jumping up and down like a lunatic when I scored. I was delighted but as I ran past one of their players, Bobby Hutton, he muttered: 'You lucky little shit!'"

It was a good season for North Shields. They had enjoyed an epic four match battle with Whitby Town in the FA Cup:

"The first game was played at Appleby Park and there was a riot – a proper riot. The fans had a pitched battle in one corner of the ground; I was flabbergasted."

They eventually lost to Whitby and they also had a major tussle with Bishop Auckland in the FA Trophy before losing in the second replay. Keith had played in every game that season until he committed an indiscretion which cost him another suspension as well as a thorough dressing down from Bobby Elwell; he called a referee a cheat and was punished with a red card. Bobby Elwell marched him into the referee's room and made him apologise; he felt like a naughty schoolboy brought before the headmaster. The referee acknowledged his apology but the red card stood and the consequences were another six weeks suspension and another lesson learned. The team was still challenging for the Northern League championship, they were in the League Cup and the Northumberland Senior Cup.

Keith's suspension did not help the cause as North Shields battled through a fixture backlog caused by their epic FA Cup and FA Trophy battles, and when the suspension was completed on the eve of the Northumberland Senior Cup final he was expecting nothing better than a place on the bench for his comeback game. As a young nineteen year old without his own transport, he packed his kit and got the number 12 bus to St James's Park for the match and, to his surprise, Bobby Elwell selected him to play in the game which was against Blyth Spartans:

"It was teeming with rain and we were playing a Blyth team which included David Barton, Micky Carroll, Steve Baxter and Paul Walker. They were all quality players and I had not done any training for the six weeks I was out. We lost 1-0 and I was actually crying in the dressing room afterwards. We played Whitby three days later in the final of the League Cup and the same thing happened; we ended up losing 2-0. The season went flat after those two blows and we finished sixth in the league. A season which had promised so much just fizzled out."

The atmosphere in the North Shields dressing room was excellent. Bobby Elwell had added to an excellent squad by bringing in Keith, Tess Baines and a goalkeeper, then he signed Derek Ord, a winger with a fabulous left foot, but from challenging for everything they ended up winning nothing. Bobby Elwell resigned as the manager, but Dave Robertson stayed on and Vic Hillier replaced Elwell:

"They called Vic 'The Assassin' but in fact he was a nice man. The only thing I didn't like about him was the fact that he worked for the Social Security!"

Vic brought players in and while things were not quite so enjoyable or successful as they had been under Bobby Elwell, Keith's own form was good and the club wanted him to sign a contract. As a young and still inexperienced player his knowledge of contracts was distinctly limited but he was tempted by the inducement of a signing on fee at a time when he was out of work and he signed on the dotted line. At the time he was playing Sunday morning football for Ray Mulroy at the Birds Nest and Ray was not happy because his signature on the North Shields contract meant that he was not permitted to play Sunday football:

"At the time big Ginger Burns was a director of North Shields and he looked after me. What a character he was! We used to go to his boozer

which was 'The Jungle' in North Shields, and stay until two in the morning. There were some right turns in that place, I can tell you."

The season was an average one because a lot of Bobby Elwell's squad had moved on; effectively, the best players had left the club and the quality was not quite the same. Keith kept playing consistently well, however, and it prompted Vic Hiller to arrange for him to have a trial with a professional club. Unfortunately it was Bristol City but despite the geographical problems that posed, Keith felt he had to give it a try as it was his first opportunity at that level. The former Leeds United and England defender Terry Cooper was the Bristol manager and Clive Middlemass was his number two:

"I set away at eight o'clock on the Sunday morning and I did not reach Bristol until half past seven at night. It was a helluva journey. I actually only played in one game which was for the Reserves against Plymouth Argyle on the Wednesday night. We travelled from Bristol to Plymouth in a little minibus with wooden seats and my backside was numb before I got there. I played well enough and they offered me another two weeks but I didn't fancy being all the way down there to be honest. There was an amazing incident the night before I left when I went to watch the first team play a match in the LDV Vans Trophy and the first person I saw when I reached the turnstile was big Ginger Burns. I was amazed and he said he had just come down to see if I was OK. How many people would travel all that way just to see if somebody was all right?"

Ginger and Keith watched the match and then returned to the big man's hotel where they went on the drink until three o'clock in the morning. Keith's landlady had moved him out of his room and up to the attic to accommodate another young triallist, so he stumbled up to the top of the house and into bed. Suffice to stay that the Bristol area actually suffered a tornado that night and Keith awoke the next morning unaware that anything untoward had taken place! The trial was over, leaving Keith disappointed, but not devastated, that nothing came of it. When the season was over North Shields were keen for him to sign another contract but he had misgivings as he was missing his Sunday morning football:

"When I was playing for the Birds Nest our arch rivals were Dunston Social. We were due to play them this day but for some reason we could not get our team out. It was such a key game that something had to be done. We used to put up our own posts and we kept them in somebody's back garden so we hit on the idea of hiding one of the crossbars in another garden so that when the Dunston team turned up we could say that somebody had pinched it and the game would have to be called off. The Dunston lads were foaming because they knew the crack but they couldn't do anything about it. We actually won the league in a play off at their place that year, and the incident of the missing crossbar is still talked about."

Once again, the lure of a few pounds signing on fee plus a slight increase in expenses helped the unemployed Keith Mills to make his decision and he signed for another season:

"As well as the deal I signed to play another year, I received a special payment. Big Burnsie came round to my house and presented me with twelve pieces of fresh cod! He said it was my loyalty bonus; I asked him where the chips were!"

It was another average season for North Shields, but in February Vic Hillier informed Keith that Clive Middlemass, who had left Bristol City and was now managing Carlisle United, wanted him to go across to Cumbria for another trial. He made the trip but he was suffering from a back injury and was unable to play, so Middlemass took him back when he was fit and invited him to stay for a month with the blessing of North Shields. After two weeks Middlemass told him he had done well both in his commitment to training and in his performances on the field, and that he intended to offer him a contract at the end of his trial period. He played for a Carlisle Reserves team, which was supplemented by

Keith in the Blyth Spartans colours, fourth from the right in the front row, sitting next to manager Ronnie Walton.

local players, against Barnsley and one of the local imports was a fellow striker called Gary Marshall. They each scored twice in a 7-1 win and that cemented Carlisle's interest in signing him, but they were strapped for cash and were unable to meet North Shields' asking price of £5,000. Instead, the Cumbrians signed Gary Marshall who cost them nothing and at the age of 25 Keith's prospects of a professional career came to an end:

> "That knocked my lights in. I was really disappointed. I realised that Shields were looking after their own interests which was fair enough, but it stopped me having my chance and I will never know whether I could have made a career for myself as a professional footballer. At least I can say I played in a Football League match against Peterborough."

Keith stayed at North Shields because in spite of the Carlisle business he still felt that was where he belonged. Not so Vic Hillier, who moved on to be replaced by the former Newcastle United forward Jim Pearson. Jim brought a feel good factor to Appleby Park and he also brought in good players to add to the air of optimism around the club. Derek Bell, Barrie Wardrobe and Paul Ferris all joined:

> "Paul Ferris was always injured. If ever a person chose the right job it was him when he became a physiotherapist."

A group of local businessmen were interested in taking over the football club and there was resistance from the existing directors. A power struggle ensued and things became difficult; the club was not allowed to use its clubhouse because of the conflict and there were escalating problems. Blyth Spartans, who were managed by Tommy Dixon, put in seven days notice for Keith but once again his status as a contracted player proved to be a stumbling block. North Shields were entitled to ask for a fee, and Blyth's financial situation was such that they could not afford to pay it. In fact, Keith was content to stay put; he was happy with Jim Pearson and he was the club captain, but the infighting at the club was unsettling everyone; Jim Pearson decided to call it a day and the business people who had wanted to invest and take over the club withdrew, leaving the original regime in charge. Len Murphy, the club chairman, informed Keith that Blyth had come back in for him and that North Shields had decided to let him go, so after six years at Appleby Park he was sold to Blyth Spartans for £1,000 and he went to Croft Park to play for Tommy Dixon.

Blyth were going through a difficult period. They had financial worries and their best players had left. Tommy Dixon had taken over at a dispiriting time, but his assistant was Ronnie Walton with whom Keith immediately established an excellent relationship. The club was boosted by the recruitment of a group of young players from the area who had been released by Ipswich Town; Darren Nicholls, Dave Hunter and Craig Liddle. The immensely talented Nigel Walker was still there as was Nigel Saddington. There were encouraging signs despite the problems and Keith was enjoying life with the Spartans. The good relationship he had forged with Ronnie Walton proved to be a bonus when Tommy Dixon left and Ronnie took over. He was an excellent manager and under his guidance Blyth won the League Cup and the Northumberland Senior Cup, finished runners up in the league and also won the Cleator Cup:

"Things were looking good, though I did have one narrow escape. We were playing on Boxing Day and it was an eleven o'clock kick off. I had just got home at six o'clock in the morning and when Ronnie Walton picked me up I was still half drunk. When we got to the ground the lads realised I was pissed and I have no idea how Ronnie did not twig. Anyway, there had been high force winds through the night and a part of the stand roof had been loosened. The referee thought it was hazardous and he would not play the game. That was the luckiest experience I ever had and I still can't believe Ronnie Walton didn't realise the state I was in. I got away with it somehow, but I don't know how"

The Blyth squad was gradually being built up into a strong one and Keith was a part of the club for four years until one pre-season Ronnie Walton said he was letting him go. He said that he thought Keith was a bad influence on the young players, though Keith told him the youngsters would tell a different story if Ronnie asked them. The manager had made his mind up and had even done a deal to sell Keith to Newcastle Blue Star, so he was both upset and panic stricken when Keith refused to move to the Wheatsheaf and said he was going to play for Colin Richardson at North Shields instead:

"I had no problems whatever with Rob and Steve Carney who were running Blue Star. I actually got on well with Steve who is a close lad and he only lets a few people in. I was one of them and we had an excellent relationship, but I was not going to be told by Ronnie Walton where I was going to play and I refused to go. In the end I decided not to go back to Appleby Park either; it just didn't feel right, so we had reached an impasse."

The issue was resolved when Ronnie Walton had a change of heart and contacted Keith to say that he had made a mistake and wanted him to stay so, although he was unsure of Ronnie's motives, he buckled down to pre-season and got himself into prime condition. Unfortunately, after just three games Keith broke his leg in a freak accident:

"I jumped up to head the ball and I thought the player behind me had landed on my leg, but he hadn't. I had just fallen awkwardly. I was stretchered to the treatment room then the ambulance took me to hospital. Gary Hayes came with me and they just put me in a room. My leg started to itch and I put my hand down the casing they had used to immobilise it. When I took it out my hand was covered with blood and Gary ran for the nurse; within ten minutes I was in the operating theatre. I had a compound

fracture of the fibia and tibia and a fractured ankle. I had to have three operations and basically lost the whole season."

Yet another change of regime at Blyth saw Peter Feenan installed as manager and he told Keith that as soon as he was fit he would be a part of his plans. With this encouragement he once again trained hard in pre-season and as part of the process of stepping up his match fitness he went to play for Ray Mulroy at Walker Central. In a game against Heaton Stannington, Walker were giving the Heaton lads a pasting and were leading 9-0 when Keith pushed the ball past the late Eddie Temple. Eddie's attempted tackle caught Keith on the point of the break in his leg and broke it again:

"I never spoke to Eddie for a long time after that which was wrong. He should not have lashed out the way he did but there is no room for bitterness in football. Thankfully we made up our differences and started speaking again before Eddie's very sad death."

The injury meant another lengthy lay off, but Keith was still only 29 and he felt that he had several playing years left in him. He has never had a quitter's mentality and the thought of giving up the game simply never occurred to him. He felt he wanted to work hard again to recover from the devastation of the second injury and that is exactly what he set about doing. He got back into the Blyth team and was planning his next season with the Spartans when Peter Feenan left and Harry Dunn became the manager:

"I feel that if a player has been loyal to a club for six years as I had, he is entitled to be told face to face if the manager does not want to keep him. All I got from Harry was a phone call saying that I was not wanted. I have to say that Harry has done brilliantly at Blyth in his current spell and good luck to him, but I found the way I was dispensed with a little disappointing."

Keith spoke to his old friend Bob Moreland who printed the story of his release in the 'Evening Chronicle' which alerted other clubs to his availability, and he ended up at Newcastle Blue Star with the Carney brothers. Dave Thompson signed for Blue Star on the same day and they knew many of the other players at the Wheatsheaf; although they were not a team of superstars they were decent players and good characters and when Dave and Keith were offered £40 a week to sign they were happy to accept it. Two days before the season started they were both told that the original offer of £40 was no longer on the table and the best they could be given was £25 a week. Despite the reduction both players opted to stay and certainly in Keith's case it proved to be a good decision because it led to possibly his best and most enjoyable season in non league football. There was a great camaraderie among the players; they played together and socialised together and the team spirit was excellent, though there were some excessive moments:

"Jimmy Anderson and old Derek used to lock up at the end of the night, but one time we didn't want to leave so they gave us the keys. We were still drinking at two in the morning, then we all decided to get stripped bollock naked and race each other up and down the pitch. We drank all the beer; there was not a drop left, and Jimmy and them went ballistic when they found out what had gone on!"

Rob Carney brought in a backer called Tom Brown who owned the traffic management company RTM, and he used to bring the lads a Mars Bar each. If the team won there was an additional bonus for Keith of a packet of twenty cigarettes!

"It was a very happy time. The money was not great and even out of the £25 we received we had to donate a fiver to transport costs, but nobody complained. We should have won the league and I really enjoyed myself, but Rob decided to release me because he thought I was a bad influence. Let me just say that I always turned up for training because I regarded it as a night out. I trained hard then went on the drink straight afterwards. Anyway, for better or worse he let me go which was a shame because it was a great time for me."

The next manager to come calling was Peter Quigley from Dunston Federation. Keith had other options but he went to meet Peter, who sat him down and spoke to him like a Dutch uncle. He made him a decent offer and, more important, he made him feel wanted but there was a caveat that he had heard of Keith's reputation as a bad apple and made it clear that if there was any stepping over the line he would be out. Keith accepted the conditions and signed for the Fed. Peter Quigley's number two was Tony Heslop, a man who could stand on the stage and make people laugh, and Keith found it easy to settle in at Dunston where he stayed for a number of years:

> "I have to say that I have never heard one of Peter Quigley's team talks. I was always in the toilet having a smoke! Peter used to tell Tony Heslop he thought I was nervous because I always went to the toilet before the game, and Tony told him to look above the toilet door and see the plumes of smoke going up like a new Pope had been elected!"

Peter Quigley left Dunston because the management committee wanted to sack Tony Heslop and Peter felt that it was a point of principle that he should leave as well. Nevertheless, Keith is adamant that Dunston was the best club he played for. The people who ran the club had his great respect and he had a particularly high regard for John Thompson who had the great virtue in Keith's eyes that he kept one of the best pints of beer in the North East! When Peter resigned and Bobby Scaife was appointed as his replacement, Keith felt that after four years at Federation Park it was time to move on.

For many years Bedlington Terriers had been keen to sign him but he had always resisted their overtures, feeling that it was not the club for him, but eventually he did join them:

> "Leaving Dunston was the worst decision I made in my entire football career. I was at Bedlington for a few months, but I found it hard to accept that Keith Perry could leave me out after I played three or four good games in a row without an explanation. That was not the way I was used to playing my football and I told him I was leaving."

He had a brief spell at Durham City with another manager he regarded highly, Tony Harrison, but unfortunately it was not a good time for Durham and they were relegated. During his spell at Bedlington they had played Dunston and the manager's son, Nick Scaife, was sent off for an offence which he had not committed. Keith, along with Steve Boon, agreed to attend the disciplinary hearing when it eventually took place to speak on Nick Scaife's behalf and after the meeting Bobby Scaife asked him if he would be interested in returning for a second spell at Dunston. Keith jumped at the opportunity and in the consequent four years he spent at the club they won the Northern League Cup three times and generally competed successfully, but in truth Keith was now reaching the veteran stage at the age of 36 and he could no longer command a regular place in an increasingly strong Dunston side.

Footballers need to be playing so he moved to Whitley Bay at Andy Gowans' suggestion in the expectation of playing regular football. Unfortunately, he was suffering from a groin problem which he found difficult to shake off. He was getting through matches be he was unable to train properly. Whitley had an away fixture on a typically cold day at Consett and when Keith was left out of the team and was not even on the bench he knew the writing was on the wall. So it proved, with Andy Gowans telling him after the game that he was letting him go:

> "I had a real go at him. Andy is a good friend of many years standing, but I told him I could have gone elsewhere and I resented being sat in the stands at Consett on a freezing cold day and then being told I was not wanted. We are still friends and I suppose the fact that he went on to win the FA Vase with Whitley justified his decision in his eyes."

After that unhappy experience Keith decided it was time to call it a day as far as the Northern League was concerned. He carried on playing for Walker Central in the Northern Alliance for another three years, but the years had caught up with him and the young players around him were becoming too quick.

The final phase of Keith Mills' career as a footballer is still unfolding. Like a growing number of other very accomplished players he is now enjoying a new lease of life playing Over 40s football:

> "I am competing alongside players who were team mates or opponents twenty years ago and it is like playing in an older person's Northern League. The players don't have the legs but they still have the football brains. I play at Heaton Stannington with the likes of Davie Norton, who has one of the sharpest football brains you can imagine, Billy Cawthra, Bobby Wombwell and Neil Howie are all there. It is wonderful to see the old lads and I will play as long as my bones will take it."

When that time comes, management is probably not an option. Keith actually had a three years spell in that capacity at Walker Central with Ray Mulroy, but he finds young players reluctant to listen and take on board the experience and wisdom of older people. He has two sons in their early twenties and he is happy to watch them play on Saturdays. They are good players and he enjoys watching them and having a couple of pints with them after games. It is a pleasant kind of contentment.

GRAEME FORSTER

Was the whole of the cat over the line?

If you possess a Ph D in Metallurgy and you surname is 'Forster' you can claim to have earned the nickname 'Doc' twice over, and both of those distinctions belong to the popular and well known manager Graeme Forster. There cannot be too many Doctors of Philosophy managing in the Northern League and it would be true to say that intelligence comes high on the list of attributes when it comes to analysing Graeme's qualities as a manager. Intelligence, coupled with massive passion, a marvellous sense of humour, an enormous capacity for hard work and a pinch of lunacy have combined to make him a highly successful, high profile and extremely well liked manager.

His involvement in the non league game began when he was a young player with Langley Park Juniors. Graeme was a big lad and he graduated naturally to the centre of defence where his role was simply to stop the other fellow from playing. His simple but effective style paid off and he was selected to play in a Durham County junior representative side which also included Micky Hazard who later made a name for himself with Spurs, and Terry Fenwick who also had a very successful professional career. Graeme's studies were an important factor in his development and as a nineteen year old he went to Newcastle University to study metallurgy, and the combination of working towards his degree and the attractions of the bright lights of the big city put his football career on hold until he completed his education and returned to his home village of Quebec in County Durham where he still lives.

There had been a football team in the village in the 1950s which had been very successful, winning the Durham Challenge Cup, but with the passage of time the team ceased to exist. However, their pitch was still in the village and Graeme bought it. He was persuaded to re-assemble the team which he did with conspicuous success for three years in which it won several trophies to provide tangible evidence of its ability. The Durham & District League in which the team played was then disbanded as the Durham FA concentrated its Saturday football on the Wearside and Northern Leagues with the lesser teams either reverting to Sunday morning football or going to the wall. This left the Quebec team in limbo in 1994 and at the same time Alan Scott, a former Blyth Spartans player took over from Peter Creamer as manager of Evenwood Town in the Northern League Division Two. Alan's period of tenure was a brief one and after the pre-season friendlies he relinquished the job, with the result that the night before the opening league game of the season Evenwood stalwart Gordon Nicholson contacted Graeme and pleaded with him to supply any players he could to make up the team for the following day's match at Ryhope.

He took five players along, took charge of the team, and so began his career as a manager in the second division of the Northern League with a 2-0 win. The following Wednesday evening the news of the football team's revival reached the consciousness of the local people and a big crowd turned out to watch them play Horden, but reality set in with a vengeance and Evenwood were beaten 5-1. Their next opponents were Bridlington Town, a good side which had won the FA Vase the previous season. It was an FA Cup tie and Evenwood got off to the best possible start with a goal in the second minute, but again the final score was a humbling 5-1 thrashing.

An unfortunate incident took place the following week when the club physio, perhaps disgruntled because he had not been offered the job when Peter Creamer left, telephoned several of the players and told them their fixture at Thornaby had been called off. They were able to muster just a bare eleven players and were beaten 10-0, with George Woodhouse scoring six.

Lesser or perhaps wiser men than Graeme Forster might

have been tempted to walk away at that stage, but he rolled up his sleeves, devised a defensive strategy which brought a 0-0 draw at Ashington the following Wednesday night to restore some belief and credibility, and that proved to be the turning point in Evenwood's fortunes:

> "Someone who must have known how my mind worked had said; 'The worse it gets the harder he will work,' and as a young lad full of energy I poured myself into the job. It worked, and we started to win matches. We finished my first season fourth off bottom which was marvellous when you consider that the general expectation was we would not win a game."

The second season at Evenwood, Graeme used his wide ranging knowledge of Newcastle's social scene to recruit a big name player for the club. Several meetings with the former Newcastle United and Middlesbrough defender Irving Nattrass on the River Tyne's floating night club, the Tuxedo Princess, resulted in Nattrass becoming an Evenwood player:

> "He played for us as Hebburn and it was obvious that he had an exceptional pedigree. He was immaculate in the air, his timing was first class; he was streets ahead, but his knees gave way and that was the only game he played."

With Irving as his assistant, Graeme kept chipping away, bringing in players he thought would improve his squad. He was never short of innovative ideas either, and one oddball fund raising scheme he devised was to raffle a promising young greyhound which was locally trained by Jean Taylor and competed at Brough Park stadium in Newcastle. The dog was named 'Evenwood Town' after the football club, the raffle winner would have ownership privileges for a year and the funds raised would go towards the cost of floodlights:

> "Two bus loads of us went through to Brough Park to watch it run for the first time. Jean assured us it would win and we backed it down from 4-1 to odds on. She was right and we had a great night."

Under Graeme's guidance Evenwood went from strength to strength and more shrewd signings followed. Paul Atkinson, a former Sunderland player, was recruited, Billy Askew was persuaded to play, and Evenwood had become respectable again. Once, they were playing at Ryhope and one member of the team was playing away in both senses of the phrase. During the game he was struck flush in the face by the ball and concussed. When he regained consciousness Graeme asked him for a telephone number so that he could inform his wife that he was going to hospital, and he gave Graeme the number of the 'other woman.' Meanwhile, his pal who had driven with him to the game from Darlington phoned his wife with the news. Later that night both women turned up at his hospital bedside in Sunderland! At the end of the season the player in question was voted 'Players' Player of the Year' and they presented him with two trophies – one for the mantlepiece in each house.

Despite Graeme's imaginative wheeling and dealing Evenwood never achieved promotion to the First Division of the Northern League, but they were consistently a top six Second Division side which was a magnificent achievement with the extremely limited resources Graeme had at his disposal. One thing his team could do was score goals and in September 1994 they equalled the club's 64 year old scoring record with an 11-1 win over Darlington CS, with Ivor Moxon finding the net five times.

In January of the same year the Evenwood volunteers banded together under Gordon Nicholson's supervision to clear the pitch of snow prior to a match with Billingham Town. They then marked the lines with sawdust:

> "The referee, Paul Nicholson, then asked whether it was treated or untreated sawdust! Gordon told him it was the same sawdust they had used for over a hundred years and nobody at Evenwood had treated it. The ref said that a player in another game got treated sawdust in a cut, it became infected and he sued the referee. He lost his case so we couldn't understand what the fuss was about. Gordon twice sent a bag of sawdust to the League Management Committee so they could examine it, but he never got a reply."

GRAEME FORSTER - WAS THE WHOLE OF THE CAT OVER THE LINE?

Strange things tended to happen during Graeme's time at Evenwood. There was the occasion when they were losing to a Bedlington Terriers side which had been transformed from no hopers into an outstanding side by Keith Perry and Tony Lowery, and Evenwood were one of the first teams to feel the effects of the new Bedlington. They were losing at Welfare Park despite a black cat wandering in and out of the goal nets at the clubhouse end of the ground, and when an Evenwood player sent in a goal bound shot to bring them back into the game, the ball smacked into the cat on the line and the referee did not give the goal;

> "The cat pissed off into the allotments and there was this article in the 'Times' about it where the reporter was trying to work out whether the whole of the cat had crossed the line!"

Animals are obviously part of the Evenwood folk lore because there was also another incident in the days when people were cross breeding pit bull terriers and the Dangerous Dogs Act was introduced which required them to be muzzled. Half way through a home game one of these dogs wandered on to the pitch and started running around and joining in the game. Two of the players volunteered to catch it and when they did it was restrained in a secure area. An advert in the local paper resulted in the owner reclaiming the animal which had apparently boarded a bus in Spennymoor, alighted at Evenwood and gone to the match. There is no record of whether it paid to get in but it was obviously a keen supporter.

Graeme found himself the victim of an extended baiting process for four seasons whenever Evenwood played Ashington at Portland Park. The Ashington people had introduced a scheme whereby youngsters were allowed into midweek matches free if they were accompanied by a paying adult and Graeme, who wore long hair at the time, was christened 'Meatloaf' by the kids. He was not blessed with great patience in those days and whenever the Ashington lads started singing Meatloaf songs at him he would race around the stand after them; like a Bat out of Hell, presumably.

Then there were the moles; or rather there were not moles. Alnwick Town hosted Evenwood on the opening day of the season and a new groundsman at Alnwick had worked with great diligence to produce a pristine playing surface. Well known Alnwick wag John Common acquired a barrow load of topsoil and used it to create imitation molehills all over the pitch which the groundsman raced around before the game to remove. Happy days and animal crackers.

When West Auckland Town clinched promotion to the First Division of the Northern League by beating Evenwood at the end of the 1997-98 season their general manager Stuart Alderson told Graeme that it he ever decided to leave Evenwood there would be a job waiting for him at West, where his ability and hard work were much admired:

> "I had been at Evenwood for about eight years and I felt that that I no longer had the support of a section of the committee there. Gordon Nicholson was sad to see me go but it really was time for me to move on so I took Stuart up on his offer and moved to West Auckland to test myself in the First Division of the Northern League."

West Auckland had retained most of their promotion squad and Graeme added Gary Innes who had played professionally and was a very accomplished footballer. Graeme is the Managing Director of a factory in Consett which makes metal coatings and he gave Gary a job at the factory to tie him to West Auckland. Things took off from the first. In a pre-season friendly they defeated a Sunderland side which included Kevin Ball, Andy Melville and Michael Bridges 4-1 and when virtually the same Sunderland team beat QPR 4-0 the following Saturday, it was an early indication that Graeme's team at West Auckland had something about it.

They went on to enjoy a tremendous season, especially in terms of the FA Cup in which they reached the first round proper before losing to Yeovil Town:

> "I had this pair of blue and white spotted underpants which I wore for every FA Cup match and they became famous. I had my picture in the papers waving them over my head and they became a symbol of our success. I was invincible in them!"

GRAEME FORSTER - WAS THE WHOLE OF THE CAT OVER THE LINE?

Graeme shows the world his lucky underpants.

A fine win over Hyde United was one of many highlights and it set up a fourth qualifying round tie at Kings Lynn, but not before the Hyde manager kept secretary Allen Bayles waiting for an hour and a half after the final whistle to complete his administration work while he indulged in a 'marathon dressing room bollocking' of his team. The result was a happy one at Kings Lynn, but the relationship between the two clubs was a frosty one. Before the match Kings Lynn kept the West Auckland team waiting in the corridor for three or four minutes as a psychological ploy, so Graeme responded with one of his own; he kicked their dressing room door open and bellowed at them to 'get their ******* selves out on the pitch!' It worked. BBC Radio Newcastle's excellent non league service that night began with their reporter saying that while it had been a disappointing day for Newcastle United, Sunderland and Middlesbrough, none of whom had won, it had been left to little West Auckland to bring some joy to the area. Thanks to an inspired display by goalkeeper Andrew Sams and a 59th minute goal from Paul Adamson they had reached the first round proper of the FA Cup:

> "There were these two old guys, Les and Frankie, who had been at West Auckland for years, cutting the pitch and doing jobs about the place. One of them started to cry and he put his arms around me and said how proud he was of what we had done. Then I had to go live on Radio Newcastle and give my reactions to the win. I could hardly speak I was so emotional."

The Kings Lynn people took the defeat badly and their churlish gesture of turning off the television set in their lounge so that the West Auckland squad had to dash to the nearest pub to see the live cup draw was not exactly a demonstration of the Corinthian spirit. The first round draw was a disappointment. With the likes of Fulham, Preston and Burnley in the hat an away tie at Yeovil Town of the Conference was not what Graeme had hoped for, but he put a smile on his face and accepted his fate philosophically:

West Auckland's Keith Gorman celebrates scoring the winner against Hyde United in the FA Cup.

> "I felt as if I had won the Derby and lost it in the Stewards room, but it least it gave us a chance to avenge that Cup win they had over Sunderland all those years ago! When I thought about it, Yeovil were getting big crowds in the Conference

and financially a tie against them was actually better proposition than some of the league clubs we could have drawn. As far as I was concerned personally I was due to go to Brazil to speak at an international metallurgy conference, and instead I would be in the dugout at Yeovil!"

West Auckland set off for Somerset confident in the knowledge that they had conceded just one goal in their entire cup run at that point. They stayed in Birmingham overnight to break the journey so that their preparation was right, and before the game Graeme reminded his players that Yeovil's home form was poor and they had only won on their own ground once all season, though he was also aware that they had not been beaten in their last nine matches. The lads from the North East rose to the occasion magnificently and pulled off a 2-2 draw to make it a great day for non league football in the region; Northern League champions Bedlington Terriers had walloped Colchester United 4-1 the same day and the smiles were broad across the region. They were both superb achievements and in West Auckland's case they had overcome the travails of a very long journey and drawn with a side which was effectively fifty places above them in the pyramid system. Hopes were high that they would be able to exploit home advantage in the replay and progress to the second round of the FA Cup for the first time in their history.

A packed ground at Darlington Road saw West enjoy the better of a rather uneventful first half in which they forced five corners to Yeovil's one, and although the former Cardiff City striker Carl Dale was proving a handful the West Auckland defence was solid. With goalscoring opportunities at a premium the half finished with a 0-0 score line. On the hour the place erupted when the West Auckland centre forward Jonathan Milroy beat goalkeeper Warren Pennock with a shot from fifteen yards and dreams of glory looked like coming true. However, the classy Dale would not be denied and he scored the equaliser which sent the game into extra time. The tie remained finely balanced throughout the extra thirty minutes and there was no addition to the score. Despite successful conversions by Gary Hornsby, Lee Innes and Keith Gorman West Auckland were beaten 5-3 on penalties and the FA Cup dream was over. It had been a marvellous experience for the club and the players which had put West Auckland on the map and the revenue the Yeovil game brought in allowed them to build a new clubhouse which was a lasting monument to their achievement, while Graeme Forster had the satisfaction of having guided his team to the first round of the FA Cup. As well as the excellent cup run West Auckland finished in fifth place in the Northern League; it had been quite a season.

At the start of the following season Graeme was invited to the BBC in Newcastle to talk to the London studio about the FA Cup, but the link failed and his trip was wasted. The team lost its first league game of the season at Seaham and during the course of the game someone ripped Graeme's suit. The portents were not encouraging. Their away tie at Clitheroe in the FA Vase was a disaster; the bus blew a tyre on the way to the match and they did not arrive until 2:30. The FA insisted that the tie must go ahead and West Auckland's disrupted preparation contributed to their defeat. Graeme was becoming frustrated and the club's financial situation did not allow him to strengthen his squad in order to make a championship challenge. Simultaneously Tow Law, the team which had always been closest to his heart, was trying to entice him back and eventually, disenchanted by what he perceived as a stagnating situation at West Auckland, he returned to Tow Law:

> *"I replaced Peter Quigley and I quickly realised why he was getting out! The club had lost three top players to Queen of the South, two more had retired and Keith Moorhead and Micky Bailey were contemplating hanging up their boots. As it happens I persuaded them to stay, but Keith's knees were knackered and he liked to watch Newcastle United! I thought, my God, what have they chucked at me? I had to start building a side and I think I put together the best team I ever had."*

It took time, but he brought in an excellent young player called Mark Eccles who went on to better things and he signed Scott Nicholson who he regarded as probably the best all round player he ever worked with because of his versatility. He could play equally comfortably as a central defender, a midfield player or a striker, and as a local lad he always gave 100% for the club. With players like Scott, the team began to take off:

> "The club had this notorious group of supporters called the Misfits who had a reputation for causing havoc, but I found them to be all right and I told the players we could use their support in a positive way. I used to tell them to stand behind the opposition goal and taunt the goalkeeper. We played an FA game at Castleton Gabriels and they travelled with us. It must have been the only time a Northern League team bus had a police escort!"

Castleton took the perceived menace of the Misfits very seriously and made the game all ticket so that they could segregate the trouble makers. As it happened, there were none of the scuffles which had marred the tie at Sudbury in the 1998 Vase run, or the trouble at Workington where the police used tear gas to disperse the crowd, nor was there any of the extensive damage which Rossendale had attributed to the Misfits a couple of seasons previously. Graeme made the best of a difficult situation by attempting to channel the Misfits energies in a positive way, but they certainly were unusual characters:

> "One of the Misfits had a false arm and when we played Congleton in the Vase he was firing rockets out of his sleeve. The Congleton secretary didn't know he had a prosthetic limb and he was very impressed by somebody he thought was hard enough to launch rockets out of his bare hands. Another time we were playing a Northern League team whose goalkeeper was a member of the Drugs Squad and they were all smoking marihuana behind his goal. After the game he said it was the best crack he had ever come across at a game!"

The season was going well and when Graeme brought in the very talented Steve Walker to replace the veteran Keith Moorhead, he had a very capable side which finished in sixth place in the league.

It would be fair to say at this point that Graeme's management style on the touchline was passionate bordering on the maniacal:

> "My second season at Tow Law every other manager seemed to have been before the Durham FA except me, which was a miracle. I told them they must have a set of hooligans running their teams! Over the years, though, I must admit I used to get wound up, mostly when we were losing. Gordon Nicholson once told me that the time to complain was when you had won so that it didn't sound like sour grapes and one night we played at Guisborough and won, but I thought one of the linesmen was totally inept and gave the referee absolutely no help. I wrote a formal complaint to Durham FA in support of the ref. and they fined the club twenty five quid! They accused me of behaving like a madman in the dugout, so I didn't try to help referees any more!"

Graeme and Tow Law skipper Jeff Hall receive the Northern League runners up trophy from league secretary Tony Golightly.

That second season at Tow Law was a tremendous one but it coincided with the golden era of Bedlington Terriers who had set an incredibly high standard and that 2001-02 season saw them win the Northern League championship for the fifth successive season. It was a case of the rest battling it out to finish second because Bedlington were so superior, and Tow Law finished above some very good teams to end the season as runners up. They also had a bizarre tie against

Graeme and Sir Bobby Robson with the FA Vase outside St James's Park.

Bromsgove in the FA Vase. The Midland club had been expelled from the Conference for alleged financial irregularities and were working their way back. They were a good side and when they arrived at Tow Law it was a typically grey, cold and miserable day in those parts, prompting the Bromsgrove chairman, a stereotypical man in a large sheepskin coat, to describe Tow Law as the most inhospitable place he had ever visited. The game itself was close and with the score at 2-2 the fog descended and enveloped the ground to such an extent that the referee had no choice but to abandon the match. The players trudged off and the game was re-arranged for the following Saturday. Forty five minutes later the skies cleared and it was a beautiful, clear and sunny evening.

The teams were about to get changed for the replayed game when a fault occurred on the National Grid and the whole area suffered a power cut:

"It was nothing to do with us, though somebody tried to blame the poor lass in the kitchen for putting on the chip pan and overloading the system! I contacted the electricity board who said they had located the fault and power would be restored within the hour. The referee agreed to start the game and I lit some candles in the Bromsgrove dressing room so they could get changed. It just wasn't what they were used to and we won easily! They went home totally demoralised. I think they believed they had been in that Royston Vasey place in 'League of Gentlemen.'

The other game Graeme recollects from his Tow Law days was an FA Cup tie against Matlock Town. His team had been having problems scoring goals and after scouring the area for a striker he signed Willie Moat on the night before the game, and it paid off with Willie winning two penalties in a dramatic 5-4 win with Scott Nicholson scoring the bravest of goals with a diving header among a host of flying boots. The win was worth £10,000 in prize money to the club and it was a major triumph, but while Scott Nicholson took the headlines it was not for his immensely courageous headed goal, but for his part in the assassination of two goldfish!

> *"This bloke whose house overlooked the pitch kept koi carp in a pond in his garden, and towards the end of the game when we were trying to defend our 5-4 lead, Scott Nicholson belted a clearance out of the ground. The ball landed in the bloke's pond and he claimed that the shock had killed two of his fish which had cost him twenty five quid each. He wouldn't let us have our ball back unless the club paid him £50 compensation for the death of his goldfish!"*

Tow Law were in the top three as the New Year came the following season and Graeme asked the club officials for some money to add to a squad depleted by injuries so that they could sustain their title challenge, but unfortunately there was none available. He saw the season out, but his enthusiasm had been damaged and when harsh words were said about his assistant, Andy Sinclair, which Graeme found unacceptable, he concluded that he was unable to continue in his job.

Graeme's next and most recent appointment was as joint manager of Crook Town with Alan Oliver. He had taken a season out then he went to Crook at the start of 2005-06. It was another success story, with Crook taking advantage of a sponsorship deal with the retired business tycoon Tom Cowie to assemble a side which was better than their Northern League Second Division status would suggest. The plan was to aim for promotion and while that target was not achieved it was still a remarkable season for the club which brought back memories of their stirring deeds in the days of the FA Amateur Cup. Despite being a second division side they carried the Northern League torch further than any other club by reaching the quarter finals of the FA Vase. It was a stupendous achievement which reflected on everyone who had worked so hard to restore the fortunes of a once great non league club which had been in the doldrums for many years. The off-the-field efforts of chairman Stephen Buddle as well as people like Kieron Bennett and Bill Penman among others, combined with the management skills of Alan Oliver and Graeme and the efforts of the players on the field, made it a season to remember.

Unfortunately, there was a rapid deterioration in the situation in the close season. The club were unhappy that key players from the FA Vase run side had not been re-signed and had been replaced with younger and less experienced players. Pre-season form and results were not encouraging, and on the eve of the 2006-07 season the club sacked Alan Oliver:

> *"I had gone to Crook at Alan's invitation to work with him on a 50/50 basis. The club decided they wanted to dismiss one half of the partnership and keep the other half, and ethically that did not stack up. I felt I had no option but to leave. It was not for football reasons and I have nothing against Crook Town really. I was sad to go but I felt it was right. Now Alan and I are out of a job, Crook are struggling and there are no winners. It's a shame."*

Graeme Forster will not be out of the game for long, be assured, and wherever he ends up next that club will have a manager with great passion who will work might and main to achieve success. Don't bet against those blue and white spotted underpants coming out of the drawer again in the not too distant future.

PETER QUIGLEY

A pantomime horse and one fight too many

Peter Quigley came to the end of his playing career at the age of 34 in 1984. He had been a Northern League player with teams including Whitley Bay, Durham City and Brandon United, but he regarded himself as a fringe Northern League player:

"If I had been the manager I would not have picked me, but Peter Feenan seemed to like me and he signed me for various clubs until a young lad called Willie Moat took my place at Brandon and I knew the writing was on the wall."

His final club, when he left the Northern League and Brandon, was Dunston Federation which was then a Northern Combination side. Peter had been the club's leading scorer for two seasons when they reached the final of a cup competition which was played at St James's Park, and he scored. He thought he was a top man! Leading scorer and scoring a goal in the cup final at the home of Newcastle United; he was full of himself and was really looking forward to the next season. The Dunston manager was Tommy Cooney and he obviously had a different perspective because at the end of the game at St James's he took Peter on one side and told him he wanted him to manage the team the following season. He was totally taken aback and came to the conclusion that perhaps he was not as accomplished a player as he thought!

He saw the offer as an opportunity to remain in the game. He had played every Saturday and Sunday from the age of sixteen and he was passionate about his football. He felt that if he was going to become a manager he would have to sacrifice his playing career as he knew he could not justice to both playing and managing, and so he hung up his boots and became the manager of Dunston Fed in 1984; he stayed their for 13 years.

Dunston played at Dunston Park in the Northern Combination; they had just acquired their Federation Park ground but there was no infrastructure in place:

"It was a fantastic club. If the team had been half as good as the committee we could have achieved anything. The committee people were all ex-players; John Thompson. Malcolm James, Alan Stott, Ian McPherson, Paul Dixon, Billy Montague, Freddie Foulis, Frankie Rankin and Tommy Cooney had all played together and they were an ambitious club who wanted to play in the Northern League."

There was no pyramid system in place, so in order to achieve Northern League status the club had to develop its ground to a good standard and produce a successful football team. Peter combined his role as manager with a place on the committee, helping with the vital process of raising funds to pay for the club's ambitions. He was an integral part of the group of people who took Dunston Fed forward from the relatively humble surroundings of the Northern Combination to become one of the biggest, most successful and most respected clubs in the area. He was a Dunston man through and through and was a fundamental member of the core group of people who drove the club forward.

Among his roles was taking a leading role in the annual negotiations with the football club's sponsors, the Federation Brewery. He would put together a presentation which was the basis of the club's annual pitch for funding:

"Jim Ramshaw who was the brewery chairman once said that my presentations were as good as anything a top London solicitor could put together which was very flattering, and I managed to persuade them each year to increase the sponsorship so that we were in a healthy financial position."

PETER QUIGLEY - A PANTOMIME HORSE AND ONE FIGHT TOO MANY

The committee took care to use their income wisely and Peter was realistic enough to accept that spending money on players was less of a priority than investing in the club's infrastructure. They worked on the playing surface, erected a barrier around it, laid hard standing for spectators, brought in portable units to provide dressing rooms, then moved on to build permanent dressing rooms, a clubhouse, spectator stands and to erect floodlights. As the ground developed the club moved from the Northern Combination through the Wearside League and finally into the Northern League. It was a time of great success and the team contained some excellent players. Peter found it necessary to employ some of the very best players in his factory to keep them at the club and he gave jobs to Steve Kendall, Tony 'Tiger' Halliday, Graham Mole, Chico Hamilton, and David Willis who were the top echelon of the players he had. Kenny Cramman was another Quigley employee who became first a wonderful left back and then an accomplished midfield player under Peter's guidance and played for the England semi-professional side.

Another Dunston favourite was Tommy Ditchburn, a strong, quick and versatile player who was comfortable in virtually any position:

"There was a group of them who came from Wallsend; David McDonald, a goalkeeper called Damian Boyd, Ian Bensley, Dave Willis and Kenny Cramman. They were a strange bunch. We had agreed a new deal with the breweries and we had this celebration in their building which was quite new then. On the first floor there was a lovely suite of offices which opened out onto the Lancastrian Suite and Jim was showing us proudly round the offices when suddenly all the top brass from the brewery started running through the double doors onto the balcony. I knew straight away the players must have done something; Damian Boyd, who was a fireman, had told David McDonald, who was a teacher and should have known better, to pull out this fire hose reel. When he pulled it out, it automatically gushed out gallons of water and there he was standing in the middle of the corridor of this new suite of offices belonging to our sponsors directing the hose, which was cascading water all over the brewery officials who were dressed in their finery, as well as the walls and carpets. It was a disaster; I thought it was the end of the club."

Peter frogmarched David McDonald out of the building, told him he was no longer a Dunston player, then went back inside to apologise profusely to the committee. He promised the considerable damage would be paid for but, incredibly, the brewery chiefs forgave them and drew a veil over the incident. David McDonald was compelled to write formal apologies to the football club and the brewery, and he was subsequently reinstated, much to Peter's dismay. He predicted that it would be a matter of time before he did something else stupid, and he was not wrong:

"The dressing rooms at the Fed are all tiled, with the showers at the back and an American style toilet where you can only see the person's feet. I was standing one day with the toilet to my left and the showers to my back and the physio couch in front of me, giving the team talk. I thought the lads were being supremely attentive but unknown to me David McDonald had kept a firework back from Guy Fawkes night and while he was sitting in the toilet he had lit the firework and it was fizzing at my feet. The players were sitting wide eyed waiting for it to explode and when it did the echo was horrendous. Everybody was dumbstruck. I was perplexed for a second, then I completely lost my temper. I was punching David in the toilet and the players were pissing themselves with laughing and trying to pull me off him. Needless to say he was disciplined for that, but he is an absolutely lovely lad and a good friend."

Peter began his managerial career with the Fed with Tommy Cooney as his assistant, then Alan Stott replaced Tommy. He had a brief half of a season away at Ryhope in the Northern League, saving them from relegation, but when he wanted to buy Ian Mulholland for £50 and the club would not sanction the signing until all of the committee had seen him play he regarded this as an unacceptable level of interference and he returned to Dunston as Alan Stott's assistant for two seasons before taking over the reigns again. It was a successful period in which Alan and Peter won the Northern Combination League treble and the Shipowners Cup, and when Peter took over again he won the Wearside League title twice and picked up the Shipowners Cup again, before the club resigned from the Wearside League and was admitted to the Northern League.

Peter felt that this was an appropriate time to extend and improve his own coaching skills so he took his Preliminary Badge then attended a series of coaching weekends at Lilleshall before he eventually spent a week completing his FA Advanced Coaching Course so that he had added a solid coaching pedigree to his existing ability to prepare his teams with motivational speeches. He believed it was necessary to have this range of abilities and qualifications if he was to be successful at Northern League level and he was proved right when he won the Northern League Second Division title in his second season.

Peter was now a passionate advocate of the FA Vase. He had been inspired by the fact that Dunston had reached the quarter final stage, which was an outstanding accomplishment for a second division side, but he was unhappy with the fact that Northern League First Division sides were compelled to compete in the FA Trophy against teams from a higher level, making it a non-winnable competition. Arthur Clark, who was the Northern League secretary, was also a member of the FA Trophy committee and he entered first division clubs in that competition, but Peter felt that if they could play in the FA Vase they would have a realistic chance of success which would not only bring kudos to the league but which would stimulate interest in Northern League football in the region.

A meeting was arranged at which he addressed the Northern League management committee to put his case, but Arthur Clark was obdurate on the issue and he was a strong and influential character and it was not until the FA themselves issued new guidelines a couple of years later that the Northern League First Division clubs were entered into the Vase. Subsequently, Whitby Town, Tow Law and Bedlington Terriers all reached the FA Vase final and Whitley Bay actually won the trophy, vindicating Peter's position.

Back at league level, Peter was becoming accustomed to the demands of competing in the Northern League First Division, though in his second season in the top flight Dunston did not fare very well:

"I am a great believer in giving people the opportunity to learn and develop. There is a term called skill snobbery whereby people keep their skills to themselves in order to protect their position, but I take the opposite view and I had given my assistant, Tony Heslop, a major responsibility to share the running of the team. He was the complete opposite of me; while I was serious he was very funny and he lightened the mood; we were an ideal combination. We had a bad season and the committee called a special meeting at which they told me they wanted to sack Tony. They decided to have a secret ballot, which was something they had never done in the thirteen years I had been there, and they voted to sack Tony. I refused to accept the decision and so they sacked me as well and I left on something of a sour note which was sad because it was a great club and I have nothing but admiration for them."

Peter had realised that nothing was for ever and that after thirteen years perhaps the club did need a change, but he regretted the circumstances in which it took place. He is also full of admiration for the success which his successor, Bobby Scaife, has achieved in winning two Northern League First Division championships. His bond with Tony Heslop remains a strong one and he has happy memories of their time together at Dunston:

"Tony is probably the most quick witted person I have met. I remember once at a Northern League dinner when Warren Pearson, who was with Tow Law, passed our table carrying a tray of drinks. Just at that precise moment the compere asked everyone to be upstanding to welcome the top table guests and everyone in the place stood up. Tony Heslop turned to Warren

> *and said; 'You mustn't get the drinks in very often Warren; everyone is standing up and applauding you!' It was so quick and so typical. I love the man."*

During the hiatus following his departure from Dunston Peter received a call from Tony Heslop informing him that there was a managerial vacancy at Tow Law. He had been there with Dunston in the League Cup and he did not have especially happy memories of the place, so he was initially sceptical. It had been a freezing night when the rain was lashing down and the wind was blowing a gale; typical Tow Law weather! Dunston had injury problems and could barely raise a team and it was not a game they relished. Shortly before the kick off all the floodlights on one side of the ground failed and it seemed the game would have to be abandoned. However, the referee said he was willing to play if the two teams agreed. Bearing in mind that Peter's priority that season was promotion from the second division, he had no wish to add to an already problematical fixture backlog, so he agreed to play. His players were astounded, but he managed to convince them that the referee had forced them to play! They lost the game to a Trevor Laidler goal in extra time and the whole experience had not exactly endeared the place to Peter, so when Tony made him aware of the vacancy he was not wild about the idea of working there. However, he accepted an invitation to attend for an interview:

> *"The Doc (Graeme Forster) was also there and there were a couple of other candidates and when I walked into the clubhouse one of them asked me what I was doing there. I told them that I always went to Tow Law Football Club on a Friday night for a drink instead of going into Newcastle! During the interview John Flynn asked me a wonderful question. He asked what I could do for Town Law and the community. I thought; 'Bloody hell, I'm here to run a football team not stand for mayor.' My answer was that if I put a decent team together and had some success I was sure the community would support the football club."*

As well as John Flynn, Sandra Gordon who is now the club chairman was on the interviewing panel along with the secretary Bernard Fairbairn whose father and grandfather had been secretary before him and who was steeped in the club, and it was a thorough and searching interview process. The following morning he received a call from Bernard and was told the job was his; Peter had an understanding that he would be allowed further discussions before his appointment was confirmed in the event of him being offered the post, but Bernard simply told him that he had been appointed and the other candidates had been informed. He was presented with a fait accompli and he was the manager of Tow Law. He realised very quickly that the club was not run in the same way as Dunston. He had pulled of something of a coup by signing Steve Pickering who had just been released by Sunderland, and he took him along to pre-season training:

> *"When we got there the grass on the pitch was about four feet high. They had cut a little furrow around the perimeter so that we could run around. I thought; 'I've brought this player from a professional club who is used to top class facilities; what the Hell is he going to think?' I spoke to John Flynn and he said there had been so much rain in the summer that the local farmer had not been able to get on the pitch to cut the grass! We had to run round the pitch and Tony Heslop told me to look behind me; there was this committee member who had a domestic lawn mower with a twelve inch blade and he was trying to cut the grass in the penalty area to create a place where we could train. I wondered what on earth I had let myself in for."*

On the plus side, Tow Law had the foundations of a very good football team. Peter strengthened an already strong squad by signing Jarrod Suddick, Stuart Dawson, Paul Haigh and Michael Robinson as well as Steve Pickering to supplement the excellent legacy of previous manager Stuart Leeming. He knew he was bringing in quality players, but even Peter was surprised at how accomplished Jarrod Suddick was. He knew he was good, but he proved to be exceptional, and with his extra qualities and the talent of the rest of the squad it was apparent that Tow Law was going to be a major force:

PETER QUIGLEY - A PANTOMIME HORSE AND ONE FIGHT TOO MANY

"It was a fantastic side. The back four was physically massive: the smallest was six feet one, and they were all exceptional defenders. Pickering gave us an abundance of skill on the right hand side; I moved Tony Nelson from centre forward to midfield and he was a revelation. We had Keith Moorhead and Billy Johnson and up front were Trevor Laidler and Jarrod Suddick. It was a very good team."

This was the 1997-98 season and Peter's passion for the FA Vase continued to burn bright, and while things were progressing well in the league his team was making an impact in the Vase as well. The momentum began to gather pace; they knocked out his old club Dunston Federation and then travelled to play Rossendale and won with ten men when Trevor Laidler was sent off after just ten minutes. At that point Peter began to believe they were capable of a major run in the Vase and that became his principal focus. He watched every team they were drawn against, and they did not have an easy draw by any means. They played Rossendale, Histon, Sudbury, Taunton and Tiverton and every one of those clubs has gone on to play at a higher level.

He watched and assessed the opposition and made any necessary minor adjustments to his team plan. Everything was done professionally; the players had light training on match days followed by lunch at an appropriate venue, then the team talk followed by a motivational video which was usually 'Lions in Africa,' the story of the British Lions rugby union team's triumph in South Africa in 1996. Preparations were meticulous:

"Prepare, prepare, prepare was the watchword. We left nothing to chance and it paid off. Every game we won, we won on merit and everyone played their part. Keith Moorhead had been badly injured early in the cup run and he took it upon himself to become the team's Entertainments Manager, which normally involved nudity! He would remove his clothes at any given opportunity and he was very adept at cock fighting which involved placing a cigarette under the foreskin, lighting it and attempting by judicious swaying of the hips to knock the cigarette from his opponent's appendage. He lost once and he slumped down next to me on the team bus and said: "Peter, I've had one fight too many!"

Tow Law played Taunton in the two legged semi final, and they were a very good side. The game in Somerset was a 4-4 thriller, though with better defending Tow Law could have returned to the North East with a lead to take into the second leg. When the game was due to be played the established routine which had served the team so well was observed again, but Peter came to realise that the tension of the occasion was getting to his players and it was an obvious cause for concern. He was afraid that the effect would be that his players would not perform on the day, but Keith Moorhead once again brought his skill as Entertainments Manager to bear on the situation. He had organised for two of his friends to come to the game:

"He said to me; 'Peter, is it all right if my mates come dressed as a pantomime horse?' I said it would be fine provided that at ten to three they knocked on the changing room door and came into the room. We went through our routine and the tension was awful, then at ten to three there was a knock on the dressing room door and when I opened it the pantomime horse came galloping in. The players absolutely broke up. They were pissing themselves and it completely broke the tension."

It was a master stroke and when the team took the field they were followed out by the pantomime horse. The players were relaxed and while they did not produce a vintage performance neither did Taunton and Tow Law won the game 1-0 to reach the FA Vase Final at Wembley. Keith Moorhead was now securely installed in his role as Entertainments Manager after the triumph of the pantomime horse, and when the team was invited to inspect the pitch at Wembley on the eve on the final he rose to the occasion again. The squad was allocated an hour to walk around Wembley with the tv cameras and associated media in attendance. Keith asked permission to remove his clothes and Peter gave his blessing only on condition that it was a case of total nudity. The squad gathered round him in the centre circle, Keith took his clothes off and they draped him in a Tow Law flag which had been made by a local firm, then he ran round Wembley completely naked, parading the flag for the benefit of the cameras.

A proud manager leads his team out at Wembley.

The final was against Tiverton, who were red hot favourites, and while Peter says his team 'did all right' against a much bigger club than his, they lost the game. The crucial factor was that at Wembley, tension effects players, the pitch is a big one and it is a tiring experience, and therefore the manager has to make sensible use of his substitutes. Tiverton had played in a previous final and had learned that lesson; their manager brought on three substitutes fifteen minutes from time and the fresh legs made the difference. One of the substitutes scored the only goal of the game in the last minute, and Peter vows that if he is ever in the same situation again he will make sure his subs are on midway through the second half.

Even allowing for the defeat, all the success he has achieved in football – and it has been considerable – comes second to the experience of having played at Wembley in the final of a national competition. He was very conscious of Wembley's history with the 1948 Olympic Games and all those memorable FA Cup finals and England internationals as well as the 1966 World Cup, and he was mesmerised by the experience of being a part of it:

> "I hope that when the new stadium finally opens, the Football Association realises what playing there does for people at the grass roots level of the sport and restores Wembley as the venue for the finals of competitions like the FA Vase. It is the ultimate footballing experience."

Peter's achievement in leading his team to the FA Vase Final has made him a folk hero in Tow Law for all time. When the team coach returned to the town after the final the party was switched to an open-topped bus. Peter felt that the situation was potentially very embarrassing and the players were reluctant to participate, but they need not have worried. The whole town turned out to welcome their heroes home and people from the surrounding areas came along to boost the crowds who came to thank the team for what they had achieved for Tow Law:

> "It was an awesome and breathtaking reception and I was humbled by the way they had not only followed at Wembley in massive numbers but had then given us an absolutely fantastic welcome home even though we had lost. I remembered that question John Flynn had asked me when I was interviewed for the job, and I was able to believe that I had helped the football club to give something special to the community of Tow Law."

He was elected 'Man of the Season' at the Northern League Annual Dinner, an honour which recognised both his personal campaign to make the FA Vase accessible to all Northern League clubs and Tow Law's individual success.

Peter felt that the impetus of the FA Vase run could be the catalyst not only for another tilt at the competition the following season, but also the inspiration for a genuine assault on the Northern League title. He was able to retain the bulk of his squad and brought in a few others and he was confident of another successful season. Unfortunately, Jarrod Suddick was injured and missed virtually the whole season and when another of his striker, Nigel Bolton, was also a long term injury victim it left Trevor Sinclair to

The Tow Law FA Vase Final squad pictured at Wembley Stadium.

operate as a lone striker. They still managed to finish second to an exceptional Bedlington Terriers side and they had another very respectable FA Vase run before losing to Workington. It was a successful season which might have been even better if his strikers had stayed fit. However, Peter remained upbeat and optimistic.

Tow Law then found themselves in an unexpected and serious financial plight. It transpired that unbeknown to the club their treasurer had been supplementing the club's income from his own pocket to sustain the operation and when the time came that he was no longer in a position to put his own money in, a sudden hole appeared in Tow Law's revenue stream. A meeting was arranged with the local community to explore ways of raising extra revenue and two ladies who were peripheral to the committee said they would knock on every door in the town and ask for a donation of £1 to the football club. Peter knew that the club already ran a letter draw which had been decimated by the National Lottery and he could not believe that if the local people would not contribute to that they would donate £1 without any hope of return. He realised that the club's financial situation was unsustainable, and further body blows came when he lost Jarrod Suddick, Steve Pickering, Billy Johnson and Tony Nelson, all to Queen of the South:

> *"I had no problem with the players leaving because I had always encouraged players if they had the chance to play at a higher level, but I found myself in a situation where I had lost half of my team and the club was in dire straits. There was no way forward so I resigned."*

He had a season off before taking over at Spennymoor, which was another troubled club. They had been relegated and had lost most of their players amid allegations of non payment of wages. A benefactor had come in at the end of

PETER QUIGLEY - A PANTOMIME HORSE AND ONE FIGHT TOO MANY

June by which time players were tied up with other clubs and when the chairman approached Peter to take to job he made it clear that survival was the pinnacle of his ambitions. In the circumstances it would have been unrealistic to expect more, so Peter took the job on that understanding and managed to cobble together a team which he predicted would start well but then begin to falter, because the players were not good enough to sustain success at that level. He was quite right, though the team did have a good FA Cup run which generated £17,000 but he was unable to persuade the club to give him the backing he needed;

"They sacked me, saying I did not give them value for money which was strange as it had not cost them anything."

By now Peter had been a non league manager for seventeen years and he decided it was time for a change. He started to play golf with his best friend Steve Dixon and became a season ticket holder at Newcastle United. He has not been to watch a game of non league football since the day he was dismissed by Spennymoor, and grass roots football in the North East is poorer as a result. His record is exceptional with Dunston and Tow Law and he can be proud of his achievements. He is quick to attribute credit to other people, especially John Thompson and Malcolm James at Dunston and John Flynn and Bernard Fairbairn at Tow Law, and he speaks with generosity and affection about the many outstanding players he worked with. He has great admiration for Steve Kendall, the best of all with his superbly professional attitude and outstanding ability. From the Tow Law days he recalls with special affection Jarrod Suddick, Tony Nelson, Billy Johnson and Keith Moorhead and he has a special mention too, for goalkeepers Bob Strong, the best he had at Ryhope and Dunston, closely followed by Stuart Dawson.

Peter was trained as an accountant and made a success of business life working in manufacturing where he rose to the level of Managing Director of a Danish company based in Washington where he was responsible for a work force of 350 people. When the economy changed and the company relocated to China he bought one of their products and set up in business for himself with further success. Recently he made the major decision to change his lifestyle completely.

His daughter Danielle is a very accomplished horsewoman and she has added to the practical talent by gaining the qualifications from the British Horse Society which enable her to instruct other riders. With her practical ability and Peter's business and financial acumen they are combining to establish a family business. Peter has bought a farm in County Durham and is investing every thing he has to turn it into a top class equestrian centre with fifty two stables, an Olympic size indoor riding school, a ménage and a cross country course. Danielle will run the operational side of the business catering for people who ride and own horses but need other people to offer a full day-to-day livery service, and Peter will look after the business and financial aspects of the centre. It is a very exciting and demanding undertaking but things are in place and the first customers are coming through the doors. and it looks a very good bet to succeed. That's the thing with Peter Quigley. He is bright and intelligent and he has a good business brain. He works hard and he knows how to win and his lifestyle change looks odds on to be a success. As for football, who knows. He will be very busy with his business in the short term, but he does look wistful when he talks about the game and although he has been away from it for a while his name still crops up regularly and it would not be a surprise if he returned in some capacity.

RUSSELL TIFFIN

Your cows are on our pitch

Most youngsters who kick a football dream of playing professionally for their local team and scoring the winning goal in the FA Cup Final, or playing on famous grounds around the country and abroad, maybe of playing in the Champions League or even the World Cup. Russell Tiffin was different. He realised from an early age that his playing ability would not allow him to fulfil those kinds of imaginings, but he had the intelligence and common sense to be aware that at least some of them could be achieved by another method, so in 1979 when he was eighteen years of age he answered an advertisement in the 'Sunderland Echo' which invited interested parties to train and qualify as football referees.

He took his basic examination and passed, and thus he began the long haul towards the big time by refereeing in the local parks in the Houghton & District League. Two seasons of experience at that very basic level resulted in his promotion to what was then known as Class 2, and he was on his way. Experience came rapidly because referees were always in demand and there was no shortage of opportunities. It was the kind of job where you learned quickly and one of the first lessons young Russell took on board was that he must never allow himself to be intimidated and must always make what he believed to be the right decisions irrespective of the consequences or the personalities involved, or of the levels of hostility his decisions might engender. It was a principle he was to apply throughout his career and while it occasionally brought controversy he was unswerving and consistent and for that he became massively respected.

His principles in this regard were put to the test as soon as he was elevated to the level of referee's assistant in the Northern League when he was twenty minutes into his very first match on the line at that level; a match between those arch rivals Bishop Auckland and Spennymoor United. He saw a player stamp on an opponent and flagged immediately. Unfortunately the referee did not see his signal and it was not until a minute later when the ball went out for a corner that he was able to draw the attention of the referee to the incident amid a torrent of abuse from the crowd:

> "I told the referee he would have to send the number eleven off for violent conduct; he asked if I was sure and I told him I was absolutely positive. The referee did not know me because I was new to the Northern League and as green as grass but he backed me and sent the player off. Spennymoor were one up but Bishops actually won the game 2-1 and as far as I was concerned it was a night when the learning curve was a rapid one."

In the clubhouse after the game the treasurer of Spennymoor came over and gave the officials their nominal £3 match fees and he said that in his opinion Russell would never graduate beyond that standard. He still sees him from time to time and is at pains to remind him of his prophetic and inaccurate words.

Gordon Nicholson was the man in charge of the Northern League officials in those days and when Gordon told people to jump, they jumped. Anyone with pretensions to refereeing at that level had to apply to go on the list; a far cry from the present day when it is much more difficult to recruit and retain referees. The abuse they suffer when they are learning their trade acts as a massive deterrent to today's emerging officials and the numbers are not coming through in the way they used to in Russell's early years when it was a much more difficult process, and his rapid advancement was remarkable by the standards of the day.

He achieved his next landmark in 1985 when he was promoted to the Referees List of the Northern League at the age of just 24. He had made rapid strides in the six years since he had answered the advert in the 'Sunderland Echo'. Refereeing at that level at that age was most unusual and said much about the precocious talent of a young man whose ability was becoming highly regarded:

Russell in celebratory mood.

"Even now, when you consider there are 33,000 registered referees in the country, when you reach Northern League level you are in the top 1% in the country. People might think that means the standard is terrible, but it is a fact and I was delighted to reach that level in so short a time."

To underline the point, if an official is promoted to the next level in the system and joins the Football League list as Russell has done, it places you in the top 0.5%; you have made the grade.

Russell's first match in the in the middle as a referee in the Northern League was between Newcastle Blue Star and Darlington Reserves and it took place at the Wheatsheaf ground on August 7th 1985. Blue Star won 7-0 in front of a crowd the likes of which they would die for today:

"Blue Star had a phenomenal team which had come through the Wearside League with top players like Billy Cruddas who I have crossed swords with many a time. I see Billy socially now and we still have a laugh; he keeps reminding people whether they are in the company or not of our many ding dongs, but it is done in a good spirit."

One significant change which has taken place in recent times is that officials in the Northern League First Division are now appointed by the Football Association not by the League Secretary, and when Russell reached the magnificent landmark of refereeing his 400th match in the Northern League they arranged for him to return to Blue Star, even though they were a second division side then:

"Four hundred games in the middle in the Northern League was a proud achievement for me and the way the system operates now I doubt it will ever be beaten. I am in my twenty second season in the middle at that level and that is something of which I am quite proud."

Russell is a meticulous man who takes great care to cover all the bases both in his preparation for matches and in his post-match attention to detail. He has kept note books containing details of every game in which he has officiated, with details of goals, cautions, dismissals and anything else of significance and he refers back to them on a regular basis to reflect on memories of a distinguished and satisfying career.

Back at the beginning, after his debut in the middle at Newcastle Blue Star his next match was between Chester le Street and Blyth Spartans, and he could now regard himself as a proper and established referee. He took pride in his work, and he always had Gordon Nicholson to provide guidance. Gordon was a stickler where the use of abusive language was concerned. It is an issue which the Northern League has always taken seriously, but Gordon was particularly vigilant and vigorous in his attempts to enforce the Laws of the Game in that particular respect, though things sometimes went awry:

"It was always evident when Gordon was in attendance at a match and whilst it was never an issue with me, his presence certainly intimidated some referees. I was in charge of a game at Spennymoor once when Tony Monkhouse was the manager and there was a challenge which I thought was

OK although the player was hurt. I looked over and saw Tony in the dugout and Gordon sitting just behind him in the stand and I made the mistake of moving within earshot of him instead of moving away, and he shouted; 'Are you blind; did you not see that?' I told him it was all about angles so he told me to get some ******* angles then! Gordon just buried his head in his hands. He was mortified by the language and in my naivety I had encouraged it. It was another lesson swiftly learned."

Ray Gowen and Phil Owers were in charge at Shildon and Russell freely admits that he and Phil never saw eye to eye. They were playing Guisborough and as Ray was not their Phil was in charge. Russell knew it would be better if they did not speak and they actually had a mutual understanding to stay out of each others way. Phil came across before the game and said he was not going to speak to Russell at all;

> "My face lit up and he shouted; 'What are you laughing at?' I said; 'Nothing Phil, that's fine by me." He had said what I wanted to hear, but in almost every case I can have a crack with people who may not agree with me and there are no recriminations on either side. That is how it should be."

Graeme Forster - The Doc - is a manager Russell holds in high regard. He sees him as a character in an era when such people are a diminishing breed but who give the game its essential element of fun. The other thing he respects is his honesty, reinforcing the view that if someone can talk to you face to face after a game, exchange an opinion and not harbour grudges, then the game benefits and the individual concerned deserves respect for their honesty. Graeme was managing West Auckland in a game at Jarrow Roofing where Russell was in charge and he had cautioned Andy Sinclair for calling him 'son.' Andy was most upset and objected that he could not be booked just for calling the referee his son:

> "I told him that I could and I had and said he was neither old enough nor good looking enough to be my father! Gillian Armstrong was my assistant that day and Andy also had a right go at her. It had reached the stage where I was going to have to send him off, then Graeme Forster shouted down the line to Andy; 'How! You've been told by your son and now you've been told by your mother, so shut it or I'm bringing you off!"

A game between Ryhope CA and Chester le Street on cold April day was a relegation battle and whichever team lost would go down. Russell arrived at the ground at ten o'clock in the morning to inspect the pitch and it was apparent that Ryhope did not want the game played. The pitch had not been marked and the posts were not up. There was a story that they had a problem with injuries and did not want to play, but Chester wanted the game played and had even turned up for the pitch inspection. The pressure was on and although the pitch was very wet Russell regarded it as playable, provided some work was done in one of the penalty areas. He decided to have another look at 1:30 before making a final decision. Somehow, Gordon Nicholson got wind of the situation and when the time came for the second inspection he walked into the ground wearing his wellies, strode past Russell, shook his head and walked straight on:

> "The temperature must have been about two degrees but I was sweating buckets because I did not know whether I should be putting the game off or not. I walked around for another fifteen minutes; I tried to persuade Ryhope to do some work on the pitch but they were holding back. Eventually, the game went ahead, Chester won and Ryhope were relegated. They were not happy and gave me the usual stuff about how I had destroyed their pitch and it was a disgrace, though they still said they thought I had a good game! As I was getting changed Gordon knocked on the door and said; 'Son, the next time you have a situation like this, make a decision!' Then he walked out. He had made his point and it was another lesson learned."

After six years as a Northern League referee Russell was promoted again when he was appointed as a Referees Assistant on the Football League list. He is now in his seventeenth season in that capacity and in that time, while

Russell at the Riverside.

he has not graced the greatest stadiums in the world, he has officiated on as many league grounds as he would have visited had he been a player, and to that extent the ambition he had when he responded to the Sunderland Echo advert has been fulfilled. He also went on to reach the panel list which saw him assessed for the role of Football League referee and underwent that process for five seasons during which time he refereed the reserve match between Sunderland and Liverpool which marked the opening of the Stadium of Light and was attended by 35,000 people, which was an astounding crowd for a reserve match even allowing for the fact that admission was only £1.

In 2001 Russell received a phone call from the Football League. He was a family farmer in those days and the joke in the office which allocated refereeing appointments was that all callers should let his phone ring long and loud as he might be on his tractor which is exactly where he was when he received the call telling him that he was being taken off his match that Sunday when he had been scheduled to be at Preston for a match which was due to go out live on Sky tv. Three weeks previously he had been officiating at Carlisle where the visiting manager had accused him of making a derogatory remark and when Jim Ashworth, his boss at the Football League, contacted Russell about the issue he was able to assure him that the allegation was entirely false. He was believed, but was told that he may or may not hear further about the incident, so when the call came through prior to the Preston game on April 2nd telling him there was a problem with his appointment he immediately thought it

Who is standing next to Russell Tiffin?

related to the Carlisle incident, so he protested that he was being done an injustice.

Ruth, the secretary with whom he was in conversation, insisted that the decision had been taken and could not be reversed:

> "I did not realise it at the time but she was winding me up, and I could not see the funny side of the conversation. I did not know that everyone in the office was listening to the conversation, then she said that because they had taken me off the Sky tv game they were sending me to Brentford against Port Vale."

He was extremely surprised because Griffin Park was 250 miles from his home, well outside the normal travelling radius, and when Ruth then told him that the game was not being played in London but at Cardiff he was even more bewildered. He was not very happy, until Ruth revealed that the match was actually the final of the LDV Vans Trophy which was taking place at the Millennium Stadium, which put an entirely different complexion on the conversation:

> "I nearly fell of the tractor. They had laid the bait and I had gone for it hook, line and sinker. It was very emotional for me because that was the first cup final ever played at the Millennium Stadium and it was the rehearsal for the FA Cup Final. It was a great honour bearing in mind that there were 250 assistants on the Football League list and I had been chosen."

RUSSELL TIFFIN - YOUR COWS ARE ON OUR PITCH

Russell approached the final in much the same frame of mind as a player would, training hard, doing nothing silly and doing everything in his power to see that he did himself justice on the day.

On the Wednesday evening immediately prior to the final he was appointed as referee for a match between Esh Winning and Penrith. It was a huge game for Penrith who were pushing for promotion, and it was also taking place at the time of the foot and mouth epidemic which had impacted not only on Russell and his family but was also a serious issue for a lot of Penrith people who were affected either directly on their farms or indirectly through family connections and agriculture related businesses.

Russell sent off an Esh Winning player in the 25th minute for what he described as an absolutely horrendous two footed tackle. Penrith scored shortly afterwards and some of the crowd made their feelings known in the usual sort of way. That was fair enough, but as the teams left the field at the end of the first half one person in particular shouted some vile personal abuse at Russell:

> "The comment was not connected with the foot and mouth outbreak as some of the papers reported. It was distinctly personal and offensive with regard to my family. The guy knew me and he knew about my family background: I had a daughter who had been diagnosed with cancer when she was thirteen; thankfully she has overcome the problem, but he knew about her issues at the time and he made some horrible, personal and extremely distressing comments. I was physically sick as a consequence; I forgot why I was there and I don't think anyone else would have responded differently. We had a 25 minute interval and everybody knew what had happened. The police were called, the guy left the ground and although we started the second half I was in such an emotional state I was unable to continue so I walked off the field and abandoned the game. This was four days before I was due to go the Millennium Stadium to officiate in the biggest match of my career."

The following few days were truly traumatic. The national press camped outside Russell's door 24 hours a day and every time he opened the door the cameras clicked. The story made headlines, though Russell himself had spoken to no-one about it. The local FA, the Referees Association and many people within the non league fraternity leant valuable and much needed support, but the fact that most of the press incorrectly attributed the issue to remarks about the foot and mouth outbreak and ignored the dreadful personal nature of the outburst contributed to a very low period.

He got through it somehow and travelled to Cardiff with his wife on the Friday before Sunday's final. On the day before the match he had to meet all the dignataries associated with the final knowing that he was featured in the day's national press. He was asked to relate the story, which he did, then Jim Ashworth told him that Sunday was his big day and he now needed to focus on that:

> "I have a great deal of respect for Jim Ashworth and the way he dealt with me that weekend. He lifted the burden and I had an absolutely fantastic weekend which I will never forget."

Everyone has highlights and lowlights in their life, but surely very few people have had to face such conflicting emotions as those which Russell Tiffin experienced in those fateful four days. It was a script no-one would have dared to write. Had it not been for the uplifting experience of the LDV Vans final Russell would probably have walked away from the game . A court case followed at which his protagonist admitted his guilt, and he also had to relive the experience at a full FA inquiry; it was an extremely difficult time but he took enormous strength from the camaraderie which exists in refereeing circles and the support he received from local clubs and football people, which helped him and his family to survive the ordeal. He believes that he has emerged stronger, but it was an experience no-one would have wanted to endure. People either disintegrate or gain strength in that kind of situation and thankfully Russell is a strong individual who did the latter, with a lot of help from his friends.

Thankfully, even life as a referee has its lighter moments. He was officiating at Hartlepool and he had forgotten to switch off his mobile phone as he stood in the centre circle with his fellow officials, and he received a call from the secretary of Chester le Street Town:

> "He said; 'We have a home game which is due to kick off in an hour and 500 hundred of your cows are on the pitch!' Some kids had left the gate open and the cows had wandered through to munch the lush grass. I told him I was at Hartlepool and there was nothing I could do, so he asked me what I suggested. I told him that the black and white one with the horns was a very good centre centre half and if he put a blue and white shirt on it they would not lose the game!"

Certain players have a reputation for making life difficult for referees and while the fact and the fiction can blur into myth, the mention of some names can cause a referee's eyes to glaze over. The passion of Richie McLoughlin, the manager of Jarrow Roofing, is legendary and from a referee's point of view you are not going to be in a dispassionate frame of mind if you have rushed home from work, bolted down your tea, grabbed your kit and battled through the traffic to take charge of a meaningless game like Roofing's last midweek match of the season against Consett:

> "It was an awful game. Everybody just wanted the ninety minutes over so that the season could end. The patter on the field was poor, some of the tackling was naughty, and I was not having a great game, so when Richie came on as a substitute I thought it was all I needed. He was giving it the usual six nowt with his mouth but as the game was nearly over I had no desire to book him and write yet another report on his antics. I called him over and he gave me a whole lot of abuse, and for once in my life I was giving him as good as I got so that eventually we were pulled apart. I had been way our of order and I phoned the Referees Secretary Ted Ilderton and told him what had happened. He said I was right to report it but to wait, and a couple of days later I received a copy of Jarrow's match report. To my amazement Richie had marked me 10 out of 10 which was a remarkable gesture and one which I appreciated and respected. Really, I should not have seen that report but I am glad I did because it showed the best side of the game from a bloke who wears his heart on his sleeve. It meant a lot to me."

Maybe Russell went beyond his brief that night, but it showed how passionate he is about the game and his job; not all referees allow their passions to show. He believes that his role is to referee the game according to the Laws of the Game and that is his only aim, but he accepts that because he does it in a black and white way, it has brought him his fair share of comment and controversy. He is also convinced that he is almost always right in his decision making and that his critics do not understand the Laws of the Game as thoroughly as he does. He treats incidents and transgressions on their merits and will not compromise and he points to the fact that assessors who watch him invariably back his decisions. He is not one of those referees who will keep his cards in his pocket to preserve his Northern League status or pacify supporters and club officials. He acknowledges the need for consistency but says that he can only be consistent within his own performances and cannot be compared to the actions of other referees. He is proud that he has never walked away from an issue or shirked a responsibility on the field. He knows the Laws of the Game inside out and that is where conflict can arise:

> "I come off after many games thinking I have done well. I am professional in what I do and I am my own biggest critic. I analyse every decision I make and think every game through, and out of over 400 games in the Northern League, while I suppose I must have had a stinker, I just can't remember one!"

When a high profile referee like Russell Tiffin is on the field with the big characters of the game like the Dean Gibbs and Marc Irwins, there is a perception that it is likely to be like Iraq, but the irony is that because they are such strong personalities there is never a problem. There is a mutual respect and if the top players like Dean and Marc show respect for a match official like Russell, the game is much better for it and it is as good a measure as you will get of

Russell Tiffin's impact and the respect in which he is held.

He is keen to point out that whatever the perceptions might be, referees are normal people with jobs, families and social lives, and they love the game like the rest of us. His own commitment has been constant for twenty four years as he has worked at his fitness and his game, and he is quick to acknowledge the support he has had from his wife without which he would have been unable to pursue his career. He is 47 now and he has maintained those levels of fitness and performance; he gives his time to talk to groups in an attempt to encourage the next generation to come into the game; his commitment is total. He believes that people who criticise referees for not having played the game miss the point, and argues that if they shadowed him for a week they would gain an insight and a better understanding of where he and his fellow referees are coming from. The belief that referees are a necessary evil who are needed in order that the game can take place, he regards as patronising and he points to the passion for the game which he and his colleagues share.

The years and the regulations catch up with referees and Russell knows that his days as a Northern League referee are numbered, but when the time comes he will not be lost to the game. He will almost certainly involve himself in the role of Referees Assessor which he sees as a logical step and a way or putting something back into the game. He has contributed so much that he is entitled to put his feet up, but that it not his way. He loves the game and he will not rest easy; he will want to do everything in his power to bring new match officials through in the proper professional way and it is a role for which he is perfectly suited.

MICKY TAYLOR

Bermuda shorts and a grass skirt

As a schoolboy growing up in South Shields opportunities to shine as a footballer were limited for young Micky Taylor. He attended Westoe School which was not renowned for its football; they played once a week and were hammered regularly. He was also at a disadvantage in terms of his age, having been born on August 27th. If he had been born five days later he would have been in the year below playing against smaller lads; as it was he had to compete with boys who were all older and mostly bigger than him. The school eventually gave up the unequal task and disbanded the team in his fifth year and Micky stopped playing football until he was eighteen, at which time he came to the attention of Sonny Hobson at Marsden Juniors:

"After a three year gap I got the bug again and I actually found it very easy. So much so that before the end of the season I was invited for a trial by Sunderland. It was the day they signed Ally McCoist."

Mick played in a trial game at Middlesbrough Juniors in a side which contained Gary Rowell, Chris Turner and Colin West and he found it a strange experience; in junior football he had been used to going past players at will and scoring goals, but now he was playing with the big boys in a game they lost 1-0 and it was a new kind of football he had not encountered before. However, he was invited back, then the manager Alan Durban decided to punish the first team for a defeat by playing them all in the reserves and Micky was stood down. He decided not to return, instead going back to his junior football and ending the season with a record haul of 96 goals.

That achievement brought him to the attention of the Whitley Bay manager Micky Clifford and he joined the Hillheads club where he quickly won a place in the first team and when Newcastle United sent a representative to watch another Whitley player it was Micky who caught his eye and he was invited to play in a game for their youth team:

*"It was the day Neil McDonald made his first team debut. We played in an FA Youth Cup tie and I scored a raker of a goal, but I went over on my ankle and this little fat ****** came on to replace me. I said afterwards to my mate Kevin Thompson that it was no wonder the club was in trouble if fat bastards like that were getting a game. It was only Gazza, wasn't it!"*

Mick was not invited back by Newcastle and on reflection he believes he was not good enough to succeed at that level:

"I had talent but I did not have enough savvy. The three years I had out had stunted my development as a player and while I possessed that raw talent I was unpredictable. I was not a mature enough player."

After a successful spell at Whitley Bay he joined his home town club, South Shields, for the first time and continued his football education until Peter Feenan arranged to talk to him about the prospect of joining Blyth Spartans. Mick was still short of his twentieth birthday and naïve in the ways of the football world, so he phoned a respected friend, Tony Harrison, for advice about negotiating a deal with Blyth

"I have never been a mercenary; I have always been sensible in that regard. Only once in a drunken haze did I ask my Sunday team at Sherburn for a rise before I would go back, and I got it, but it was the drink talking and it was not typical of the way I negotiated. Money has never been my God."

MICKY TAYLOR - BERMUDA SHORTS AND A GRASS SKIRT

Mick Taylor - Boy Wonder!

The decision to sign for Blyth Spartans brought him into contact for the first time with a more professional side of the game; the proper preparation and coaching. Peter Feenan was a top class coach who encouraged Mick and brought out the best in him. He played up front with Tony McFadden and David Buchanan and while they were scoring goals Mick was charging around like a young bull upsetting defences. His first contribution to the cause was to be booked for a foul on Kenny Lowe.

He really enjoyed his time at Blyth where their FA Cup tradition manifested itself in a run which took the club to the First Round Proper and a tie against Scarborough. Peter Feenan demonstrated his tactical awareness by making the surprise decision to give Mick a marking role against Scarborough's very dangerous left back Neil Thompson. It was not a decision which went down well with the Blyth hierarchy and when the players reached Croft Park they discovered that Peter had been called into a meeting with the chairman Jim Turney and Spartans guru Jackie Marks, the outcome of which was a dressing room announcement by the manager that he had been sacked. Jackie Marks took over and dropped three of Feenan's team, Derek Ord, Ronan Liddane and Mick. The post match newspaper reports quoted Jim Turney as saying that Peter Feenan had been dismissed because some of his players were not good enough, and the implication was obvious. It was a slight which Mick was to use as a motivation throughout his career.

Blyth drew the match and when the coach stopped in Felling to pick up one of the three dropped players on the way to Scarborough for the replay he was 'mortal drunk.' The identity of the player remains a secret but it was not Mick Taylor! It was a big night; there was a large crowd and Scarborough had a very professional set up; they proved to be too good for Blyth and won 3-1 with the man Peter Feenan had identified as the main threat, Neil Thompson, scoring twice from left back, which was ironic to say the least.

A parting of the ways had become inevitable and Mick moved down the coast to join Vic Hillier at North Shields. He had a decent spell there, but Vic was not really Mick's type of manager so he moved across the water for a second spell at South Shields. Shields had not won a trophy for several years so when they lifted to Monkwearmouth Cup a celebration function was held at Roker Park. The comedian was a man called Les Ritchie and Mick and his mates were not impressed. Fuelled by the substantial use of half price beer tickets they ruined the comic's act by heckling and delivering his punch lines. He walked off and the secretary Mick Gordon went across to the offenders and told them they would never play in the league again. The committee were sitting with their backs to the stage prior to the presentation, with the rest of the audience, including a substantial female representation, facing the stage. Mick persuaded Willie Wilson from the Ryhope squad to join him on the stage where they removed their shirts and waved them over their heads in an impromptu dance, whereupon Mick Gordon intervened again to reiterate his threat to have them banned.

Two days later the Shields Gazette ran a front page story alleging that two Shields players had stripped down to their boxer shorts, and printing the names of two players who

MICKY TAYLOR - BERMUDA SHORTS AND A GRASS SKIRT

Mick and Ian Taylor receive their Player of the Month awards at South Shields.

were not actually involved in the incident. Not for the first time, the press had got it wrong. Shortly afterwards Mick was called to a disciplinary hearing along with Paul Craik, who had been an innocent bystander. Paul was grilled for forty five minutes before Mick was called in. He admitted heckling the comedian and apologised, but flatly denied the allegation that he had stripped to his boxer shorts. As it happens, he never wears boxer shorts, but when he dropped his trousers at the disciplinary hearing to prove it, it was the final straw. The committee said they had never been subjected to such impertinence and he was banned from football in the North East sine die!

He was able to play for Gateshead who operated in a national league, and they took him on. He scored the goals in a 2-1 win over Southport which saved the club from relegation and when a young John Carver took over the management of the club with Derek Bell, Mick 'had a ball.'

Non league footballers are working men who have to balance the demands of their jobs with the requirements of their football, and sometimes it is a difficult balancing act, so when Mick was given a promotion at work which involved extra responsibility and a substantial pay rise, he had to make adjustments. One of the Nissan executives intervened on his behalf with the Durham FA, pointing out that he now held a position of responsibility with the company and had turned the corner in his behaviour and attitude. The ban was lifted on appeal and he was able to resume his playing career. He signed for Nissan's own team, partly out of gratitude for their help in the lifting of the ban, but mostly because he was aware that there was to be an end of season trip to Spain! The spell with Nissan was not especially fruitful and when another promotion at work coincided with a falling out with the team manager he stopped playing football for eighteen months. He had other priorities.

After his self imposed sabbatical he joined South Shields for the third time:

> "I was offered the assistant manager's job, so I contacted Billy Cruddas for advice. He told me not to be daft, that it was not for me, and he offered to sign me for Durham City. He had signed Kevin Wolfe, John Reach, Peter Bragan and Justin Robson, but most significantly I got together with Dean Gibb and then the real lunacy started!"

It was the foundation of the Durham City team which was to win the Northern League championship and the beginning of a riotous time in the dressing room. The famous bubble bath story, for instance, is one which is well known in non league circles. Mick and Dean Gibb filled the team bath with bubble bath solution and swished it around until the dressing room was a mass of bubbles, then they hid in the bath to listen to the players' reaction. They were not disappointed!

The Old Ferens Park ground was located in a fairly affluent part of the city and neighbours were known to make occasional complaints about noise in general and profane language and inappropriate behaviour on training nights in particular:

> "We were practising running on to crosses one night and Dean and I hurtled out of the dressing room bollock naked and started hurling ourselves at the crosses. Billy Cruddas went light and the club received a letter from a neighbouring couple who were regular complainers. I thought they were asking if we could do it every week but I was wrong!"

They were hugely enjoyable and very successful times at Durham and they culminated in the team winning the title in 1994. Mick formed a potent strike force with Colin Howie and in terms of what he contributed to Mick's game he was the best he played with, but a long standing knee injury prevented Colin sustaining his high standards through no fault of his own.

Mick fell out with Billy Cruddas on the Easter Bank Holiday Monday of the season they won the title, and Billy warned him prior to the decisive game against Tow Law the following Saturday that Mick owed him. Mick's partner in crime and fellow striker Dean Gibb was injured in the third minute, so Mick had to rise to the occasion, which he did in spectacular fashion by scoring four times in a five goal victory which clinched the title. It was a triumph for all concerned and the contribution that Dean and Mick made to team spirit with their outrageous behaviour cannot be over estimated. After a game at Whitby the pair of them failed in an attempt to climb out of the sun roof on the coach, so they compensated by removing their clothes and hiding on the luggage rack:

> "We were lying there and anyone who cared to look could see the tattoos of Mickey Mouse and Minnie Mouse on my arse, and Dean's little pinkie protruding through the netting."

Then there was the time when the pair of them unlocked the door to the driver's sleeping compartment on the coach returning from an away game. They helped themselves to as much drink as they could conceal about their persons, crawled inside the hatch, locked the door so that no-one else could get in, and drank the lot.

The championship win entitled Durham to move up the pyramid system to the Unibond League. There was an agreement that they could ground share with Spennymoor until their brand new stadium at New Ferens Park was completed, but the club suffered a body blow when the league changed their mind. It was an outrageous and indefensible decision which caused enormous controversy and resentment, but the politics washed over Mick who was only interested in playing football and had envisaged problems with his work commitments if he was to play in a national league with its time and travel implications:

> "I was bothered that the club had been denied its rightful place in the Unibond because of an injustice, but from a purely personal point of view it was not a disaster."

It turned out that Durham actually ground shared with Chester le Street. Billy Cruddas brought in a couple of players Mick felt were not improvements to the squad and it was a less happy time. He started the first season at New Ferens Park and played in the inaugural match before serving a suspension. The game was against Stockton and it was George Woodhouse who had the distinction of scoring the first goal at the new ground.

Another falling out with Billy saw Mick move back to South Shields despite his brother Joe advising against it, saying they were woeful:

> "I signed on the Thursday and we were sitting in the dressing room when Bobby Graham, the manager, said he had to answer the phone and we should sit quietly and talk amongst ourselves. It was like being back at school, then after training I was asked to go upstairs with John Rundle and Bobby and sit in on a Fans Forum. They asked Bobby how he was going to win the league and he told them to ask me because I had already done it! I was gobsmacked."

He made all the right noises about supporting the chairman and backing the manager and he thanked the club for giving him the opportunity to return to play for his home town, but when he got home he phoned brother Joe who again advised him that it was a bad move. The following night he contacted the manager and told him he had made a mistake. There had been a lot of interest from other clubs and he signed for Bedlington at the instigation of Dean Gibb. South Shields got their money back plus a couple of Terriers players, but Mick could not play for a month because of the league's transfer rules:

> "Bobby Graham thought I wanted to move for more money, but as the Lord is my witness I did not know what I would be paid when I signed for Bedlington. Keith Perry at Bedlington knew a player and while the club was not as professional as Durham in the way it ran things, it was successful."

An away tie in Bedlington's Holy Grail, the FA Vase, illustrated the point about the club doing things differently. They were playing Romford in Essex and the team met up at Newcastle Central Station. They took a train to Kings Cross, crossed the city on the tube, took a local train to Romford and then caught a service bus to the ground! It could only happen at Bedlington. It was a bizarre match. Two of the floodlights failed, Mick went on as a substitute, then another light went out but he scored the equaliser in the last minute to cement his place in the team. Bedlington progressed to the quarter finals where they were beaten by eventual finalists North Ferriby.

Mick's experiences in the FA Vase were unfortunate. He had turned down the chance to sign for Whitby who won the Vase that season. Peter Quigley asked him to sign for Tow Law the year they reached the final; and he declined, and by the time Bedlington reached the final he had left, so he denied himself three consecutive opportunities to play at Wembley in the final. That takes a bit of doing!

He left Bedlington principally because of a groin problem which was preventing him from doing himself justice, and he played another spell at Nissan, helping them to promotion to the first division of the Northern League, but he was actually beginning to think in terms of winding down his career at the age of thirty four. He fell out with Stan Fenwick at Nissan because the night they won the league:

> "Stan was moaning on about something and I was elated and emotional because we had won the league, so I told him he could stick his team up his arse."

The next season he signed for Chester le Street and scored fifteen goals in four pre-season friendlies. Things were going superbly, then Gary McDonald came back from holiday. Gary was a scoring machine, but the two of them failed to gel as a partnership and Mick's form fell away and he was dropped by Paul Bryson. He was not prepared to end his career on a low note, so he laid off the drink, trained hard, and won his place back in the side for the FA Cup tie against Thackley.

Mick ready for action.

A refreshed and reinvigorated Mick Taylor played superbly and Chester won the game, after which he told Paul Bryson he was leaving. The following day he played for Plains Farm Club and again excelled, and one of his team mates tipped off the Durham City manager Brian Honour that Mick was back to his best. He signed for Durham, who were struggling, and embarked on what he calls the best period of football he played in his career:

> "I knew my career was coming to an end and that I could not **** about any more if I wanted to do myself justice. It went very, very well. I had ongoing problems with my groin and sometimes I could not play but 'Jackie' Honour knew that and he accommodated me."

He missed a particular game with the groin problem and the following week he was disappointed to find himself on the bench for an FA Vase tie against Mossley. Durham were losing two-nil with sixteen minutes to go when Jackie sent him on with instructions to get him a goal. The outcome was to be Micky Taylor's finest hour. He scored an incredible hat trick to win the game for Durham and write his name into the record books. The club had reached the semi finals on an extremely restricted budget, which reflected great credit on the management team of Brian Honour and Derek Bell, but also had a great deal to do with the special talent of Mick Taylor.

All things come to an end, and after the heroics of the FA Vase Brian Honour left and Billy Cruddas returned to the club. He invited Mick to help him out, but bearing in mind that Brian Honour's dismissal had come about because of his support for Mick in what was a genuine misunderstanding with the chairman, and because of his friendship with Brian, he felt unable to stay and help. He thought it would be disloyal. Two weeks later the chairman, Stuart Dawson, asked him to return and he went back briefly but found the situation unsustainable and rejoined Brian Honour at Bishop Auckland.

This was Unibond League football which raised again the issue of Mick's work commitments, but Brian Honour was content for him to play when he could and he actually found the Unibond style of play ideally suited to his game, to the extent that he played successfully at that level in his fortieth year and thoroughly enjoyed it. Brian wanted him around the club despite his advancing years and he was helping out off the field as well, until a switch to permanent day shift at Nissan forced him to curtail his involvement and Mick brought the curtain down on his playing career.

Many of the more picturesque Mick Taylor stories involve the removal of his clothes and when his wife asks him why he continues to do it, his argument is that if God had meant him to wear clothes he would have been born wearing an Armani suit. It is not a convincing argument but Mick is happy with it. Many of his exploits have involved his long term Sunday team, Sherburn Club, and his naked parade through the lounge and concert room carrying the County Cup is a typical effort which is recounted elsewhere in this book.

Jackie Ord and the Muppets, as he affectionately calls the committee, looked after him over the years despite his extravagances. At a function following Sherburn's defeat by Blackhall in the County Cup final the players were

Mick goes for goal.

instructed to wear shirts and ties, but no-one mentioned trousers so Mick turned up in a pair of Bermuda shorts. People really should read the small print when they are dealing with Mick Taylor. It was a lesson the Nissan people failed to heed as well when the team went to Spain and the club chairman Harry English again issued the shirt and tie edict but failed to offer any instructions regarding trousers so Mick arrived wearing a grass skirt!

In the middle of the 2005-06 season Mick called into the Voyager pub for a pint and he met his good friend Gary Crutwell. The hot topic of conversation was the fate of South Shields football club which was teetering on the brink of closure. Mick was still a high profile football figure in the town thanks to regular snippets about his matches which appeared in the Shields Gazette courtesy of Mick Worrall, and as a South Shields lad and a former player his name was being bandied about as a possible manager in the unlikely event that the club could be saved.

Gary Crutwell and Tom Manson entered into discussions with the South Shields owner, John Rundle, and their strategy was to agree a take over package which had as a pivotal feature Mick Taylor taking over as manager:

"I told Gary I was really, really not interested in being the manager, but I was very happy to help in any other way. The deal with John Rundle was almost done but Gary was most insistent that I had to be involved. He is a great friend and he won me over with his passion."

They were putting proper building blocks in place and Mick agreed to attend a meeting which resulted in his first visit to Filtrona Park for some time and when he walked in he was reminded of just how big a football club South Shields was. He joined in the negotiations with John Rundle and agreed with Gary to give it a go until the end of the season;

> "What people don't realise is that being a footballer is nothing like being a manager. I might have had a harum scarum reputation as a player but I also had eighteen years of training and experience in management at Nissan. The players respected me and respected my judgment, and I am was asking to give me anything they were not capable of producing."

South Shields was saved with Gary Crutwell and his partners in charge. Darren Frazer became the new chairman with Mick Taylor, assisted by his brother Joe, in charge of team affairs. They finished the season strongly and set their stall out for a promotion push on 2006-07.

Mick Taylor was rehabilitated. He is a mature individual with work and family responsibilities which he takes very seriously and he was making rapid strides in football management. The days of complete lunacy were over but not regretted because they are a part of what he was and where he has come from. It is wonderful that South Shields has been saved and set on the road to possible future success and Darren, Graham, Mick and the rest of the new regime were working extremely hard to make it happen, but there was always the spectre of Mick's full time work commitments hovering over him and he came to the painful conclusion that although he was enjoying success as a manager with Shields top of the league, he simply could not devote the time to the job that he knew it required, so with reluctance he handed over the reigns in October 2006. He can feel proud of the contribution he made in a short time and the club's future looks a healthy one, though without Mick Taylor on board there might not be quite so much hilarity about the place.

EVAN BRYSON & TERRY RITSON

A suitcase full of money and an audience with the Queen

Early days at Redheugh Boys Club.

It all began at Redheugh Boys Club in 1957 when the old school canteen at Tyne View School on Morrison Street was converted into a centre where local boys could use their leisure time to play snooker and table tennis thanks to the financial support of Clarke Chapman, a major local employer who had financed the conversion. A group of local Rotary Club members also leant support along with the Borough's Director of Education. The aim of the club was to provide a recreational facility for lads living in a deprived area of Gateshead, and almost fifty years on there is ample evidence of its success. Evan Bryson, who was responsible for the introduction of football at the club, is contacted regularly by former members from all over the world who have made their mark in their chosen walks of life:

> "The Rotary Club was very helpful in the early days when we really needed money. They organised golf days and other fund raising activities which kept us going, but we always operated on a shoestring."

Evan was in on the ground floor as a volunteer helper and he believed that if the club was to be successful it had to offer a wide range of sporting facilities to meet all needs, and along with football the club extended what was on offer to include basketball, athletics and boxing:

> "The first club leader was an ex-boxer called Billy Charlton who was and excellent man and a great humorist. One of our boxers was a big lad called Dave Cannon who fought as a heavyweight and Billy took him to a big tournament in London where he got a right hiding. Both his eyes were shut and his nose was flattened. There was blood everywhere and Billy decided to throw in the towel. 'Don't do that, I'm going to knock him out,' Dave protested. 'Knock him out? You cannot even see him!' said Billy, and he hoyed in the towel."

The range of varied activities on offer still exists, but it is football for which Redheugh Boys Club is renowned. They began by playing on a pitch on Lobley Hill Road, then moved to South Terrace:

> "The Rotary Club donated a double decker bus which we converted into changing rooms before our first match, but three blokes broke in with welding gear and dismantled it ready to take away. When I found it I called the police and they were caught but the magistrate wanted an early finish so he dismissed the case against them on a technicality and all we got was the price of the scrap. It was not the best of starts."

The early days were hard and money was tight. The club was run by volunteers and Evan's enthusiasm was a major factor in driving things forward. The lack of funds meant that they had to cut corners in a way that would not be possible today, and returning one night from the county trials in a small van bulging at the seams with seven players, Evan turned on to the A1 at the Cock of the North pub in Durham and was immediately stopped by the police. Not only was the vehicle grossly overloaded but the lights were defective and the van was leaking fluid which Evan explained was antifreeze. One of the policemen said he had never seen antifreeze looking like that and Evan replied that he would look like that if he had spent ten years in a car radiator! Fortunately, the police took pity on him when he explained that the lads were all members of Redheugh Boys Club and he was sent on his way with a warning to wash his number plate as the patrol car had been 'right up his arse before he could read it!'

It was never the intention to become a breeding ground for the professional side of football, but the club has produced a high quota of very good players and it was inevitable that some would go on to make a living from the game. The first was Tommy Robson in 1959 when, after an unsuccessful trial with Newcastle United, he joined Northampton Town and later played for Peterborough and Chelsea before returning to Newcastle in exchange for a fee of £35,000. Others followed, the most notable being Ian Branfoot, Don Hutchison and, of course, Paul Gascoigne.

Many of the Boys Club members came from rough backgrounds and had poor home lives, and sometimes their circumstances stressed them out to such and extent that they would react on the pitch without provocation, and it was always difficult to strike a balance when it came to discipline in the club. The leaders sometimes had to deal with aggressive fathers who wanted to make sure their boys were selected and it is a problem which has now permeated junior football at all levels irrespective of social background and status to such an extent that the behaviour of parents is probably the biggest single issue facing the game at junior level at the present time. All clubs have codes of conduct for players and parents, but some are more rigorous in their enforcement of the rules than others.

The first football team at Redheugh Boys Club was an under 18 side and once it was established it acted like a magnet to other local boys who wanted to join, and the club expanded rapidly. Evan Bryson has always been at the forefront and has devoted his life to the cause of voluntary service in Gateshead where he has spent almost fifty years working in the community helping young people to get a proper start in life. His dedication received official recognition in 2004 when he went to Buckingham Palace to receive the MBE 'for services to youth work in the county of Tyne and Wear.'

> "The medal was presented again at a local ceremony and there was this big policeman on the stage to receive a police medal. I did not

EVAN BRYSON & TERRY RITSON - A SUITCASE FULL OF MONEY AND AN AUDIENCE WITH THE QUEEN

know that he was a policeman and when he asked me if we would receive videos of the ceremony I said we would and told him I knew a bloke who made fakes who would do him as many copies as he wanted! He gave me a real old fashioned look."

From the earliest days a pattern emerged of young people who stayed with or rejoined the club when their days as members were behind them, which gives an indication of the spirit and well being of Redheugh and Evan Bryson is entitled to much of the credit for that. With the passing of the years he has remained heavily involved and constant but he has handed to day to day running of the club over to younger and more energetic people, principal among whom is former Boys Club member Terry Ritson.

Terry's involvement began in 1970 when he was still a junior player. He had been playing for Lobley Hill Juniors when a neighbour who happened to be a scout for Northampton Town stopped him in the street and told him that he had arranged a trial for him, but it was not at Northampton; it was at Redheugh Boys Club! He was instructed to present himself at the club and meet Tommy Leonard, so he went down and he met a bunch of lads who were to become lifelong friends, including Mick Hughes, Jimmy Donaldson and Ian McPherson. He had the trial and was accepted into the fold under the collective guidance of Evan, Tommy Leonard, Alec McPherson and Allan Blackburn. The impact of Redheugh Boys Club on young Terry Ritson was immediate and lasting, and he is still there. Sadly, Allan Blackburn, one of those founder members of the club who was such an influence on Terry and the others and who later held the roles of both Chairman and President, passed away in 2006 and he is greatly missed.

Terry played football at Redheugh for two years as a member of the under eighteen side and when the time came for him to move up to senior level he opted to stay on at Redheugh and eventually he became involved in running teams, which he has now done for over twenty five years during which he has derived enormous satisfaction from his part in continuing the Redheugh story. At first it was a case of training there while he was playing senior football elsewhere:

"It has always been the kind of place where you were always welcome to go back and use the facilities. No-one was ever turned away and I think that has been a major factor in the success of the club."

Gradually Terry became more involved, and in 1980 he found himself running a team for the first time. He was helping Denis Washbourne run the Under 14 side:

"Evan, Alec and Tommy had a bit of a reputation as hard guys and we went to play at Whickham Juniors. While we were getting changed the Whickham lads were pointing at them and calling them the Redheugh Poliburo, and that has been their nickname ever since."

The three top men ran the club with strict discipline; there was no smoking, no foul language. The rules were unwritten, but everyone was aware of them and they were obeyed, and those principles are still in force. The youngsters appreciated the need for discipline and there was a great feeling of belonging. Young players wanted to be in the team, so they accepted the ground rules as well as aspiring to the high standards of football for which the club also had a reputation. Those basic rules and disciplines meant that the club had very few failures among its membership, and an impressive number of old boys have gone on to achieve conspicuous success in their adult lives.

As the years went by, rival clubs were starting to run teams in other age groups and Redheugh had to follow suit in order to compete. Under 14s and Under 16s were added to the two Under 18 sides and by 1984 they had four teams. That was a very significant year for Redheugh, because they took part in the prestigious Ayr youth tournament, which attracts youth teams from all over Britain, and they won it at the first time off asking which was a fantastic achievement. Peter Featherstone, who now helps Terry out, was a member of that winning squad, but he was injured after just twenty minutes of the first game and played no further part!

The tradition of people staying on beyond their youth days which has become an integral part of the way Redeugh Boys Club does things has several factors behind it. First and

EVAN BRYSON & TERRY RITSON - A SUITCASE FULL OF MONEY AND AN AUDIENCE WITH THE QUEEN

The Redheugh Boys Club squad which won the Ayr tournament at the first time of asking in 1984.

foremost, there is no closed door policy so the opportunity exists for people to stay on or return to the club if they wish to do so. The other major factor is that over the years the club has regularly taken teams away from Gateshead, often into Europe to take part in competitions, and that has had a marvellous bonding effect. Often the lads would be away from home for the first time and almost without exception they were making their first trips abroad. They were properly guided, supervised and generally looked after on their trips by Evan and his colleagues in the early years and later by Terry and his team. They learned about living together, making compromises and building lasting friendships, and they knew that the Boys Club was responsible for providing the opportunities, which increased their love and respect for the place.

Trips to Belgium were a regular occurrence which had all sorts of beneficial effects, and there were many tales to tell because although the oversight and discipline were thorough the lads were expected to enjoy themselves:

"Lads are lads and things happened which the leaders were not aware of; there were toothpaste fights in the rooms and sometimes skin and hair would fly, but underneath it all there was a great bonding process taking place. One incident shows the kind of lads we had at the club, when a hotel owner in Belgium whose name was Ivan lost his wallet containing a substantial amount of money. One of the lads, Jimmy Donaldson, found the wallet and immediately handed it in to the leaders who returned it to Ivan. Jimmy never thought for a moment of keeping it, and that said a lot about him and about the standards and respect the club had taught to all of the lads. Honesty was one of the bedrock principles."

EVAN BRYSON & TERRY RITSON - A SUITCASE FULL OF MONEY AND AN AUDIENCE WITH THE QUEEN

The Redheugh Boys Club in 1985 with Don Hutchinson third from left on the front row.

The men who ran the club led by example and the example they set was followed by the members. There was a mutual trust, and parents were happy to send their boys to Redheugh knowing they were in safe hands and were being properly prepared for life.

While Belgian trips were essentially holidays the lads also played some football, mostly against men's teams:

> *"Evan brought me off one time because I was kicking them too hard! My big mate Mick Hughes had reminded me that we were under instructions to behave on the field as well as off it, but they were kicking lumps out of us. I decided we had to kick Hell out of them as well, and I was taken off."*

After one game the lads went back to the hotel and one of them spotted the referee's bike parked outside, so he let the tyres down. Evan and the committee caught the culprit and gave him a dressing down before making him blow the tyres up again. It was just as well they did because the referee also happened to be the local gendarme! Those trips were a marvellous part of life at Redheugh and it was a great shame in many ways when they had to be abandoned in the wake of the dreadful Heysel Stadium disaster.

Typical of the way things work is the club dress code which requires the players to wear a white shirt and a club tie for important occasions. It is a strict rule and there has been an incidence of a player being dropped after having been selected to play in a cup final because he turned up in jeans. It is about pride and standards, discipline and respect. Peter Featherstone invested £1000 of the club's hard earned money in club ties but it was a decision which was justified by events. At last season's presentation night every single player from the eight year olds upwards wore a club tie bought by his parents or himself.

EVAN BRYSON & TERRY RITSON - A SUITCASE FULL OF MONEY AND AN AUDIENCE WITH THE QUEEN

As the years passed the club continued its growth and expansion and by 1988 there were eight teams operating, beginning with Under 12s. It was not always easy to recruit managers or raise funds, but somehow the club continued to meet it targets and obligations though not without the occasional alarm. On a trip to Spennymoor in the County Youth Cup, Terry and Evan travelled together and after losing the game they set off on the homeward journey in Evan's van. The shock of defeat must have been too much for Evan because he started driving down the wrong side of the dual carriageway! Evan's driving is the stuff of legend and after another game at Chester le Street he had further mishap:

> "There were three drivers in the van and they all told me it was clear to go. I didn't know there was a contraflow system in operation and when the treasurer, who had a gammy eye, told me to go he negotiated me straight into the side of a brand new Honda. The driver was really upset because I had bashed his door in and when I told him it was just a dint he had me pinched by the police. I was fined £100 for dangerous driving."

Alec McPherson was typical of the people who ran Redheugh. He looked after the Under 18 'B' side for thirty years without complaint when the first team was the priority. He had what could be described as the remainder who could vary in quality, but he always gave them his best efforts and they did the same in return. They were losing a game at Jarrow and Alec was on the touch line as usual wearing his trademark trilby hat. The team was 4-0 down at half time and the goalkeeper was having a particularly difficult time, so during his half time team talk Alec demonstrated the art of goalkeeping by throwing his trilby on the pitch and diving on it! He was a man with great enthusiasm and a passion for his work. A semi final at Temple Park in South Shields was won and after the game everyone piled on the coach for the journey home, but Alec had been handing in the team sheet and they inadvertently left him behind. He rang his wife Grace and explained what had happened and that he only had a shilling for the phone call so could she contact the club and get someone to pick him up? 'Never mind that,' said Grace, 'What was the score?!'

By the 1990s the club was still expanding and improving and although not all of the lads went on to scale the heights in the game the Redheugh spirit was still a positive influence. With a record of seven County Cup wins to look back on and a substantial catalogue of success at the Ayr tournament and elsewhere, there was a great deal of which they could be proud. The phrase 'a Redheugh lad through and through' is one which Evan and Terry employ frequently and it has a special resonance. One such character was John Thew who attended every game and joined the club on its tours. He always carried a rattle and a bell and he made his presence felt. Before a game at Dunston Park, which was the team's temporary ground during the Gateshead Garden Festival, Terry dropped the team off before setting off to collect a couple of stragglers. John climbed aboard the minibus with his bells and rattle but when they returned to the ground there were cars double parked along the street and there was nowhere to park. Terry stopped the minibus in the middle of the road to assess the situation and as he moved off again John fell out of the back door and clattered on to the road. There was a clanging of bells and a rattling of rattles as he landed in a heap and some of the opposition from Cleveland Hall who witnessed the incident ran across to pick him up. Unfortunately, John was a very substantial man weighing almost twenty stones and he could not be lifted. Terry feared for his well being, but he eventually picked himself up, dusted himself down, rang his bell, twirled his rattle and walked off the watch the match unperturbed!

It was a matter of honour among the Politburo that the many trophies their football team won were looked after properly and treated with respect, but things can sometimes go awry even in the best ordered of societies. On the way to Langley Park to defend a cup they had won the previous season, John had parked his large frame in the seat immediately behind Terry who was driving the minibus once again. When they arrived at the ground they discovered to their consternation that John had been sitting on the trophy and had done it major damage. It was bent and twisted out of shape, making it imperative that Redheugh won the game and retained the cup so that it could be taken for repair. Thankfully, they were successful and John and trophies were kept well apart from then on.

EVAN BRYSON & TERRY RITSON - A SUITCASE FULL OF MONEY AND AN AUDIENCE WITH THE QUEEN

The Redheugh Boys Club with Paul Gascoigne third from the right on the front row.

Paul Gascoigne is by far Redheugh's most famous son, though others such as Ian Branfoot and Don Hutchison have had considerable success in the professional game, and Gazza's imprint is firmly on the pages of Redheugh's history book: His talent as a player shone like a beacon and his talent for impish and sometimes outrageous behaviour also manifested itself at an early age. Gazza and another lad called Keith Spraggon went to Ipswich for trials in Bobby Robson's time at Portman Road and the same week Redheugh Boys Club had reached the final of the NABC Percy Beattie trophy in which they were due to play Perth Green at Eppleton's ground. Ipswich gave their word that the boys would be back in time to play, so when Terry finished work he drove straight to Newcastle Central Station to collect them and link up with the rest of the squad at Eppleton. When they arrived in the dressing room the rest of the players were out looking at the pitch so Keith and Terry joined them, but Gazza remained in the dressing room ostensibly to sort out his kit. When Terry returned five minutes later Gazza had swapped everyone's gear around so that all the players had the wrong size shirts, shorts and boots. He just sat in the corner with an impish grin on his face; he was thirteen at the time and it was a sign of things to come. Evan and Terry have nothing but praise, admiration and gratitude for Paul Gascoigne who has been a magnificent friend to Redheugh:

EVAN BRYSON & TERRY RITSON - A SUITCASE FULL OF MONEY AND AN AUDIENCE WITH THE QUEEN

"When Paul was at Lazio he rang me and said he wanted to do something for the club and after some discussion it was agreed that he would buy us a new minibus. The bus was ordered and a sign indicating that it had been donated by Paul Gascoigne was painted on the side. Gazza said he would come and present it when he was at home for Christmas and he was as good as his word. After the presentation he told me he had a suitcase full of lire in his hotel room which I could have to pay for the bus! I had to persuade him that a more conventional arrangement would be better and he said his Mam would sort it out. Three days later the bill was paid. The lad is an absolute diamond."

Gazza's anxiety to help his old club was typical of him, but the fondness he has retained for Redheugh has been shared by people too numerous to mention. People who have been successful in football and those who have made their mark in other walks of life. It has been a special place for fifty years and Terry sums up what it means to everyone who has been a part of it when he says he does not need money to be a millionaire because he has been made rich by the many, many friendships he has as a result of his association with the club:

"There are so many people I cannot remember all the names, and faces change as people grow up, but folk from all over the country stop me and remind me of their time at Redheugh, and that makes it all worthwhile."

People like Evan Bryson and Terry Ritson are special; they devote themselves to providing opportunities for young people and they do it with no desire for reward, but sometimes the good people are recognised and in 2004 Evan was awarded the MBE for his work at Redheugh. Typically, he took Terry with him to Buckingham Palace for the investiture along with Ian Branfoot and Wilfie Reid:

"Ian had a lot of contacts in London from his coaching and managing days and he agreed to arrange our accommodation. He also arranged with his mate Alan Pardew for us to watch West Ham play. We were in Pardew's private box and the next day we saw the Queen and Evan was presented with his medal by her. It was a totally marvellous experience."

Unbeknown to Evan, it had been Terry who had nominated him for the award as an acknowledgement of all that he and his colleagues had done, and it was therefore fitting that Terry should be at the Palace when the Queen bestowed the medal on him. Evan and Terry have given over 85 years of combined service to Redheugh Boys Club and they are part of the fabric. Unlike Evan, who is a single man able to make his own decisions about how he commits his time, Terry is a family man and he is quick to pay tribute to the willing support he has received from his wife which has allowed him to make his own remarkable contribution to the club.

Evan Bryson after receiving his MBE from the Queen, accompanied by Ian Branfoot.

EVAN BRYSON & TERRY RITSON - A SUITCASE FULL OF MONEY AND AN AUDIENCE WITH THE QUEEN

Redheugh now runs eighteen teams including a girls' side. After all the years at Morrison Street they have taken a lease on new premises at Eslington Park playing fields; the Football Foundation has been consulted and a bid is being made for grant aid to develop the site. The problem of securing matched funding needs to be tackled and there are people on board who are concentrating on that aspect of Redheugh's future, and the next couple of years should see a massive upturn in the club's fortunes. The new facilities will be a fitting reward for fifty years of effort and dedication and the club will have a home worthy of the people who have dedicated their lives to its cause.

The club are planning a major function in June 2007 to mark Redheugh's fiftieth anniversary and as well as providing the opportunity for a huge reunion it will take some of the pressure off Terry Ritson following a conversation he had in Hyde Park a couple of years ago. Terry and a group of Redheugh people and their wives had travelled together to London for a theatre weekend and a visit to 'The Phantom of the Opera' and during a Sunday morning stroll through the park he was asked to name his best ever Reheugh select team. There was much discussion and debate and eventually he named his team. A couple of weeks later he was approached by Peter Dixon in the Teams club who complained because he had not been nominated, and that was the start of an ongoing series of complaints from a whole host of ex-players who thought they should have been included. So when the major celebration takes place in 2007 Terry intends to display sheets with the names of all the club's former players and invite the guests to name their own best sides, in the hope that the complaints will stop!

> *"I have taken so much stick over it and I still do. Even Gazza was not picked because he left us before he played for the Under 18s so he did not qualify, so it was a hard task and it's all about opinions anyway."*

The Boys Club today is as strong as ever in terms of numbers and atmosphere and the people involved remain faithful to the ongoing spirit and principles. A man who brought his son and daughter to play for the club articulated what it was that made the place special when he said that he had been to other clubs where their priorities are different. He said that the friendliness of the people and the atmosphere it creates set it apart. Terry and Evan are at pains to explain that everyone is welcome irrespective of their background or culture. It is a special place run by special people.

JOHNNY INNES

The East End Historian

Johnny Innes was a terrific footballer in his time as anyone who saw him and his brothers or played alongside them in the dim mists of time will verify. He is also a considerable authority on the post war history of non league football in the East End of Newcastle. Still an avid fan of the game, he enjoys nothing better than watching non league and reminiscing in a supremely entertaining manner. Anyone who knows Johnny will tell you that he is a true character in his own right, and he has also known all of the great characters who have adorned the game in the East End for the last fifty years and more. He is very reluctant to talk about his own part in the history of the game in that part of Newcastle where he was brought up and played his football, but he is very keen to record the top teams and the main movers and shakers of his time.

One of the clubs he holds in high affection is the Birds Nest which came into existence at the beginning of the 1963-64 season when the Birds Nest Social Club, which was located just off Walker Road, took over the fixtures of the Red Lion pub in the North East Sunday League. Ray Donnison was the driving force behind the Birds Nest and like many another in grass roots football in the region, he was a tireless worker who devoted countless hours of his spare time to his club.

The progress of the Birds Nest was staggering in its rapidity as they won five consecutive league championships, moving up from Division Five to become champions of the Premier Division; a remarkable feat. To underline their consistency and quality they won the championship of the North East Sunday League Premier Division, which was by definition the best Sunday league in the area, without suffering a single defeat, which was a magnificent achievement. It is also an accomplishment which has not been equalled before or since in the history of the league, which was formed in 1949. Ray Donnison's principal helper was Brian 'Coker' Coulson, who is still involved in East End football with the Monkchester Road based Northern Alliance Premier League side Walker Central.

To win titles as consistently as the Birds Nest did you need good players, and they need to be players who can gel as a team and complement each other. You also need goalscorers and in that respect the Nest was served magnificently by Billy Wright and Geordie Jackson. Billy was an awesome centre forward; big and brave and with a better touch than he was sometimes given credit for. He was a prolific scorer in the Northern League with Whitley Bay as well as with the Birds Nest and he later became a referee and a council member of the Northumberland FA. On the field he and Geordie Jackson were perfect foils for each other and they plundered goals galore.

Successful teams also needs character and characters and the Birds Nest had both. Johnny recalls, for instance, Joe Boyd and a conversation long after their playing days in which someone accused Joe of not having been able to play. Quick as a flash came the reply; 'No, but I could stop those who could!' Little Ronnie Carr, the winger they nicknames 'Killer' was another character along with another small lad called John Tweddle. What the pair of them lacked in stature they made up for in class. The names roll of the tongues of those old enough to remember, and there was not as bad player among them:

> *"There was Peter 'Lob' Stephenson who always played better with a couple of bottles of Brown Ale inside him. Lob was a real old fashioned winger who could drop the ball on a tanner and he was perfect for Wrighty and Geordie Jackson."*

The fantastic level of success and consistency which the Birds Nest achieved was impossible to sustain and a few

The Birds Nest, North East Sunday League Champions.

barren years in terms of real success followed, before the advent of a worthy successor to Ray Donnison in the shape of Ray Mulroy, who was assisted by another well known local football man, Derek 'Darkie' Gair. Together they plotted a course to promotion from the second division so that the Birds Nest returned to its rightful place in the Premier Division. Derek moved on but Ray stayed to guide the club to two further Premier League titles and the County Cup. The Birds Nest had revived its tradition of success which is there in the record books for all to see, but sadly habits change and the Birds Nest club itself was to close a few years later.

At the bottom of Raby Street in Byker stands the St Peters 'Bottom' Club which first began to run a football team in the 1963-64 season. From the start they were a club which took a pride in playing good, attractive football and they never won the volume of trophies the quality of their football deserved. Johnny himself was one of the pioneers at the Bottom Club and his brother Eddie was one of the star players as were quality footballers like Eddie Mitchell, Stan Carty, Tommy Lowery and Bob Sample. Bob was typical of the type of player the Bottom Club recruited; strong and pacy with good control and two good feet. On his day he was unstoppable.

After many years of playing entertaining football without actually winning anything significant, success finally came the way of the Bottom Club in the 1977-78 season when a former Birds Nest player called Billy Small, assisted by Billy

St Peters Athletic - the 'Bottom Club'.

Young, put together a side which added strength and physical presence to their traditional finesse, and they won the Frank Brennan Cup, creating something of a record in the process by including in their side three brothers, Joe, Jimmy and Paul Buzzeo. Unlike the Birds Nest, St Peters continues to flourish as a social club and they still have a decent football team, served by club stalwart Tom Lowery who has been involved with the team since its inception 44 years ago; he is a man of great character and determination who loves his team.

Daisy Hill in Walker has been a member of the North East Sunday League from the earliest days, and can lay claim to having been the first Sunday team from the East End. In the heyday of the league in the sixties and seventies they had a large following and they swept the board with victories in the Premier League, the Frank Brennan Cup and the Association Cup. They were a team of local lads from Daisy Hill itself including John Coxon, Colin Greenwell, George 'Bomber' Thompson, Dave 'Whitey' McClelland, Bobby Cain, Cliffie Waldock and the greatest of them all, Kenny Oliver:

"Kenny was something special. He was a joker who was converted from being a winger into an outstanding full back. He was another one who liked his Newcastle Brown. There was never any Brown Ale left on the table when Kenny was there. If there was anything unfinished he would doon it."

JOHNNY INNES - THE EAST END HISTORIAN

Sadly, he passed away and the Ken Oliver Memorial Trophy was established in his memory, though it is no longer contested. Anyone who ever spent time in Kenny's company left with a smile on their face.

Clubs are about players, but they are also about the people who run them behind the scenes, and Daisy Hill were very well served in that respect. Their most influential character was the late Charlie Taylor who was also the chairman of the North East Sunday League and an official of the Northumberland FA, and another of the stalwarts was Eddie Cardose who began his association with Daisy Hill as a boyhood supporter, went on to become a member of the committee, and is still involved today. Les Stephenson was the secretary for many years; a quiet man who never pushed himself to the fore but who carried out his responsibilities with great efficiency. One of the hallmarks of Daisy Hill has always been the loyalty of the men who ran and played for the team and no-one exemplified that better than Jimmy Gourley, an outstanding player who was sought after by every Sunday team in the area but who rejected all offers and advances, and remained steadfast Daisy Hill throughout his playing career.

Wallsend Buffs is the next port of call on Johnny Innes's stroll through the history of the game in the East End, and there is a link between the RAOB team and St Peters 'Bottom' Club, a couple of whose players visited the Buffs in their formative days in an attempt to arrange a friendly match. The word got around and a several of the RAOB's Saturday players decided to form a Sunday morning team as well. The friendly was duly arranged and the Buffs suffered a 7-1 hiding. One of the unfortunate members of the team in that opening fixture was Brian Watson who later made a considerable name for himself in the professional game, first as the Youth Development Officer at Carlisle United under Bob Moncur and later with Newcastle United in the same capacity:

> *"Anybody who knew football knew Watty. He was a genuine guy who got most of the best of the young local talent to St James's Park due to his connection with Wallsend Boys Club along with Peter Kirkley and Brian Clark."*

The Buffs were a happy go lucky bunch who would meet up at the 'Morgue' club, better known as Willington Quay and Howdon CIU. Carefree they may have been, but they could also play and with John Atkinson, Kenny Poulter, John Montgomery and Darkie Gair involved as well as the legendary Jimmy 'Sport' Martin as the driving force, they had their share of success.

There are two St Peters Social Clubs within striking distance of each other in Byker and to distinguish them one is called the 'Bottom' Club because it is located at the bottom of the bank and the other is the 'Middle' Club because it is half way up. The 'Middle' Club, which is now Johnny Innes's watering hole, first launched its team in the 1969-70 season under the managership of Kenny Watson. Another of Johnny's brothers, Jimmy Innes was a key member of the team along with Les Leech and Dave Brierley, who scored goals for fun in a team which enjoyed great success as it made rapid progress through the divisions of the North East Sunday League. This part of Newcastle is an area which loves its football and the 'Middle' Club was always a very well supported team; they routinely took two busloads of supporters with them to away games, heavily laden with crates of Brown Ale!

Byker St. Peters: Frank Brennan Cup Winners 1983.

Sammy Turner and Seppy Vose stood out as real characters in the 'Middle' Club set up. They were called the 'SS' and they were further examples of the dedicated people who populate grass roots football:

> "No job was too big for the 'SS' and they thought nothing of clearing all the snow off the pitch to make sure games went ahead. They had hearts of gold."

The late 1970s witnessed a decline in the team's fortunes, before a new committee was formed which was very successful in raising funds and relaunching the team in a successful way. The key appointment which proved pivotal to their success came when Ian Playfair was made manager, and under his guidance they won promotion to the North East Sunday League Premier Division as well as winning three different cup competitions in successive seasons. Ian assembled an essentially young side by signing Tony Cornfoot, the Walker brothers, Steve Wright and Frankie Deverdics, and to mould them into a successful unit he added the invaluable experience of Billy Barlow and Alan Hewson.

At the junction of Heaton Road and Shields Road stands one of the best known social clubs in Newcastle. The Heaton RAOB club. Heaton Buffs is big and successful and it was natural that it should have a football team, so the task of raising the necessary funds was undertaken by George Smith, Kenny 'the Animal' Shaw and Bucky Lancaster who all worked tirelessly in the cause. When the team was up and running they washed the strips, ran the line, swept the dressing rooms and, in Johnny's words, 'generally sorted out the crap.' One of the heart warming things about these three diehards was that they never envied or begrudged any other team in the locality their success, and they were always there to encourage other East End sides in their key matches.

The number and quality of Sunday League sides which had success in the East End is remarkable and perhaps the best known and certainly one of the most successful over the years was Byker Legion. The club stood at the top of Shields Road and the football team was at the top of the tree for many years. To be fair, they were known for several years as the 'nearly' club because while they were a very good team which always finished high in the league and made excellent progress in the cup competitions, they were beaten finalists on many occasions, and the ultimate success of lifting silverware eluded them for many years until everything came together and they won the League, the Frank Brennan Trophy and the Association Cup:

> "They were run by the greatest character of them all, Big John Wilson. He was a colossal man who would fight tooth and nail for his club and his players. His great partner and accomplice was Andy Kinchley and they had some exceptional players through their hands like Billy and Mick Colwill, Ian Mutrie, Bill Tarbitt, Peter Stephenson,, Micky Coogan, Kenny Webster, Billy Cawthra, Paul Dixon and too many others to name."

Big John Wilson was a gentle giant once the game was over and his team had won! During the action he was known to chase opposition players around the pitch if they went over the top or injured his players. When he left the Legion he took his team to Benton Social Club where he won both Sunday cups before going on the do the same at North Heaton Sports Club. Due to his work commitments he handed his team over to Ian Playfair who achieved his success at the 'Middle' Club with many of John's squad.

'The Jubilee'.

Walker Jubilee Club on Proctor Street adjacent to Walker Park was another of the may East End success stories of the 1970s, with their quota of cup victories and progress through the league, though it took them until 2001 to reach the dizzy heights of the Premier League. Ken Moreland was the chairman in the seventies and he was a fund raising legend. He sold domino cards and squibs in the shipyards where he was worked as a scaffolder:

"He used to send tickets up to the crane drivers in the crane drivers' buckets. Nobody escaped Kenny! He also had good lads working alongside him in Norman Rutherford, Steve Gibson, and Bob Barlow, and they had good players as well. Coker Coulson played, with Jimmy Barber and Tommy Gibson. Dave Fleming was a cultured wing half and they also had big John Studholme who was as blind as a ******* bat!. Up front they had Brian Oliver who was a ringer for Frank Overmars."

They had great battles in the cup ties against the top teams like Whindyke and Killingworh Club and they won their share of trophies before having a run of dormant years prior to their revival under Tess Lunn and Geordie Jackson who guided them to promotion to the Premier League before putting together a team of young players which in 2006 won the Association Cup, beating the league champions Blakelaw 4-0 in the final.

Next up, the Chillingham Hotel on Chillingham Road in Heaton where Brian Thompson made his mark after several years at the Prince of Wales pub around the corner on Shields Road. In the five years of his tenure they won the Tyneside Sunday League three times and they also won three cups. Johnny Innes comes back time and again to the people behind the scenes as he outlines the stories of the great East End teams – the unsung heroes, and the 'Chilly' was another club blessed with such people, particularly their chairman Harry Knighton, treasurer Eddie Jenkins, along with John 'Scouse' Alvers and John Yeats.

Mention must also be made of the Walker Fosse team which had its heyday in the sixties when John and Wilf Carr were heavily involved along with Cec and Malcolm Hodgson.

The Chillingham Hotel.

Tommy Orrick who played in the North Shields team which won the FA Amateur Cup in 1969 was a Fosse player as was Billy Horden, and that gem of a player Ray 'Spike' Owen.

Johnny sets great store by the characters who have made their mark on East End football:

"Alfie Allen, who ran the Glendale pub team before the CIU club sides emerged, was a marvellous example of a one man band. He used to hump the strips in a rucksack on his back, and the balls and the first aid kit went in a plastic bag. Alfie had a dodgy leg but that did not stop him carrying everything up the bank to the Glendale through the snow on a freezing cold winter's morning."

Alfie was a cobbler at Legender's shop on Heaton Road and he was renowned for his ability to repair footballs which he did for all the teams in the East End.

Billy Todd used to run teams in Wallsend, and the best known of his teams was Wallsend Gordons for which Johnny Innes himself played. Billy Todd was actually running the Wallsend Slipway apprentices team, but within a year he had changed the name to Wallsend Gordons after the square in the town where he lived, and entered them in the Tyneside Amateur League. He also ditched the apprentices and replaced them with East End lads he knew like Darkie Gair, Kenny Shaw, Billy Berry, John Montgomery and John Atkinson as well as top goalkeeper Billy Allen. He had to tread warily, because the Wallsend Slipway management was unaware of his shenanigans. He had dropped their name and disposed of all their players but his team was still playing on their pitch! They were very successful, but Billy made the mistake of bringing in big guns like Ray Young and Tony Cassidy when the cup finals came around. Nevertheless, he won a hatful of trophies and he was a devoted non league man:

> "Toddy's classic quote was; 'If you don't play football for Toddy, you don't play football' and he was a major contributor to the East End scene. He was also the most controversial manager I ever met! Once he named a team and he left me out. I was sub, so Billy Allen took his shirt off and told him to find another goalie! I had been having storming games every week, but that did not bother Toddy. He used to organise the transport for away games and when it came to the end of the season midweek cup matches he would tell us all to meet outside the Wallsend Buffs club. Legend has it he was putting the bill for the bus down to the Buffs club, but I don't think that is true!"

Rugby coach Steve Black was a member of the Middle Club Jolly Boys when he was seventeen and he was young and daft. There was a committee meeting taking place one night and he was under the seats with his pal, banging on the skirting boards with his hands. He said they had been sponsored to go around the room as many times as they could following the coal seams!

> "Blackie was a crazy kid. When he was running the second team he got hold of this megaphone and he was standing on the line shouting; 'Six pass to four, four pass to seven…..four ******* pass it to seven or I will bring you off. He was nuts."

Another of Johnny's cohorts was Derek 'Darkie' Gair who was the archetypical 'football daft' Geordie lad and who first emerged as a manager when he shared team selection duties with St Peters Athletic (the official name of the 'Bottom Club' team) with Peter Carr and Johnny in 1965. Remarkably, having taken the team to the Premier Division, they were relieved of their duties and Derek left to take over at various other clubs, and he never failed to achieve success. North Heaton Sports, Byker St Peters, Walker Jubilee and the Birds Nest all benefited from Derek's input. He had a wonderful talent for creating a 'laugh a minute' dressing room atmosphere and Bob Elwell was quick to recognise his value and worked with him on Saturdays with Bishop Auckland, South Shields, Spennymoor United and Blyth Spartans. Derek's crowning glory was the part he played in the success of Bedlington Terriers who won five consecutive Northern League titles and reached the final of the FA Vase. He is still involved, helping out at West Allotment Celtic.

Until recently Johnny Innes's involvement in East End football has been all about Sunday teams, because that was where the great players, the great characters and the huge success were all to be found. The teams were based in the working men's clubs of a heavily industrialised area, and the they played in the North East Sunday League. Some still do and although it has to be conceded that the West End has dominated the Sunday league scene in Newcastle for many years, there are encouraging signs that the East End is on the way back through teams like Walker Jubilee, the Willows Club and St Peters. However, the nature of the East End itself has changed in recent decades with the decline of the shipbuilding and manufacturing industries in the area. Working Men's Clubs have closed or are operating in reduced circumstances, and the heyday of the Sunday league teams has passed, for the present at any rate. Thankfully, the void has been filled and there is a new surge of optimism with the emergence of Saturday football as a renewed force.

The sea change began in the late 1980s when a team called Newcastle Benfield Saints was formed and took up residence on the Sam Smith playing field, which was formerly the sports ground of the Byker based Ringtons Tea company on Benfield Road. Their progress is in the tradition of the great Sunday teams of a bygone era, and it is perhaps no surprise that they began life as a Sunday morning team themselves, representing the Corner House pub in Heaton. They had great success and that fed their ambition to become a successful Saturday team which could reach the level of the Northern League. They quickly made their mark in the Northern Alliance, secured grants to improve their ground to Northern League standards and in 2003, having won the Northern Alliance title they were promoted to the second division of the Northern League. A consecutive promotion saw them achieve their ambition of playing in the Northern League Division One and to have achieved what they have in so short a space of time is phenomenal. The East End has a Saturday team which can already compete with the best the area has to offer and there is every indication that with the people in charge they will rise and rise and give the East End another team of which it can be proud. Hats off, then, to chairman Jimmy Rowe, John Colley and their man for all seasons Danny Gates. Newcastle Benfield are here to stay, and with West Allotment Celtic and Team Northumbria having joined them to provide three East End teams in the Northern League, and with a revitalised Heaton Stannington also knocking on the door, Saturday football in the East End has never been healthier:

> *"My ambition is to see one of these teams bring the Northumberland Senior Cup back to the East End for the first time since Walker Celtic won it in 1920. It is time it came back."*

The oldest Saturday team in the East End is Heaton Stannington, named after their original ground in Stannington Avenue, but residing on Newton Road for several decades. Heaton Stann. is forever associated with the late Bob Grounsell, former player, secretary and president who served the club in various leading roles for half a century and after whom their ground is now named. Aside form Bob 'Gunner' Grounsell, the other great son of Heaton Stann. was Eddie 'Tremendous' Temple who, like Bob, was a devoted Heaton man from his early days as a player to his later range of roles as a major contributor to the club's cause.

Heaton Stannington has a proud history, having been founded in 1910 and they played in the Northern League until their resignation in 1948. They have had their problems and their fallow years, but they have remained steadfast and they are currently in the process of improving their facilities with an eye on a return to the Northern League. They are building new dressing rooms and the ground looks, as Eddie would have said, 'tremendous.' Bill Colwill is the secretary these days and the club is run energetically on both its social side with its excellent revamped clubhouse, and on the football side under the management of Derek Thompson and they are geared for success on and off the field; ready to become the fourth in a quartet of East End clubs in the Northern League.

There could be another waiting in the wings. Walker Central, like Newcastle Benfield, are new kids on the Saturday afternoon block. They were founded in 1988-89 and founder members included Ray Mulroy, Brain Clark and 'Coker' Coulson. They have an excellent set up with a good range of facilities and their clubhouse is among the best around. They run sixteen teams and they have become a respected East End institution which meets a genuine football need across the age spectrum in the area where it is located. They are currently playing in the top division of the Northern Alliance and with a fair prevailing wind they, too, could become a force in the Northern League in the years to come.

When it comes to talking about his own career Johnny Innes is very reluctant, but people who were around at the time say he was as good as there was. It has been possible to glean from the man himself that he played for Parsons at the age of fifteen and while he was there he was the only person in the side who was not a Parsons employee which speaks volumes for the regard in which he was held as a player. He joined the Red Lion pub team in Shieldfield as a young man in 1958, which turned out to be their last season:

> *"We were playing the Blue Bell and we needed two points to avoid relegation. We were 1-0 up at half time and although the Blue Bell equalised we won the game 2-1. We were over the moon but it was later revealed that the game had been bought and paid for! It didn't matter because the Red Lion folded and the Birds Nest took their place."*

He went on to play for the Evening Chronicle with Bob Morton and his brother Andy. Their centre half was Billy Inchmore – the Bull:

JOHNNY INNES - THE EAST END HISTORIAN

> "Billy hated to play against Bobby Jardine for the Crown. We played them in a cup game at their place and I told him his physical presence would frighten Jardine; he did great until six minutes from time and we were winning 1-0, then Bobby Jardine went Bang, Bang and they beat us 2-1. They swept the board that year."

He was one of the founder members of the team at the 'Bottom Club' where he remained involved in various capacities for seventeen years:

> "We played the Black Bull once and I had finished; I was the treasurer, but we were a player short so I gave my pocket full of money to Billy Dryden to look after and played. We beat them 2-1 and I played a blinder. That was my finish until I got involved in the Over 40s with Walker Celtic."

Well, it was Walker Celtic, but it nearly was not. The team was formed when Ernie Brown, Derek Gair and Johnny decided to start a team so they presented themselves at the league meeting in Sunderland. When they were accepted they said they were called Newcastle East End, then they went into a huddle and told the chairman they had decided to call themselves Monkchester Rovers, then Johnny and Derek vetoed that idea because they thought Ernie wanted to be 'Roy of the Rovers' so they finally settled on Walker Celtic. They assembled an excellent side for which not only Johnny but Ronnie Carr, Geordie Jackson and Billy Wright all played.

The Walker Celtic team was managed by Ted Copeland and in 1990 they were invited to take part in a tournament in Germany in place of Bradford City who had been banned:

> "It cost us £70 each, all in. We travelled by way of Bradford in this posh coach where we had to pick up the Bradford City junior side which was coached by Leighton James. We drew the first game but it was obvious we needed a goal scorer so we roped in Leighton James. We went through to the finals then we won this greet big gold cup!"

Another time Johnny was in charge of Walker Celtic and he named his team. His half back line was Billy Small, Micky White and Davy Brown so he said: 'Half backs; Small, White and Brown:

> "One of the lads said; 'Me Mam used to send me to the Co-op for that - a small white and a broon' – so I told him I had been using my loaf when I picked the team!"

That is typical of Johnny Innes; he is a quick witted man with a wonderful sense of humour and a fabulous and sometimes colourful turn of praise. He is steeped in the traditions of non league football on Tyneside and his knowledge of the East End scene is encyclopaedic. He won't tell you so himself, but he was an outstanding winger in his time and he was a major force in the running of several successful teams in the area. His dream of seeing the Northumberland Senior Cup return to the East End is bound to be fulfilled as the Saturday clubs continue their development, and he takes pleasure in the upturn in fortunes of the area's Sunday teams as well. Johnny Innes is a true character and a real football man. There are not many to touch him.

TOMMY COONEY

A policewoman and a spot of Morris dancing

The Prince Consort Hotel team with Tommy Cooney second from the right on the front row.

As a nineteen year old Gateshead lad who had cut his football playing teeth with St Mary's Juniors, Tommy Cooney graduated to senior football with the St Mary's team which played in the Northern Combination League. He earned quite a name for himself as a player in his early days and his brother, who drank in a pub on the town's Prince Consort Road, told him that the pub intended to start a football team. As a player with a growing reputation, albeit in a minor league, he was able to persuade his Saturday afternoon team mates from St Mary's to link up with the new Sunday morning team at the Prince Consort pub, and they were successful right from the outset.

They were admitted to the second division of the North East Sunday League in 1959 and had a successful run for a couple of seasons, before progress of a different kind intervened and the pub was demolished to make way for the town's new Civic Centre and the team had no option but to move on. Tommy ended up at the Blue Bell in Felling which had an outstanding team and in his first season they reached the final of the All England Sunday Cup. Tommy's reputation was continuing to grow and he was a player in demand. He was approached by his friend Frank Peareth who was the captain of Dunston Social, and he was persuaded to join them:

> "I was the only player in the team who was actually from Gateshead. The rest were real Dunston lads who had grown up together like big Billy Ward, Tommy Robinson who went on to captain Gateshead, John Shanley, Dave Liddle, Frankie Rankin, Dave Webb, Tommy Dixon and George Bagnall; they were all top players."

A lot of the Dunston team also played Saturday football for Huwoods, who were not a high profile side but they were an outstanding team and they included Brian Oakley and Billy Roughley who worked at the factory.

The success of the Dunston Social team during Tommy's era was phenomenal and he was happy to stay there for several years. As he grew older the Five Bridges Hotel opened in Gateshead town centre and he used to drink there. It was natural that a football team should be formed and Tommy was involved from the first days in what proved to be another team which enjoyed consistent success from its beginnings, moving rapidly through the divisions of the North East Sunday League to reach the Premier Division.

The Five Bridges prepare to do battle.

By the time he reached his early thirties Tommy was no longer able to command a regular place in the Five Bridges team, so he helped to form a second team based at the same venue which became known as Rank Hotel. It was intended initially as a team for the hotel staff, but Tommy was able to use his connections to draft in better players which brought about a steady improvement. They became a very good team and they achieved a notable landmark when they defeated the Fairholm side to bring to an end the run of 106 consecutive victories which had earned them a place in the Guinness Book of Records. Fairholm were a formidable team with Stuart Leeming on the left wing while Kenny Usher and several other top players from the Westerhope area were also in the side. For a team like Rank Hotel to rise from obscurity to inflict that rare defeat on them in a cup semi final was a fine achievement. They went on to win the trophy, but the management of the Five Bridges Hotel upgraded their leisure facilities and introduced a membership scheme which meant that Tommy and his colleagues were no longer able to play for the Rank Hotel team.

They moved to another pub, the Queens Head on Bottle Bank, and carried on with some small success before that was closed for a major refurbishment. The upshot was that Tommy and company were on the move again and this time they went to the A1 Allerdene Social Club in Harlow Green in 1972 and Tommy began what has been an unbroken 34 year association with the club.

He became involved with the Allerdene because his brother in law was the steward, so that when the Queens Head closed it was a logical move. His playing career had come to an end so he began to manage the team; the end of his career coincided with Peter Quigley's retirement as a player and Peter linked up with him at the Allerdene to share the management responsibilities.

The pattern of instant success which had been a hallmark of his playing days was again evident in Tommy's managerial time at Allerdene. They got off to a flying star and they have been, quite simply, one of the most successful teams in the Gateshead and District League throughout the 34 years of his involvement. They have never been out of the top division, always finished in the top half and usually

TOMMY COONEY - A POLICEWOMAN AND A SPOT OF MORRIS DANCING

Rank Hotel, 1972. Tommy is in the centre with the ball at his feet.

challenged for honours. It is a remarkable record of consistency. Many teams have their purple patches but it takes a very special level of commitment and dedication to achieve success over more than three decades, and as manager and now chairman Tommy Cooney had been the leading figure throughout.

Aside from Tommy's own massive contribution in his various roles, one of the main reasons behind the Allerdene's success has been the fact that the players have been friends off the pitch as well as team mates on it; it has never been a matter of just turning up on a Sunday morning and playing football. Another factor has been continuity; Tommy has always been there, players have remained loyal and new people have been integrated on both the playing and the administration sides in a seamless way. Paul Kennedy is the manager now although Tommy is still a major influence,

and the team is continuing to thrive. The current squad includes four players from the Tow Law team which reached the final of the FA Vase at Wembley; Tony Nelson, Paul Haigh, Kevin McGarrigle and Ian Aitken and their experience combined with a good crop of young players ensures that the club's record of success has every chance of being extended.

One of his higher profile players at the Alllerdene was Peter Harrison who had played professionally in Belgium and who was later to be at the centre of a series of allegations surrounding his work as a players' agent. He was a significant capture for the Allerdene because he had not long finished playing professionally and was still an outstanding player by Sunday league standards, even those set by as good a team as the Allerdene. Towards the end of the season a friend of Peter's came to visit from Belgium. This friend came over in a vehicle which Tommy described as 'a dodgy car which was not properly registered:'

> "He was a big, robust man who had a lovely nature and a great sense of humour. We all knew about this car, so we arranged for a stripper dressed as a policewoman to come to the club after the game. The bloke was really enjoying himself and throwing back the Brown Ale like it was going out of fashion, then this police lady came in and asked to speak to him. Peter was telling him that he was in very serious trouble and really winding him up, and he was starting to get really worried. Then she started to strip off and we all fell about laughing. It could not have worked better."

Allerdene A1 Social Club team. League champions' dropping only three points all season and conceding just eleven goals.

The Allerdene was like most local Sunday morning teams in the sense that they had a loyal band of supporters who followed them home and away. They included a lad who was not the brightest, but he was there for every game and he would do anything to help out. He was not very good at the menial tasks he was given but he was very willing and loyal. One Sunday morning Tommy had to give the pre-match team talk so he asked the young man to put the nets up. He managed to hook the net at one end around the posts and crossbar successfully, but confusion took over when he reached the other end of the pitch and he managed to lay the net flat in the ground between the posts and the penalty area. Everyone assumed that the job had been done properly, and it took some quick work to rectify the situation before the game could start.

Sometimes the names have to be changed or omitted to protect the innocent, or not so innocent, when tales of local football are being related, so suffice it to say that Tommy had a brief spell helping a struggling team in Gateshead which organised a prize draw in order to raise the funds they needed to keep going. When the time came to make the draw and pay out the lucky winners there was not enough money left in the kitty so, unbeknown to Tommy who was not present, they hit upon the idea if fiddling the draw so that the club won the first prize. Two of the committee were appointed to make the draw and one of them was instructed to keep ticket number 192 in his hand. A hush descended on the premises as the result of the draw was about to be announced, then calamity struck. The committee man dropped the '192' ticket back in the bag. His colleague acted with great presence of mind, pulled a random ticket out of the bag and announced that the winning number was '192' before dropping the ticket back in the bag before anyone could see it. It was actually number 68 which won but sometimes drastic measures are needed to keep struggling teams going!

Tommy also had an impressive record as a player and a manager in Saturday football. As a player his clubs included Evenwood Town:

> "They called us the Toonies up there because the bulk of the team were bedded in Evenwood cement. Two of them – Tony Woodhouse and Bob Tookey – had played over 600 games for them. The manager was Billy Bell who was a football maniac in the best sense, and he would never accept any excuses for not turning up for training or matches. There was this incredibly cold and bleak Saturday when we were due to play Billingham Synthonia in the FA Cup, so we phoned Billy to check that the game was on. He said we had to travel and that the pitch was

TOMMY COONEY - A POLICEWOMAN AND A SPOT OF MORRIS DANCING

Dunston Mechanics, winners of the Northern Combination League Cup at St James's Park.

ideal, which it could not possibly have been; the weather was absolutely freezing. When we reached West Auckland which is a couple of miles from Evenwood we saw this massive pall of black smoke and when we reached the ground we saw Billy wearing a pair of goggles. His face was jet black – he looked like a minstrel! He had bought a load of tyres, distributed them all over the pitch, doused them with petrol and set fire to them. The blaze was terrifying and by kick off time the pitch was ankle deep in mud. We played, and lost 3-1 so Billy's efforts had been in vain!"

It was after his Saturday football playing days came to an end that Tommy first went into management. He had captained Whickham for the last two years of his career, leading them to a League Cup Final win over Wallsend at St James's Park before he hung up his boots. He had always felt that he could make a success of management, so when Whickham asked him to return to the club in that capacity he agreed. Unfortunately, the coffers were empty and they were a struggling Northern Combination side, but he managed to put a side together. There were problems because several of the players lived in the Stanley area and had no transport, so he had to drive through on training nights to collect them and take them home afterwards. It was a demanding and time consuming process. He had to compromise, too, on playing standards because of the club's financial position and success was not easy to achieve, but the small committee worked very hard and Tommy cut his managerial teeth in moulding a decent side which won the Northern Combination League Cup. It was hard sustain the success, however, and eventually he lost his job, mainly because he was still inexperienced and lacking in toughness in management, and he tried unsuccessfully to keep happy a large squad of players who were turning out for no payment.

His next move was a highly significant one when he joined Dunston Mechanics as assistant to John Thompson who was the manager. The Mechanics evolved into Dunston Federation and in time Tommy took over as manager. They won the League Cup and in due course he was joined by his

159

TOMMY COONEY - A POLICEWOMAN AND A SPOT OF MORRIS DANCING

good friend Peter Quigley and the rise of Dunston continued. He steered the team to promotion to the Wearside League and eventually into the Northern League:

> "In all their time Dunston have only had five managers and four of them are still at the club. The only one who has gone is Peter Quigley. John Thompson, Alan Stott, Bobby Scaife and I are still there."

The dual role of managing Dunston on Saturday and the Allerdene on Sunday became too much of a burden, and with Peter Quigley doing an excellent job at Dunston, Tommy decided to concentrate his management skills on the Allerdene, while maintaining his links with Dunston:

> "I love my Sunday football. The social side is very enjoyable, and we go away on trips which are great fun. I am more passionate than ever now that I am retired from work and I have been heavily involved in a project with the Football Foundation to bring development revenue to Dunston as well being heavily committed to the Allerdene, so I keep busy. Saturday football is different from Sunday. On a Sunday I run the show as chairman and basically all you need is a pitch and a team, but on Saturday you need a proper organisation and excellent facilities if you are going to play at a good level, and that takes a lot of time, hard work and money."

Sunday football is played mostly in public parks with facilities which can sometimes be fairly basic by comparison with the enclosed grounds, fenced off pitches, floodlights, hard standing and comfortable changing rooms which are enjoyed by Saturday afternoon teams. The North East Sunday League began life on Newcastle Town Moor where players hung their street clothes on nearby railings and put up their own goal posts, and there were several back-to-back pitches. In some respects things have not changed very much nearly sixty years later. The game between the Allerdene and Washington Steps was typical of the sort of setting that Sunday league teams can be required to endure. The teams were playing at the Northumbria Centre in Washington and another match was talking place on an adjacent pitch with the goalposts at one end sited back-to-back.

During the course of the game there was a goalmouth incident in which the ball went past the Allerdene post and came to rest just outside the penalty area of the adjoining pitch. Play was taking place at the opposite end of the field, so the Allerdene players called out to the goalkeeper to retrieve their ball. Happy to oblige, he strode out of his penalty area to pick up the ball but as he did so the ball in his own match was cleared downfield to his end of the pitch. It passed him and made its way inexorably towards the goal. Realising the danger, he threw the Allerdene ball in the direction of the goal and began to chase frantically after his own ball. Both balls ran towards his goal with the Allerdene ball leading the way, then his ball collided with the Allerdene ball, causing them both to cross the line. He made a frantic but unsuccessful attempt to prevent this from happening but his despairing dive only resulted in two footballs and an severely embarrassed goalkeeper ending up in the back of the net.

The Allerdene and Washington players and supporters dissolved into fits of raucous laughter while the distraught goalkeeper tried to explain what had happened to the referee. The official was unmoved by the keeper's predicament and to his consternation and fury, he awarded a goal. Mayhem ensued and the referee was surrounded by in incensed goalkeeper and his ten team mates who protested vehemently, but in vain and the goal stood.

There does not seem to be any obvious link between Sunday football and the olde English pursuit of Morris dancing, but Tommy Cooney became known as the Morris Man at Allerdene club following an elaborate joke which was played on him by some of the members:

> "I worked at a Civil Engineering office in Newcastle where my senior engineer was a member of a Morris dancing team and he was constantly pestering members of staff to join the team. My long term friend Alan Lumley knew how much the prospect of getting involved in such an activity filled me with horror and he continually encouraged the bloke to pester me to join."

TOMMY COONEY - A POLICEWOMAN AND A SPOT OF MORRIS DANCING

Attempts to recruit Tommy failed, but there was a better outcome when an engineer from Nepal joined the company and, being new to the area and having nothing to fill his social hours, he was quickly persuaded to try his hand at the traditional English pastime. He found it greatly to his liking and despite his very different cultural background he was enlisted into the team and became an active and popular participant in displays all over Northumberland. It was a nice little story which attracted the attention of the 'Evening Chronicle' which ran an article about him.

Tommy was on holiday with his family when the article was published and he knew nothing about it until he returned home and went to the Allerdene club, where the doorman said:

"Aa didn't knaa ye wor a Morris dancer,"

and pointed to the notice board where a copy of the article was posted. Some wag had doctored the accompanying picture so that Tommy' head replaced that of the Nepalese gentleman and the text had also been altered appropriately:

> "There was this picture of me in this Morris dancer's outfit grinning like a fool, and I was quoted as saying that I intended to introduce Morris dancing at the club discos and to include it in the football team's training sessions. Everybody had a good laugh at my expense and some people still refer to me as the Morris Man."

Derek Francis was one of the greatest characters ever to wear an Allerdene strip and he was always ready with a wisecrack and could be relied upon to be the life and soul of the party. Midway through one season he disappeared from the scene because he had been admitted to Ward 'E' of Gateshead's Queen Elizabeth Hospital for a major operation, which the committee kept quiet so that very few people were aware of the serious nature of the problem.

As fate would have it, during Derek's stay in hospital a riot took place at 'E' wing in Strangeways Prison with some of the prisoners taking to the roof as part of the protest. The incident received massive media coverage and a picture of the prisoners on the roof was printed on the front page of the 'Sun' newspaper, and it emerged that one of the ringleaders of the riot was the living image of Derek Francis. It was too good an opportunity to miss and the phantom photo crew at Allerdene struck again, posting the picture on the notice board with the footnote; 'We thought you were in 'E' ward, not 'E' wing!"

The lads took the picture to Derek's hospital ward and when he saw it he laughed so much that he almost re-opened his post operative stitches; it was a wonderful incident which had an extremely beneficial effect on Derek's rehabilitation; he went on to make a marvellous recovery and was soon back wearing the Alleredene's number five shirt.

Sunday morning football can be a tough training ground for fledgling referees, and even the most experienced officials can sometimes find themselves in difficulties which are not necessarily of their own making. Following an Allerdene game at Birtley Village ground, which is situated in the middle of a recreation park, Tommy checked the team dressing rooms to make sure they were empty then walked along the passage, calling out to make sure that no-one was still in the building before he locked up and returned to the Allerdene club for his Sunday morning pint.

Meanwhile, back at the Birtley Village ground match referee John Cuthbert was cheerfully towelling himself down after a post match shower and making his way back to his changing room, when he realised that he has been locked in. It was Sunday midday and those were the days before mobile phones, and he was in the middle of a quiet park in winter. His first course of action was to search the small building in the hope of finding some tools to facilitate his escape, but all he could find was a spade and a toilet brush. He thought he might be able to force a window but they were all to high for him to reach and in any case years of minimal maintenance rendered them impossible to open.

John was further frustrated by the fact that the main door had a twelve inch vision panel but it was glazed with heavy duty wired security glass which meant that the premises were virtually sound proof. His only option was to attempt to break the security glass, so he set about is with his spade and toilet brush. They were tools which were totally unsuitable for the task but he had no choice and by 2:30 he had managed to punch a small hole of about four inches

TOMMY COONEY - A POLICEWOMAN AND A SPOT OF MORRIS DANCING

diameter in the glass, but because he was short of stature he was unable to look out of the hole and shout for help. Necessity is the mother of invention, and he gained the extra height he needed by balancing a small wooden box on top of the line marking roller and from that precarious vantage point he began trying to attract attention.

An hour and a half later, at four o'clock, he was hoarse from shouting and no nearer being released, when his luck changed at last. Six youngsters appeared on the pitch outside and started having a kick about, so John shouted at them but they could not make out where the noise was coming from until their curiosity brought them to the dressing room door and John was able to explain his dilemna. He asked them to go to a pub on Front Street in Birtley where he knew an acquaintance of his who worked for the Council would be drinking, and ask him for help. To their credit the lads tracked the man down and he was able to contact the key holder who drove to the park and released John from his temporary prison. By this time it was six o'clock in the evening and John had been incarcerated for six hours! A lesser man would have held a lifelong resentment of Allerdene and Tommy Cooney, but being the type of character he is John bore them no lasting ill will and refereed several subsequent matches for them. So, the next time you think the referee should be locked up, you could do worse than get in touch with Tommy Cooney.

If you have enjoyed reading this book you will probably like to know that the first book in this series (published in 2001), We Just Love Football by Barry Hindson and Paul Dixon is available to buy at £9.99.

For more details or to order a copy log on to www.nonleaguedaily.co.uk/shop or call Baltic Publications on 0191 442 4001.

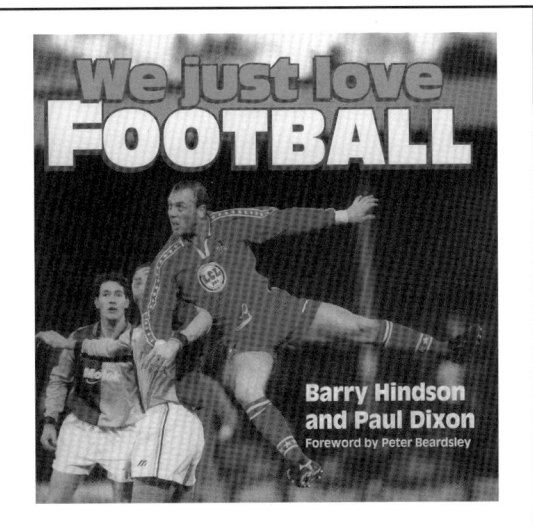